Bounded Rationality and Economic Evolution

Bounded Rationality and Economic Evolution

A Contribution to Decision Making, Economics and Management

Clem Tisdell
Professor of Economics
The University of Queensland
Australia

Edward Elgar
Cheltenham, UK • Northampton, MA, USA

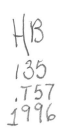

HB
135
.T57
1996

Published by
Edward Elgar Publishing Limited
Glensanda House
Montpellier Parade
Cheltenham
Glos GL50 1UA
UK

Edward Elgar Publishing, Inc.
6 Market Street
Northampton
Massachusetts 01060
USA

Reprinted 1999

A catalogue record for this book
is available from the British Library

Library of Congress Cataloguing in Publication Data
Tisdell, C.A. (Clement Allan)
    Bounded rationality and economic evolution : a contribution to decision making, economics, and management / Clem Tisdell.
    Includes bibliographical references and index.
    1. Economics, Mathematical. 2. Econometrics. 3. Decision-making–
–Mathematical models. 4. Management—Mathematical models.
    I. Title.
    HB135.T57   1996
    330'.01'51—dc20   96–15867
                                                        CIP

ISBN 1 85898 352 5

Printed and bound in Great Britain by
Antony Rowe Ltd, Chippenham, Wiltshire

Contents

Figures

Tables

Preface

Economic rationalism can be considered to be both a hallmark and a legacy of political economy as developed in the nineteenth century. Its early exponents included utilitarians such as Jeremy Bentham and James Mill. Such rationalism involved a strong belief in the rational calculating nature of humankind especially in economic matters but not exclusively so because Bentham also applied utilitarianism to crime, punishment and the law. The strong belief of many political economists in the rationality of humankind suggested to some that it could be used for the perfection of society.

The dominating influence of rationalism on economics continued in the twentieth century and in many respects was strengthened as a pillar of economic theory. For example, advantage was seen in the development and refinement of theories of rational behaviour without resort to the classical assumption of measurable utility, economic equilibrium became the centrepiece of neoclassical economics and was inextricably linked with the presence of unbounded rationality of economic agents and vice versa, and more recently the rational expectations hypothesis has become widely used in macroeconomics. Nevertheless, during the twentieth century concern was increasingly expressed about the concept of rational economic man.

The consequences of knowledge limitations (uncertainty), learning and social conflict for economic behaviour were increasingly studied. Without giving a history of this subject, let me note that Keynes pointed to the limits of rationality, especially in relation to expectations, in *The General Theory of Employment, Interest and Money*. Frank Knight made significant contributions on the subject of uncertainty and economics. Furthermore, limitations of using rationality as a predictor of social behaviour were highlighted by G.L.S. Shackle and by Oskar Morgenstern.

In the 1950s and continuing into the 1960s, Herbert Simon emphasized the bounded or limited rationality of economic agents as a result of their limited knowledge and their inherent finite mental capacities, that is limits to decision-making processes themselves. Because decision making is subject to limitations and involves in itself economic dimensions, unbounded rationality is either impossible or, where it is possible, it is often uneconomic to attain it. In fact, the latter implies that to try to attain unbounded rationality would be irrational. This led Simon to the view that much economic theory based on economic man was not useful for the management and administration of organizations and could be deficient as a predictor of economic behaviour.

Furthermore, a parallel development has been a growing interest in transaction costs and informational constraints as influences on organization and management and on economics, including their impact on the use of markets. R.H. Coase made early contributions on the subject and more recent advances have been made, for example by O.E. Williamson (see Chapters 11 and 16). At the same time, evolutionary economics has expanded as a field of enquiry with important publications by S. Winter and R. Nelson, G. Dosi, L. Soete and others. A systematic review of evolutionary economics is provided by G.M. Hodgson in *Economics and Evolution* (Polity Press, Cambridge, 1993). Here, I suggest that the presence of bounded rationality implies that many economic processes are best viewed as imperfectly predictable evolutionary processes.

Bounded rationality, learning, transaction costs and evolutionary consequences are combined in this book to provide insights into economic and managerial phenomena unavailable from neoclassical economic theory. The book is based primarily on articles published by me in the period 1966–95, the details of which can be found at the end of this book. These articles have been modified but not changed in substance to provide a connected and integrated whole. This was not difficult given the relative consistency of their coverage.

Although chapters are interconnected, each chapter in this book can be read as a self-contained whole. Some contain more mathematical details than others. These may be skimmed or skipped by the less mathematically inclined. However, none of the mathematics used is very technical.

The earliest article in this collection has been incorporated into Chapter 8 and was written while I was a Visiting Fellow at Princeton University, and a Consultant to its Econometrics Program appointed by Professor Morgenstern. I wish here to record my deepest gratitude to Oskar Morgenstern for his personal and specific encouragement of my research. This book may not reach his high standard but his early encouragement has undoubtedly had its influence over many years. It can only be a token of my appreciation. I also met Kenneth Arrow when I was a Visiting Scholar at Stanford, and had contact with William

Baumol when I was a Visiting Fellow at Princeton in 1965, and their own work has continued to be an inspiration to me.

I have had many helpful suggestions and considerable assistance from fellow academics, students, typists and so on, in relation to the individual articles incorporated into this book. I am grateful for this. Even though I shall not be able to mention them all by name, I especially wish to thank those who assisted with the preparation of the final typescript for this book.

In conclusion, I thank Edward Elgar for agreeing to publish this book and Mariel, my wife, for the patience she has shown during my preparation of the manuscript and various versions involved in the production of it.

Clem Tisdell
Brisbane

PART I

Background

1. Bounded Rationality and Economic Evolution: Broad Implications for Economics and Management

INTRODUCTION

We do not live in a perfect economic world and are unlikely to do so. Our world is characterized by the absence of unbounded or perfect rationality and by the presence of socio-economic frictions or resistances and of diversity in the behaviour of human beings, their groups and organizations. Consequently important economic and managerial implications follow, many of which are explored in this book. Most individuals and groups are less rational than suggested by the traditional economic view of rational behaviour and many may even be less rational than suggested by recent conceptions of bounded rationality. However, this does not spell chaos for economic and managerial theory. On the contrary, it provides new insights to increase the richness and generality of theory and to enhance its value for predictive purposes. New theories are needed and they indicate that novel approaches to policy formulation are frequently called for. For example, improvements in the design of organizations or institutions are often needed to enable institutions to respond or adapt more effectively to the changing world. This is because of constraints on their knowledge and their ability to respond to available knowledge. In such situations, organic rather than mechanistic models may prove to be more relevant for policy purposes.

AN EVOLUTIONARY ECONOMIC WORLD

In a world of limited knowledge, of learning and of impediments to unbounded rationality, processes of economic evolution help shape the socio-economic world. The nature of economies, their industrial structure and their institutions (economic and otherwise) are, for example, moulded by such evolutionary processes. Economic processes involving trial and error, experimentation and learning are important and they sometimes randomly (but not necessarily unpredictably) shunt socio-economic institutions, structures and environments on to irreversible paths. The nature of experimentation engaged in by actors and the impediments faced by them influence the evolution of economic systems and organizations and the nature of their responses to the changing world. The performance and evolution of socio-economic systems may be altered in principle by changing the range and nature of the experimental or exploratory behaviour of its participants or by constraining their scope for consequential actions. Therefore, institutional design affects socio-economic change and the evolution of socio-economic systems and becomes an important focus for policy formation. In this theory, institutions assume a much more significant policy role than in neoclassical economic theory.

NEOCLASSICAL UNBOUNDED RATIONALITY VERSUS MODELS OF 'IMPERFECT' BEHAVIOUR SUCH AS BOUNDED RATIONALITY MODELS

Unbounded Rationality of Individuals

Models involving less than perfect rationality can be extremely diverse, as will become clear from this book. Unbounded rationality implies that, as far as individuals are concerned,

1. they have perfect knowledge of their possibility sets including the relationships between their available strategies and the outcomes associated with these, and that
2. they have a complete transitive preference ordering of their possibilities;
3. they choose their most preferred option from their possibility set.

The neoclassical theory of consumer behaviour, as, for example, expounded by Hicks (1946) and by Samuelson (1947), is based on such assumptions but, as pointed out in Chapter 3, the assumption of unbounded rationality is stronger than necessary for neoclassical demand theory to be applicable.

Unbounded Rationality of Groups

The unbounded rationality assumption is basic to much neoclassical economic theory. The firm, for example, is asserted by Hicks to maximize its profit or its net present value, its preference depending linearly and positively on its profit. Organizational aspects of the firm or business are abstracted from in neoclassical economic theory and its choice problem is seen as being no different from that of an individual. Because frictions and impediments to organization in firms, particularly large firms, are considerable, this abstraction is increasingly being questioned. Significant advances have been made in economic and managerial theory by taking organizational impediments into account, as illustrated in this book.

The difficulties involved in individuals acting with unbounded rationality are considerable even when they are in a position to control perfectly the outcomes of their choices. But these difficulties are compounded in group situations when outcomes depend upon the joint behaviour of individual members of the group. In such situations, individuals, economic agents or players only partially control the outcome of their strategies, choices or actions because these also depend on the choices of other individuals, economic agents or players. For example, social or group interdependence is striking in the case of markets involving duopoly or oligopoly.

A definition of unbounded rationality of groups is needed to complete the economic conception of unbounded rationality. Adopting the approach of von Neumann and Morgenstern (1944), unbounded group rationality requires Paretian optimality to be achieved for the group. This implies that unbounded rationality by a group requires its members to select a set of strategies or actions such that, given the constraints imposed by their collective decision possibility set, it would be impossible to make any member of the group better off without making another worse off. Von Neumann and Morgenstern (1944) abstract from the complicated situations faced by groups to concentrate on conflict between individual self-interest and collective rationality. Participants in the group or game are assumed to be imbued with a vast amount of knowledge, outstanding ability to retain and process information, and organizational impediments involving transaction costs are virtually ignored. Consequently the advent of the theory of games, concepts of unbounded rationality and economic man were extended to a wider economic domain than ever before. This is significant because the theory of games as applied to economic behaviour has now become a standard part of many microeconomic texts (for example, Varian, 1990, 1993).

Bounded Rationality

Herbert Simon (1955, 1957, 1959) was an early critic of the concept of rational economic man. He argued that 'satisficing' rather than maximizing behaviour better characterizes much human behaviour and proposed (Simon, 1961) that the concept of economic man be replaced by that of administrative man. Simon argues that bounded rationality is the rule. Individuals have limited knowledge, data is costly to collect and to store, and much economic behaviour involves search and trial and error processes, with individuals being prepared to settle for satisfactory outcomes rather than requiring an optimal one. Basically, this is because the decision possibility set is usually imperfectly known by the decision maker and search and exploratory behaviour is needed to obtain an improved idea of what can be achieved. Many of the chapters in this book emphasize the importance of such behaviour and its implications.

Given that information collection and its processing is not costless, it follows that the neoclassical economic model of unbounded rationality would rarely if ever represent truly rational behaviour. This follows from Baumol and Quandt (1964). They consider optimally imperfect decisions given that the collection of information involves a cost as does its processing, calculation and refinement in order to make decisions needed for optimizing. In their view, it is only rational to engage in these decision-making processes up to the point where the expected additional benefit from these activities equals the expected additional cost involved. Normally, therefore, imperfect decisions will be optimal or rational, taking account of all the circumstances involved. This is so notwithstanding the fact that in many cases considerable uncertainty exists about the expected net benefits from refinement of decisions.

On the whole, game theory and associated economic models do not come to grips with problems of asymmetry of information or knowledge in groups, the costs and desirability of communicating information in groups, transaction costs involved in group behaviour or the evolution of institutional frameworks which modify or regulate group behaviour. All these important factors play a major role in the evolutionary pattern of industries and business firms. In recent times, a range of writers have recognized the importance of one or more of these elements as significant factors affecting group behaviour. In this respect consider Marschak (1954), Radner (1961, 1962), Williamson (1986) and Nelson (1987), for example. Such factors when combined with the persistence and inertia of economic patterns (difficulties in reversing economic structures or the hysteresis involved) play an important role in economic evolution.

More on Optimally Imperfect Decisions

Even where extra knowledge has economic value, it can be irrational from an economic viewpoint to seek it. It is optimal from an economic point of view to maximize one's net gains from the activity of knowledge generation (Baumol and Quandt, 1964). In many cases, this implies that it is optimal to improve one's knowledge about a matter up to the point where the expected marginal cost of doing so equals the expected marginal benefit of doing so. Usually this means that the optimal decision is to stop short of gaining perfect knowledge about knowledge having economic value.

Four possibilities are illustrated in Figure 1.1. There, *MB* indicates the relevant marginal benefit curve from knowledge generation and *MC* represents that for marginal costs and the variable $\hat{x}$ represents complete or perfect knowledge and $\bar{x}$ indicates the optimal economic amount of it. In case (a), the marginal benefit of knowledge falls to zero before perfect knowledge is achieved and it is not rational to seek perfect knowledge in this case. In case (b), net gains from knowledge generation are also maximized by stopping short of perfect knowledge. In case (c), perfect knowledge of the relevant knowledge set is optimal whereas in case (d), it is optimal to generate no knowledge about the relevant knowledge set. Case (c) is likely to be rare.

Rational Expectations and Optimally Imperfect Decisions

It may be pertinent to add some comments on the Rational Expectations Hypothesis, as put forward originally by Muth (1961). Boland (1982, p. 73) claims that 'those models employing the Rational Expectations Hypothesis assume merely that every decision maker has acquired information only to point that its acquisition is economical'. Thus rational decisions of the type just considered underlie the formation of rational expectations. Supporters of the Rational Expectation Hypothesis claim that the expectations of firms tend to be distributed for the same information set about the prediction of the relevant theory (Muth, 1961).

Thus it is important for the theory to consider the likelihood of firms or individuals arriving at the same information · set. Since the most economical amount of search is likely to be limited, there is no reason to believe that all will end up with the same information set. To some extent, search involves random procedures. The same amount of search by different individuals does not ensure the same amount of knowledge. If, for example, two individuals spend the same amount of time (but a limited amount of time) in gathering background material (information) for a project, it is likely that they will come up with information sets that only overlap. Furthermore, depending upon these different situations the optimal degree of search varies between economic entities. It would be worthwhile exploring the factors which influence the degree of overlap of information sets obtained by different firms or individuals. However, even if individuals or firms do end up with the same information set, what are the chances that their predictions will be the same? To what extent can Carnap's (1950) or Keynes's (1921) view of logical probabilities be accepted? Personally, I believe that there is much greater diversity of

Figure 1.1 Different degrees of optimal knowledge generation determined by economic considerations

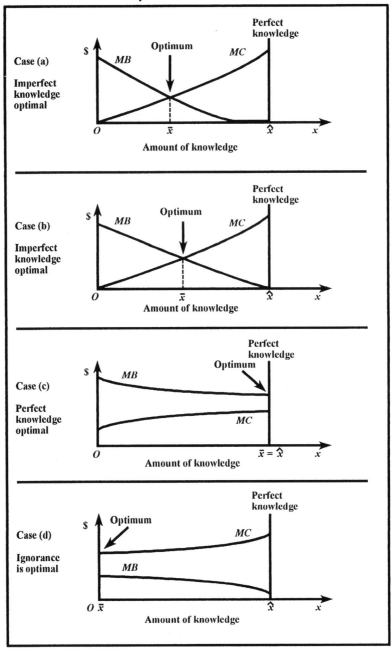

expectations (and diversity of information sets) than assumed by the Rational Expectations Hypothesis and that it is unwise to build theories which do not encompass the full range of diversity (Tisdell, 1968, or Chapter 5 of this book).

Balancing of Information

Another type of decision involved in the generation of knowledge is a decision about how to allocate limited resources between the collection of different types of knowledge. Microeconomic models can at least help us to conceptualize the type of choices that need to be made and to see at least how they are likely to be affected qualitatively by parameter variations. In Figure 1.2, for instance, curve *ABC* represents the production trade-off between two types of knowledge given the limited resources available for knowledge generation. Given that the curves marked R_1R_1, R_2R_2 and R_3R_3 represent iso-expected gain functions, the optimal allocation of resources to the generation of the two types of knowledge corresponds to that which yields point *B*. In certain instances it may be operationally possible to estimate the relevant curves. Choices about appropriate mixtures of different types of knowledge, for example, economic and physical knowledge, can be important in cost-benefit analysis (Tisdell, 1986).

Figure 1.2 The optimal mixture of different types of information

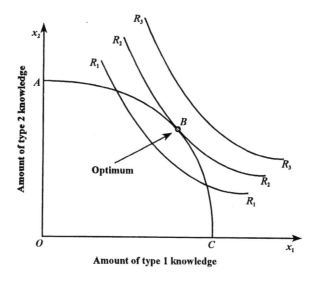

In principle, an expansion path for the collection of mixed information might be specified. However, as is clear from the discussion surrounding Figure 1.1, it will be rarely rational (economic) to collect complete information of any type or to proceed along the expansion path until perfect information is achieved.

Main Differences between Neoclassical and Evolutionary-Type Theories

Some of the main differences between neoclassical economic theory and more modern theories (as I see them) are summarized in Table 1.1. Naturally my view of the differences are stylized but overall sufficient difference exists to establish a new paradigm or set of paradigms. A hallmark of modern economic theory is its emphasis on the importance of institutions, of evolutionary phenomena and of the bounded rationality of individuals and groups. All of these factors combined imply that dynamic processes must be studied in order to predict or understand economic outcomes.

DIVERSITY OF BEHAVIOUR, INSTITUTIONAL STRUCTURES AND EVOLUTION

Uniformity of Behaviour in Neoclassical Theory

Neoclassical economic theory assumes relative uniformity of economic behaviour. Marshall (1920), for example, makes considerable use of the representative firm and Hicks (1946) used the average or representative consumer in his analysis. Furthermore, in neoclassical economics, institutions in themselves have few if any interesting economic implications. Institutions are but irrelevant shadows in this theory, of no fundamental significance for the working of economies. In Hicks's theory, institutional structures, impediments and conflicts within firms do not deter firms from maximizing their net present value or profit.

Diversity of Behaviour is Important in Evolutionary Theories

However, most evolutionary economists are of the view that economic behaviour tends to be diverse and that this diversity has important economic and policy implications. Furthermore, institutional structures have significant implications for economic behaviour, are varied and play an important role in the way in which economies perform and evolve.

Table 1.1 Contrasting characteristics of the foundations of neoclassical microeconomic theory and 'modern' economic theory

Characteristic	Neoclassical	'Modern'
Perfect or relatively complete information	Yes	No
Information gathering and storage costly	No	Yes
Decision making costless	Yes	No
Capacity of individuals for decision making limited	No	Yes
Preferences complete	Yes	No
Transaction costs absent	Yes	No
Economic behaviour relatively uniform or appropriately modelled by a 'representative' type	Yes	No
Historical context and hysteresis important	No	Yes
Experimentation and search behaviour important	No	Yes
Capacity of groups to engage in rational behaviour, e.g. to achieve Paretian optimality, is limited	No	Yes

Sources of Diversity of Economic Behaviour by Individuals

The sources of diversity of economic behaviour are many. At the level of the individual, they may, for example, arise from differences in any of the following:
1. motivations,
2. perceptions of the decision possibility set,
3. types of exploration paths employed in trying to determine the decision possibility set, that is, differences in search behaviour and in resulting experiences,
4. degrees of enthusiasm to engage in search and maximizing behaviour and
5. inferences drawn from observations.

Thus, as often observed in managerial or industry economics, some firms are laggards and others are leaders in adopting innovations. Some individuals may basically engage in adaptive behaviour whereas others engage in proactive behaviour or behaviour that is close to maximizing behaviour.

Sources of Diversity of Group Behaviour

Just as individuals exhibit variety, so too do institutions. They do so not only because they consist of different collections of individuals (capable of varied behaviour) but also because of variations in the nature of their institutional structures and their rules or procedures. These change slowly for the most part (although at discrete times, they may change radically) and as Nelson (1987) suggests, they are of considerable importance for the evolution of economies, industries and firms.

Variety in Behaviour Does Not Imply Volatility

Although behaviours of individuals are varied, this does not mean that they are necessarily volatile. Patterns of behaviour if they are reasonably 'successful' tend to persist or to be reinforced. Furthermore, they may endure for psychological reasons. In addition, institutional constraints on behaviour tend to last. It is difficult because of the inertia (for example, transaction costs) involved to change institutional structures and practices rapidly. This is not to say that a sea-change does not sometimes occur. It is the persistence of patterns of behaviour which permits economic predictions to be made using the evolutionary approach to economic theory despite the existence of diversity.

The Desirability of Diversity of Behaviour

Given that diversity of behaviour of individuals and institutions is important, the question naturally arises of whether this variety is beneficial from a social point of view. Such diversity is in fact socially beneficial in a number of economic situations, but not always. In some situations, it is economically disadvantageous (Tisdell, 1968) or patterns of variety present in the economy may not be the optimal ones. Furthermore, some extreme forms of socio-economic diversity can be disruptive of the cohesion of societies and may hinder their 'advancement'. However, the benefits of diversity in an evolutionary society are many and this theme is emphasized in parts of this book.

DYNAMICS, COMPARATIVE STATICS AND EQUILIBRIUM

The major part of neoclassical economic theory relies on comparative statics, that is, the comparison of economic equilibria. For example, comparisons of equilibria of the consumer, of the producer and of markets are important in neoclassical economic theory but much less attention is given to the processes involved in reaching equilibria.

Comparative Statics and Uniformity of Reactions in Dynamic Economic Models

This means that the speed of convergence to equilibrium of the economic situation under investigation is often ignored. This limits the policy relevance of comparative statics (Tisdell, 1972). Nevertheless, neoclassical economists have given considerable attention, at least for markets, to the question of whether an equilibrium or more than one equilibrium exists and to whether or not market equilibria are stable. While the stability question involves consideration of dynamics or processes, it need not involve a deep or wide consideration of such matters. In the last respect note the correspondence principle as developed by Paul Samuelson (1947). The theorem points out correspondences between the stability of a market equilibrium and the properties of the comparative statics of this equilibrium. A market is stable for Walrasian market reactions if and only if an increase in market demand results in an increase in the level of the market equilibrium price, and vice versa. Similarly for Marshallian market reactions, market equilibrium is only stable if an increase in demand leads to an increase in the equilibrium quantity supplied in the market and vice versa. These conditions are both satisfied for normal demand and supply curves. However, for different assumptions about market reactions, markets may be unstable even when supply and demand curves are normal. Such instability occurs, for instance, for some simple cobweb relationships when market supply and demand curves are normal, for example if the steepness of the supply curve is less than that of the demand curve.

An important aspect to note is that neoclassical economists as a rule assume uniform types of market reaction by market participants. Mixed reaction functions are not emphasized. Usually, for example, all market suppliers are supposed to be Walrasian price adjusters responding to differences between quantities of the commodity demanded and supplied or Marshallian supply adjusters responding to differences in the demand price and the supply price of the commodity. A mixed situation, for instance, in which some participants are Walrasian adjusters and others are

Marshallian adjusters, is not usually considered. Other diverse behavioural possibilities can also be imagined. Furthermore, even for those market participants who show the same type of reaction, their rate of reaction can differ. These variations are all possible sources of diversity of economic behaviour. In the case of cobweb-like market models, sources of variations can include differences in the ways in which price expectations are formed, for example the range of previous prices which enter into the estimates and the weights placed on these in making predictions about future prices, and differences in reactions to these expectations.

If it is accepted that variation is an important aspect of economic life, it becomes important to study the disparity involved because diversity plays a major role in the unfolding of economic processes and their consequences. For example, what proportion of market participants are likely to adopt one form of market reaction rather than another? To what extent is there stability in the mixture of market reactions? What causes the combination of reactions to change? As the distribution of reactions alters, what consequences does this have for market stability? A change in the distribution of reactions can sometimes alter a market situation from an unstable to a stable one. These are all matters neglected in neoclassical economic enquiry but are suitable for empirical investigation and have welfare and policy consequences of considerable interest.

Dynamic Reversibility – Lack of Hysteresis in Neoclassical Modelling

As usually expounded, neoclassical economic theory exhibits complete dynamic reversibility. This implies that historical experiences do not influence future relationships. Thus there is complete flexibility of wages, demand patterns, and so on. In other words, 'ratchet-like' effects are absent or more generally hysteresis does not occur. However, in an experiential world, this is often not so and hysteresis does occur in economic situations. Economists noting the importance of hysteresis at a relatively early time include Keynes (1936) in relation to wage flexibility and Duesenberry (1949) in relation to the consumption function.

Discontinuities and Catastrophe Theory

Another feature of neoclassical economics is its emphasis on the use of differential calculus and the occurrence of smooth continuous rather than abrupt changes in economic variables. Marshall (1920), for example, proclaimed that nature does not change by leaps and bounds, *naturam facit sultam*. It is being realized, especially in relation to ecological and environmental economics and economic development, that this may not be so and that more attention should be given to discontinuities and abrupt change. This is not to say that no economic models incorporate abrupt change. The kinked demand curve model of oligopoly provides an example of an economic model in which price cutting can trigger an abrupt change in market conditions.

In mathematics, catastrophe theory (Zeeman, 1976) allows for both hysteresis and for jumps or discontinuites in relationships. In economics, such a phenomenon can, for example, be very important to environmental economics. Its existence creates a difficult policy problem when there is little forewarning of environmental catastrophe or by the time forewarning is available, it is too late to avert the catastrophe.

Chaos and Economics

Partially because of mathematical developments stimulated by research in biology, chaos theory (Gleick, 1987) has become of increasing interest to economists. In 'chaotic' situations, small variations are capable of causing very large differences in the unfolding of events or the evolution of systems. This possibility can be established for several types of mathematical relationships. When systems are very sensitive to small variations, study of such variations and their consequences is important to decide how worthwhile it is likely to be to control these variations. While it seems likely that some economic situations can be usefully modelled using chaos theory, the bulk of economic relationships may not exhibit the degree of sensitivity suggested by chaos theory.

FRICTIONS, IMPEDIMENTS AND MISCELLANEOUS MATTERS

In general, one obtains the impression from neoclassical economics that economic systems containing fewer frictions and involving improved knowledge are likely to function in a socially superior way. However, in reality such improved functioning is not always the case.

Knowledge as a Destabilizing Force

In some cases, for example, improvements in knowledge can be a destabilizing force. This is, for instance, clear from the theory of games. In some games, if each player has perfect knowledge of the strategy to be played by other players no equilibrium or solution is possible unless mixed strategies are adopted. The adoption of mixed strategies implies that actual strategies used are determined randomly but according to some probability constraints. Such randomization is necessary to obtain any solution.

Frictions or Dampeners can be of Positive Economic Benefit

Second, the presence of frictions or factors that dampen responses to changing situations can be advantageous in promoting stability and convergence to equilibrium where this is desired, or in avoiding the opposite: instability and explosion of the relevant economic system or subsystem. This is most easily illustrated by a simple cobweb model. If suppliers predict the same price for the next period as for the previous one, then for a given demand situation, convergence to equilibrium is more likely, other things equal, the less responsive is supply to price.

A somewhat similar phenomenon exists in relation to controversy concerning 'rules versus discretion' in policy. Discretion involves policy adjustment as information changes, that is, flexibility. Rules generally involve less variation or a greater degree of steadiness. Rules impose a degree of rigidity on decision making. But it is suggested in this book that this can be beneficial, especially when information and changes in information are imperfect, or subject to uncertainty.

Transaction Costs

In addition, observe that neoclassical economics has generally ignored transaction costs involved in market exchange and impediments to optimization in organizations such as firms. Impediments to optimization within organizations or institutions can include asymmetry in the information available to participants, costs in transmitting information and in gaining access to information within organizations, differences in the goals of participants and lack of a collective objective agreed on by all. Such matters and their consequences for management and economics are given considerable attention in this book.

PLAN OF THE BOOK AND PHILOSOPHICAL VIEWPOINT

Decision making and the behaviour of individuals or single economic entities are explored first and the discussion is then extended to organizations and groups. Finally, wider issues such as those involving markets and the evolution of industries are considered. In the latter respect, innovation and research and development are given particular attention.

A pluralistic approach to economic theory is adopted. This means that neoclassical economics is not completely rejected but rather looked upon as just one source of illumination of our complex world. However, we need other sources to improve our knowledge, thereby developing additional benchmarks and theories to provide insights into and predictions about economic phenomena. This provides an important way to improve our knowledge, even though we are never likely to obtain perfect knowledge.[1]

NOTE

1. Some of the material in this chapter is from a guest lecture which I gave at the University of Potchefstroom, Orange Free State, South Africa, in 1984.

REFERENCES

Baumol, W. and Quandt, R. (1964), 'Rules of Thumb and Optimally Imperfect Decisions', *American Economic Review*, 54, 23–46.

Boland, L.A. (1982), *The Foundations of Economic Method*, London: George Allen & Unwin.

Carnap, R. (1950), *Logical Foundations of Probability*, Chicago: University of Chicago Press.

Duesenberry, J. (1949), *Income, Saving and the Theory of Consumer Behaviour*, Cambridge, Mass.: Harvard University Press.

Gleick, J. (1987), *Chaos*, New York: Viking.

Hicks, J.R. (1946), *Value and Capital*, 2nd edn, Oxford: Clarendon Press.

Keynes, J.M. (1921), *A Treatise on Probability*, London: Macmillan.

Keynes, J.M. (1936), *The General Theory of Employment, Interest and Money*, London: Macmillan.

Marschak, J. (1954), 'Towards an Economic Theory of Organization and Information', in Thrall, R.M., Coombs, C.H. and Davis, R.L. (eds), *Decision Processes*, New York: John Wiley, Chapter 14.

Marshall, A. (1920), *Principles of Economics*, London: Macmillan.

Muth, J. (1961), 'Rational Expectations and the Theory of Price Movements', *Econometrica*, 29, 315–35.

Nelson, R. (1987), *Understanding Technological Change as an Evolutionary Process*, Amsterdam: North-Holland.

Radner, R. (1961), 'The Evaluation of Information in Organizations', in *Proceedings of the Fourth Berkeley Symposium on Probability and Statistics*, Berkeley: University of California Press, 1, 491–530.

Radner, R. (1962), 'Team Decision Problems', *The Annals of Mathematical Statistics*, 33, 857–81.

Samuelson, P.A. (1947), *Foundations of Economic Analysis*, Cambridge, Mass.: Harvard University Press.

Simon, H. (1955), 'A Behavioral Model of Rational Choice', *Quarterly Journal of Economics*, 79, 99–118.

Simon, H. (1957), *Models of Man*, New York: John Wiley.

Simon, H. (1959), 'Theories of Decision-Making in Economics', *American Economic Review*, 54, 253–83.

Simon, H. (1961), *Administrative Behaviour*, New York: The Macmillan Company.

Tisdell, C.A. (1968), *The Theory of Price Uncertainty, Production and Profit*, Princeton: Princeton University Press.

Tisdell, C.A. (1970), 'Implications of Learning for Economic Planning', *Economics of Planning*, 10, 177–92.

Tisdell, C.A. (1972), *Microeconomics: The Theory of Economic Allocation*, Sydney: John Wiley.

Tisdell, C.A. (1986), 'Cost-benefit Analysis and the Environment and Information Constraints in LDCs', *Journal of Economic Development*, 11, 63–81.

Varian, H.R. (1990), *Intermediate Microeconomics: A Modern Approach*, 2nd edn, New York: Norton.

Varian, H.R. (1993), *Microeconomic Analysis*, 3rd edn, New York: Norton.

von Neumann, J. and Morgenstern, O. (1944), *Theory of Games and Economic Behaviour*, Princeton: Princeton University Press.

Williamson, O.E. (1986), *Economic Organizations: Firms, Markets and Policy Controls*, Brighton: Wheatsheaf.

Zeeman, E.C. (1976), 'Catastrophe Theory', *Scientific American*, 234(4), 373–88.

PART II

Decisions by Individuals and Learning

2. Concepts of Rationality as Foundations of Economic Theory

INTRODUCTION

Concepts of rational behaviour dominate not only microeconomics because economic agents (consumers, firms and suppliers of resources) are supposed to act rationally, but have become of increasing importance in macroeconomics as theories of rational expectations have become more widely used in macroeconomics (for example, Sargent, 1986; Lucas, 1987; Leslie, 1993, Chapter 3; Sachs and B. Larrain, 1993, pp. 462–8). As observed in the previous chapter, the assumption of unbounded rationality is a fundamental one in neoclassical economic theory.

This chapter explores the plausibility of this assumption as an explanation of the behaviour of individuals and considers modifications to it. However, problems raised for rationality by group or social interdependence are not considered here but dealt with later in this book.

The decisions and actions of individual agents are important for economics in themselves and as building blocks for theories of the operation of market systems. For example, in neoclassical economic theory market supply and demand curves are derived respectively by aggregation of the supply curves of individual sellers and the demand curves of individual buyers. The supply and demand curves of individual buyers and sellers are obtained by supposing that these individuals engage in rational behaviour. Thus this approach to theorizing is essentially a reductionist one which ultimately relies on rational behaviour by individual economic agents.

After discussing philosophical views about rationality and economists' conceptions of it generally, the scope for using the unbounded rationality assumption is explored in depth. There is more scope for applying it than seems to be the case at first sight but, as observed, there are a large number of situations in which it cannot possibly be applicable. In those cases, bounded rationality may be possible. However, even this type of behaviour may not always be possible or may not occur. This, then, adds weight to the view that behaviour of individuals is likely to be diverse and that this diversity is worth exploring and taking into account in theorizing.

PHILOSOPHICAL VIEWS ABOUT RATIONAL BEHAVIOUR

In their theorizing, economists employ a variety of concepts of rational behaviour, and some of these are outlined, criticized and compared with selected alternatives. All the concepts fail to deal adequately with the rationality of beliefs of actors. For instance, in some models, such as (subjective) expected utility models, the rationality of the beliefs of the actors is ignored and their beliefs taken as data. In order to act rationally, actors must merely act consistently with their beliefs, however ill-founded these might be. By contrast, in other economic models, such as those of perfectly competitive markets, actors are assumed to have perfect knowledge, so that the problem of forming rational beliefs on the basis of limited information is assumed away. It is also interesting to note that while the deliberative aspect of rational choice is central to some economic models, such as those involving cost-benefit considerations, in other models, such as those relying on revealed preference, the deliberation of actors is ignored.

The bulk of existing economic theory depends upon the hypothesis that individuals choose and act rationally, even though a range of rationality concepts are used. Broadly, economists interpret this hypothesis to mean that individuals choose optimally on the basis of their own preferences and subject to external constraints upon their alternative choices. However, differences of opinion occur between economists as to the import of 'optimally'. For instance, does it imply an optimal choice relative to an actor's (possibly distorted) perception or limited information, or an absolute optimum such as might be achieved with perfect information if calculation is rapid, logically consistent and costless? One's attitude to the use of the concept in economics is likely to vary with the particular interpretation which is adopted.

Economists have taken opposing views about the value of the rationality hypothesis for economic theorizing. For instance, whereas Machlup has come out strongly in favour of the postulate, Shackle contends that rational behaviour is virtually impossible and is an inappropriate basis for economic theory. Machlup (1969, p. 117) says,

> The fundamental assumption – whether it be regarded as a conventional postulate, a useful fiction, or a well-known fact of experience – maximizing behaviour, that is, of utility maximizing reactions of households and firms is recognized as a useful and

probably indispensable part of the theoretical system of economics. The assumption has frequently been hypostatized into the symbolic figure or 'personal ideal type', the Economic Man.

On the other hand, Shackle (1972, pp. 245–6) contends that rational choice is impossible if an actor's knowledge is fragmentary and disconnected. He says,

> Rational choice, choice which can demonstrate its own attainment of maximum objectively possible advantage, must be fully informed choice. But there can be no full information except about what is past, or else about what is exempt from the world of time altogether. The paradox of rationality is that it must concern itself with choosing amongst things fully known; but in the world of time, only that is fully known which is already beyond the reach of choice, having already become actual and thus knowable.

Shackle's concept of rational choice is one of unbounded rational choice. Since most economic actions are designed to influence future events and the future is uncertain, rationality is not an appropriate assumption in Shackle's view for most economic theory. Although the unbounded rationality assumption has practical limitations in economics, I shall contend later, in contrast to Shackle, that full information is not necessary for perfect unbounded rational behaviour.

Rationality, Deliberative Action and Rationality of Beliefs

Philosophers, like economists, hold differing views about what constitutes rational behaviour, but on the whole they seem to be much more concerned than economists about the deliberative aspect of rational choice and about the rationality of the beliefs which actors hold. This is not to say that all philosophers have this interest in rational behaviour. For instance, Karl Popper's situational logic pays little attention to the rationality of beliefs. Popper expresses the view[1] that the actions which an actor performs are likely to be appropriate given his goals and the way in which he perceives his situation. To understand why individuals act in a particular way and to predict their behaviour, one needs to know about their goals and perceptions. The individual's perceptions may be, but need not be, based upon rational beliefs.

However, confirmation theorists or inductive logicians insist that actors' beliefs must be rational if their behaviour is to be rational. The rationality of actors' actions depends on their beliefs and the rationality of their beliefs depends upon the information available to them at the time of acting. The rationality of actors' beliefs must be judged relative to the amount of information which they have at the time of acting.

Allowing that the information which is available to the decision maker is likely to be limited, some philosophers, in determining the rationality of behaviour, concentrate on the nature of beliefs which are held on the basis of the available information. Oppenheim (1953), for example, suggests that if choice is to be rational, beliefs which are the basis for choice must be warranted by the evidence which is available to the decision maker at the time of choosing. But this is not sufficient. For individuals' choices to be rational, their warranted beliefs must be held on the basis of the information which is available to them at the time of their choice. In Oppenheim's view, if individuals hold beliefs which would be warranted on the basis of their available information but which are not in fact formed upon this basis, then their choice cannot be rational. The conscious and deliberative aspect is seen as an important ingredient of choice. Beliefs must be warranted (which implies, among other things, that they must not be inconsistent) and choice must be made in consistency with these beliefs.

Oppenheim (1953, p. 350) summarizes his concept of rational choice in the following way:

> Someone's choice of a goal is rational if and only if the information available to him at the time of his choice and his standards of evaluation support the following belief which he has the disposition to hold at that time on the basis of that information: There exists at least one course of action open to me whose effect complex includes the actual goal and which, together with all its other significant effects, is no less valuable to me than any of the significant actions I could do instead, together with their respective significant effects.

Oppenheim's concept differs from the concept of perfect unbounded rationality which is used in much economic theory and which is discussed below. In Oppenheim's case, limitations on the amount of information which is available to the decision maker are taken into account and the deliberative aspect of choice is emphasized. A rational choice requires individuals to be aware of their reasons for choosing in a particular way. If they do not attend to those reasons at the time of their choice, because, for example, the choice has become repetitive, they must nevertheless be able to elaborate their own reasons in retrospect. In some economic models of rational choice, for instance in those models based on revealed preference, the deliberative aspect of rationality is given no attention. Oppenheim's conception implies that a rational choice is an optimal one relative to values which individuals have and the information which is assumed to be available to them.

Consistent Behaviour, Neurosis and Effectiveness of Choice

The view has been considered by philosophers that much neurotic behaviour is in fact rational. Neurotics may choose in a consistent manner even though they are misinformed. For example, the revealed preferences of neurotics may be transitive and they may choose optimally in relation to these 'preferences' (revealed orderings) given their basic beliefs about the world and the information available to them. Peter Alexander (1962) and Harvey Mullane (1971) reject the notion that neurotic behaviour can be rational. They reject it because this behaviour is unlikely to achieve the object which neurotics intend and/or neurotics are not aware of or cannot of their own volition become aware of their reasons for choosing in the way they do.

Mullane (1971, p. 421) suggests that:

(1) Behaviour is rational if it is likely to achieve what the agent intends and is unlikely to lead to other consequences the undesirability of which outweighs the desirability of what it is intended to achieve.

(2) To behave rationally a person must behave for a reason that is also his reason for behaving in that way. It must be his reason in the sense that he must be able to become aware of it, as his reason or at least be able to become aware of it if he thinks about his behaviour.

There is an important difference between Oppenheim's concept of rationality and Mullane's. Behaviour is only rational in Mullane's sense if it is effective in achieving the goal which is sought by the agent. By contrast, behaviour may be rational in Oppenheim's sense even if it is ineffective in attaining the goal which is sought by the agent. Although agents' beliefs may be warranted on the basis of their available information, this information may be so limited and distorted that their warranted beliefs result in their choice of an action which fails to meet their goals most effectively.

VIEWS OF PHILOSOPHERS ABOUT RATIONALITY COMPARED TO THOSE IN ECONOMICS

While economists assume in most of their economic models that agents choose rationally, there are broad differences in their conceptions of rationality. In some models, no attention is paid to the deliberative aspects of rationality and to the goals which are pursued by the agents. In other models, decision makers are assumed to know their alternative choices and their consequences. There is no discussion of the way in which they build up beliefs.   In revealed preference approaches[2] (say, to determining the demand for commodities by consumers) the main aim of the economist is to discover the ordering of alternatives which the individuals act upon in practice.   Some economists suggest that such an ordering is likely to be transitive and complete and consider consistent choice in relation to the revealed ordering to be a sign of rational choice.   However, even in the absence of changed tastes, consistent choice may not be rational in terms of the philosophers' concepts mentioned above.   For instance, neurotics may be consistent, but may consistently fail to act in their own best interest.   Again, individuals' beliefs may be unwarranted but biased in a way which leads to no observable inconsistency in their choice.

If one is merely interested in predicting behaviour, the assumption of consistent choice may be sufficient for this purpose.   A considerable body of economic theory is merely aimed at predicting economic behaviour. However, the assumption of consistent choice leaves some social or welfare problems unresolved.   From a welfare point of view, it does make a difference whether or not consistent individuals act in their own self-interest and this depends on the rationality of their beliefs.   However, individuals' beliefs may be rational and yet they may be so ill-informed that they are unable effectively to act in their own self-interest.   By contrast, rational people in Mullane's special sense are so well-informed that they always act effectively in their own self-interest, that is to achieve the goals which they themselves wish to achieve given the limitations on their available choices.   Are actors sufficiently well-informed to be rational in Mullane's sense?   If they are well-informed, can they be rational in Mullane's sense?   These matters will be considered as economic conceptions of rational choice and discussed in the remainder of this chapter.

ECONOMISTS' CONCEPTIONS OF RATIONAL CHOICE BY INDIVIDUALS

Simon (1957, Part IV) has suggested that economic models of choice by economic agents can be usefully divided into those which assume unbounded rationality on the part of economic agents and those which assume bounded rationality.

Extreme models of unbounded rationality suppose that economic agents know all their alternative choices and all relevant consequences which follow.   In this extreme case, which underlies most general equilibrium theories of the economy, economic agents are assumed to be omniscient. Their information is complete and they have no problem in discovering the best choice from their point of view. In retrospect, they are never disappointed by their choice. Agents choose their most desired alternative from those available and face no effective barriers of search and calculating cost in discovering it. Let us call such models of choice, *models of perfect unbounded rationality*. Economic models of perfect competition are of this type.

However, the information available to agents is usually limited or distorted, and calculation and thought do impose effective costs and limitations on choice. One suspects that perfect unbounded rationality is uncommon. Nevertheless, economic theories which assume perfect unbounded rationality cannot be immediately dismissed. The predictions of a theory may be correct or may be sufficiently accurate for the purpose of particular applications, even though the assumptions of the theory are not satisfied.[3]

Hicks (1956, p. 55) defends the concept of perfect unbounded rationality in economics on the grounds that it is characteristic of individuals in aggregate. To Hicks, perfect unbounded rationality is a general approximation, an 'average' concept, and no individual need act exactly in accordance with the theory.

Other arguments can also be advanced in favour of the concept. Theories of unbounded rationality make stronger assumptions than are frequently required to ensure the choice of the most desired alternative.[4] The assumptions about knowledge and preference ordering of the decision makers are usually stronger than necessary. For instance, a complete and entirely transitive preference ordering of possible choices is not necessary for choosing one's best alternative and for knowing that one is choosing such an alternative. For instance, an intransitive ordering of a set of possibilities which are unattainable makes no difference, nor would an inconsistency in a subset of available alternatives which are rated as inferior to another attainable set rule out the best choice. For example, given my preference for comfort and convenience in transportation, given my income and given prices, my preference ordering of the various types of horse-drawn transport may be incomplete and inconsistent and yet this need not prevent me from rationally choosing motor transport in preference to horse-drawn transport. Under prevailing conditions, my preference for motor transport dominates that for all types of horse-drawn transport and this I know without considering the details of my preference for different types of horse-drawn transport.

Selection, Equilibrium and Rationality

Laws of social selection, competition and of survival of the fittest, it is sometimes claimed,[5] operate to ensure that rational individuals occupy key (economic) roles in society. Rational acquisitive individuals tend to amass and control most resources in the economy. Because rational individuals dominate the economy, this makes the rationality assumption appropriate for most economic analysis.

Again, economists sometimes express the view that perfect unbounded rationality tends to be achieved by decision makers in the long run. Perfect unbounded rationality has been traditionally associated with the attainment of equilibrium in economic systems.[6] When the equilibrium of an economic system is stable, as it usually is hypothesized to be, the equilibrium tends to be reached in the long run. When a neoclassical economy is in perfect equilibrium, the expectations of economic agents are fully realized and their plans are ideal in the sense that none would want to revise these after the event. However, a number of points may be worth noting. The absence of dissatisfaction with one's past decisions is not sufficient to show that these decisions were rational. One's past decisions might have been optimal by chance rather than by design. Furthermore, cognitive dissonance may be present, that is, individuals may subconsciously alter their perceived past preferences in retrospect to justify their past decisions. Consequently, they may not feel dissatisfied in retrospect.

In addition, long-run cumulative experience need not lead towards perfect unbounded rationality. If the economy (the external world) is continually changing, past experience may be a misleading guide to the future. Furthermore, the needs of decision makers alter in the long run, as they grow older or change, and this can limit the applicability of the individual's past experience. Experience is not a guide to perfect unbounded rationality in some other circumstances. One's observations or experience may alter one's preferences. Hence, individuals' 'final' preference ordering can depend upon the sequence in which they observe or experience things. For instance, the order in which I try various occupations may influence my evaluation of these. If this is so, I have no independent evaluation of my alternatives.

While Hicks (1946, p. 132), Shackle and other economists have inseparably linked economic equilibrium and perfect unbounded rationality, as has Kornai (1971), an economic system may be in equilibrium and yet decision makers may not be choosing rationally. Some of the reasons for this were mentioned above.

Expected Utility Maximization and Rationality

Some economic models assume that decision makers choose rationally, but not in a perfectly unbounded manner. For instance, a number assume that decision makers have less than perfect information (choose on the basis of uncertain prospects) and yet are at the same time unboundedly rational in Simon's sense. Most of these models rely upon the hypothesis that choosers maximize expected utility. The theory of expected utility maximization, sometimes called Bernoullian decision theory, was proposed by Ramsey (1931), by von Neumann and Morgenstern (1944 and 1953) and by Savage (1954). The theory allows for choice of uncertain prospects and is unboundedly rational in the sense that it ignores optimizing (calculation) costs and assumes that choice is in complete consistency with three axioms. These axioms govern the ordering, continuity and independence of alternatives. The ordering axiom supposes that choosers have a transitive complete ordering of all their alternative choices. The continuity axiom assumes that if there are three alternatives (A, B, C) the individual is indifferent between B and some lottery involving only the chance of winning A or C as a prize. The independence axiom implies that the addition of a previously unavailable alternative should not alter an individual's preference ordering of the existing alternatives.[7]

If these simple axioms are satisfied, individuals' 'utility' curves can be theoretically constructed by observing their behaviour under suitable experimental conditions. The utility curve is not a measure of the individual's satisfaction but provides an index for consistent ranking of alternatives in accordance with observations and with the implications of the axioms mentioned above. Given the foundations of the theory and no change in the individual's basic preferences, rational individuals must maximize their expected utility in consistency with the utility curve which is computed from their past observed behaviour.

The expected utility or Bernoullian approach relies on revealed preference plus a few simple axioms. In most formulations, individuals are assumed to act on the basis of their personal or subjective probabilities.[8] These probabilities may, but need not, accord with logical probabilities or with objective probabilities. Writers such as Keynes (1921), Jeffreys (1948) and Carnap (1950) contend that in relation to any amount of knowledge, there are particular probabilities or degrees of belief which it is reasonable or rational to entertain and that these are independent of the individual and can be deduced by logical methods. The expected utility theory does not assume that the individual's personal probabilities coincide with these logical probabilities.[9]

Because of the possible divergence between personal and logical probabilities, expected utility maximization (on the basis of personal probabilities) need not pass Oppenheim's test of rationality. Choosers' personal probabilities (beliefs) may not be rational or reasonable on the basis of the information available to them. Nevertheless, individuals may act entirely in accordance with the Bernoullian theory and be rational in the very restricted sense of acting in complete (internal) consistency with their beliefs. *A fortiori*, expected utility maximizers need not be rational in the sense outlined by Alexander and by Mullane because of imperfections in their beliefs or shortcomings in their information. It is conceivable also that expected utility maximizers may be unaware of their reasons for acting in the way that they do and in that case their behaviour would not be rational in the view of the philosophers mentioned earlier.

It is interesting to observe that many adherents of the expected utility approach do assume that initial personal or subjective probabilities are revised in accordance with logical principles as further information comes to hand. As a rule, adherents assume that probabilities are revised in accordance with Bayes's Theorem, which states a logical or rational method for adjusting prior probabilities on the basis of additional information.[10]

Bounded Rationality: The Views of Simon

Simon (1957 and 1961, p. xxiv) criticizes all formulations of behaviour which assume that mankind is unboundedly rational. Theories of unbounded rationality, which may assume either perfect or imperfect information, are unrealistic in Simon's opinion. They are unrealistic because the capacity of individuals for processing, storing and recalling information and their calculating ability are limited. Humans, like a computer or a machine, have limited capacities for problem solving.

Simon calls theories which incorporate constraints on the information processing capacities of the actor, *theories of bounded rationality*.[11] Simon believes that theories of unbounded rationality are not of descriptive and practical relevance because, apart from any limitations imposed on decision making by the outside world, decision makers themselves have limited ability to choose. Chess can be taken as an example of this. In a game of chess each player has a large number of strategies and the possible games of chess could be of the order of 10^{120}. But players do not as a rule think their games right through but at most explore a limited number of moves given the stage of the game. They act on the basis of incomplete information, because they do not have the time and the capacity to consider all possible alternatives. Players may be rational in the sense that they explore some alternatives and draw logical or reasoned conclusions from these which become the basis of their action. Nevertheless, the aim of such action or choice is not to maximize or to optimize an objective function but to obtain satisfactory results.

Simon stresses that individuals act and search on the basis of aspiration levels which are revised in the light of their success or failure in meeting these, but that humans do not search for a very best strategy. As soon as individuals discover a course of action which meets their aspiration level at the time, they choose this course and consider it to be satisfactory. However, they may revise their aspiration levels with the passage of time and alter their behaviour accordingly.

The satisficing type of behaviour described by Simon is like that predicted by some theories of optimizing behaviour which take into account the costs of search and the value of new information, as, for instance, in some theories of search by sequential sampling. Simon agrees, but still rejects these optimizing theories as an adequate explanation of behaviour. He says:

> A satisficing decision procedure can often be turned into a procedure for optimizing by introducing a rule for optimal amount of search, or, what amounts to the same thing, a rule for fixing the aspiration level optimally. . . . Although such a translation is formally possible, to carry it out in practice requires additional information and assumptions beyond those needed for satisficing. (Simon, 1972, p. 170)

In Simon's opinion the additional information is unavailable and the additional assumptions are typically not satisfied in practice. While Simon appears to be correct in stressing barriers to optimization, optimizing models may nevertheless be able to predict actual behaviour, approximately.

Baumol and Quandt (1964) and others have shown that a number of business conventions, rules of thumb and habits result in optimal choices on average relative to the limited information which is available to businessmen. Under some conditions, the procedure of adding a common percentage mark-up to costs to determine the selling price of a product is approximately optimal since the additional costs of more refined methods exceed their additional gross benefit. Nevertheless, some of those engaging in mark-up pricing may not be aware that it is an approximately optimal procedure in a world in which calculation and search have a cost. Their choice may not be based upon a rational or deliberative decision.

However, Julius Margolis (1958) claims that businesspeople do decide as a result of deliberation to adopt various conventions and rules of thumb. He says, 'The managers rather than being omniscient at one extreme, are deliberating leaders of a firm who adopt procedures and rules because of the lack of information necessary to be fully "rational"'(1958, p. 189). While Margolis believes that business conventions and rules have rational origin, they are designed in his opinion to ensure satisfactory results rather than to yield optimal results.

Attack of Shackle on Rationality and Equilibrium Theory in Economics

Shackle's attack (1972) on the use of the rationality assumption by economists is one of the most uncompromising. In his view, equilibrium economics is only viable if all economic agents are rational decision makers. But economic agents cannot be rational unless they have perfect knowledge of their decision-making environment. According to Shackle, actors' decision can only be rational if it results in the absolutely best possible outcome for them. If after the event, say because more information is available, it becomes clear that there was a better decision than the one taken by a decision maker, the decision maker is not rational in Shackle's sense. The possibility of rational behaviour relative to limited information is dismissed by Shackle, and in his view rationality is incompatible with unpredictable changes which in practice occur with the passage of time. However, Shackle's conception of rationality is rather special. It leads one to ask the type of question which Geoffrey Newman (1974) asks in his review of Shackle: is it reasonable to fuse rationality and perfect knowledge? If one answers in the affirmative then it may be true as Newman suggests that all we are left with is a romantic view of behaviour.

NOTES

1. This view is ascribed to Popper by Koertge (1974) where other philosophical views of rational action are also discussed.
2. See, for example, Hicks (1956).
3. Georgescu-Roegen (1966, p. 15) describes this view as Neo-Machian; it sees prediction as being the main purpose of science and is subscribed to by economists such as Frank Knight and Milton Friedman. Georgescu-Roegen in contrast sees the purpose of science as being able to promote understanding and Shackle (1972) considers theory to be important in affording 'a good state of mind' to men. Prediction is incidental.
4. For a more detailed discussion of the following proposition see Tisdell (1976).
5. See, for example, Alchian (1950).
6. See Hicks (1946, p. 132).
7. For a discussion of the axioms and other aspects of the theory see, for example, Alchian (1953).
8. Once an individual's utility curve is established, then, given the assumptions of this approach, an individual's personal (consistent) probabilities can be inferred from his or her behaviour.
9. For a general discussion of concepts of probability and rationality, see, for example, Tisdell (1968, Chapter 2).
10. See, for instance, Savage (1954).
11. Simon's view is clearly presented in Simon (1972).

REFERENCES

Alchian, A.A. (1950), 'Uncertainty, Evolution and Economic Theory', *Journal of Political Economy*, 58, 211–21.

Alchian, A.A. (1953), 'The Meaning of Utility Measurement', *American Economic Review*, 43, 26–50.

Alexander, P. (1962), 'Rational Behaviour and Psychoanalytic Explanation', *Mind*, 71, 326–41.

Baumol, W.J. and Quandt, R.E. (1964), 'Rules of Thumb and Optimally Imperfect Decisions', *American Economic Review*, 54, 23–46.

Carnap, R. (1950), *Logical Foundations of Probability*, Chicago: University of Chicago Press.

Georgescu-Roegen, N. (1966), *Analytical Economics: Issues and Problems*, Cambridge, Mass.: Harvard University Press.

Hicks, J.R. (1946), *Value and Capital*, 2nd edn, Oxford: Oxford University Press.

Hicks, J.R. (1956), *A Revision of Demand Theory*, Oxford: Oxford University Press.

Jeffreys, H. (1948), *Theory of Probability*, 2nd edn, Oxford: Clarendon Press.

Keynes, J.M. (1921), *A Treatise on Probability*, London: Macmillan.

Koertge, N. (1974), 'Bartley's Theory of Rationality', *Philosophy of the Social Sciences*, 4, 75–81.

Kornai, J. (1971), *Anti-Equilibrium: On Economic Systems Theory and the Task of Research*, Amsterdam: North-Holland.

Leslie, D. (1993), *Advanced Macroeconomics*, London: McGraw-Hill.

Lucas, R.E. (1987), *Models of Business Cycles*, London: Blackwell.

Machlup, F. (1969), 'The Universal Bogey', in Streissler, Erich *et al.* (eds), *Roads to Freedom: Essays in Honour of Friedrich A. von Hayek*, London: Routledge & Kegan Paul.

Margolis, J. (1958), 'The Analysis of the Firm: Rationalism, Conventionalism, and Behaviourism', *Journal of Business*, 31, 187–99.

Mullane, H. (1971), 'Psychoanalytic Explanation and Rationality', *Journal of Philosophy*, 68(14), 413–23.

Newman, G. (1974), Review of 'Epistemics and Economics: A Critique of Economic Doctrines', *Philosophy of the Social Sciences*, 4, 409–17.

Oppenheim, F.E. (1953), 'Rational Choice', *Journal of Philosophy*, 50(12), 341–50.

Ramsey, F.P. (1931), 'Truth and Probability', essay VII in Braithwaite, R. (ed.), The *Foundations of Mathematics and Other Logical Essays*, London: Routledge & Kegan Paul.

Sachs, J.D. and B. Larrain, F. (1993), *Macroeconomics in the Global Economy*, Englewood Cliffs, New Jersey: Prentice Hall.

Sargent, T.J. (1986), *Rational Expectations and Inflation*, New York: Harper & Row.

Savage, L.J. (1954), *The Foundations of Statistics*, New York: Wiley.

Shackle, G.L.S. (1972), *Epistemics and Economics: A Critique of Economic Doctrines*, Cambridge: Cambridge University Press.

Simon, H.A. (1957), *Models of Man*, New York: Wiley.

Simon, H.A. (1961), *Administrative Behaviour*, 2nd edn, New York: The Macmillan Company.

Simon, H.A. (1972), 'Theories of Bounded Rationality', in McGuire, C.B. and Radner, R. (eds), *Decision and Organization*, Amsterdam: North-Holland.

Tisdell, C. (1968), *The Theory of Price Uncertainty, Production and Profit*, Princeton: Princeton University Press.

Tisdell, C. (1976), 'Rational Behaviour as a Basis for Economic Theories', in Benn, S.I. and Mortimore, G.W. (eds), *Rationality and the Social Sciences*, London: Routledge.

von Neumann, J. and Morgenstern, O. (1944, 1953), *Theory of Games and Economic Behaviour*, 1st, 3rd edns, Princeton: Princeton University Press.

3. Further Views on the Role and Concept of Rationality in Economics

INTRODUCTION

Economists have as a rule closely associated rational choice with the attainment of equilibrium in behaviour and with optimization. I have suggested in the previous chapter that equilibrium may be achieved without choice being rational and that rational choice is possible under conditions of limited information. Yet one's knowledge may be so limited in some circumstances that there is no sensible way of determining one's optimal choice. One may be able to eliminate some choices as irrational, but there may be no rational basis for choosing between a remaining range of alternatives.[1]

In 1945, Oscar Lange, in considering the scope and method of economics, stated that the postulate of rationality (1945, p. 30)

> provides us with a most powerful tool for simplification of theoretical analysis. For, if a unit of decision acts rationally, its decisions in any given situation can be predicted by mere application of the rules of logic (and of mathematics). In absence of rational action such prediction could be made only after painstaking empirical study of the uniformities in the decision patterns of the unit.

However, Lange overestimated the value of rational behaviour as a basis for economic theorizing. More than logic and mathematics are involved in the prediction of rational behaviour. First, one needs to know the nature of that which is to be maximized. This might only be discovered after painstaking empirical study and even then success is not guaranteed; for example, actors might disguise their motives or not be exactly aware of them. Second, in order to predict the rational behaviour of individuals, knowledge of their feasible region of choice is required. Logic and mathematics alone do not inform us of this region. Third, unless the relevant objective functions show some permanency, at least in their basic properties, the theory of rational behaviour is likely to be of little predictive value. Economists claim that the objective functions of economic man do have certain permanent properties; for example, it is sometimes claimed that firms maximize profit consistently, and that the preference functions of consumers are always strictly concave. Given the permanent nature of economic agents' objective functions and their region of feasible behaviour, the postulate of practical rationality has considerable predictive power, provided the economic agents are well-informed about their possibilities, and the theorist about the agent's perceptions.

It is sometimes assumed, as in neoclassical economic theory, that economic agents are so knowledgeable that they can select a set of actions (a strategy) which cannot be bettered from their point of view. They are able to act with unbounded rationality in the restrictive sense that they know their optimal option X and choose X because they know it to be optimal.

The concept of 'as if' rationality should be distinguished from the concept of unbounded rationality. The 'as if' concept is used in some economic theories. Provided individuals consistently act as if they are pursuing an objective to maximum advantage, they are rational in the 'as if' sense and their behaviour can be predicted. Individuals may be acting rationally in the 'as if' sense in choosing the optimal option even when they do not choose it because they know it to be optimal.

The hypothesis of unbounded rationality has been attacked by Simon and others as inapplicable to economic life. In my view, it is more relevant than is commonly realized. Unbounded rational behaviour is possible under conditions of limited knowledge both of preferences and of the external world. In some circumstances where unbounded rationality cannot be attained immediately, it may be approached by search and attained in time. It may also be characteristic of groups on average or be ensured by selection processes.

Nevertheless, there are clearly circumstances in which unbounded rational behaviour is impossible, now or in the long term; I shall mention some of these circumstances. In the next section I consider possibilities for unbounded rational economic behaviour, on the assumption that the interdependence of individuals in groups is unimportant. Even with this assumption, rationality postulates cannot always predict behaviour. I then relax the unbounded rationality assumption.

RATIONAL BEHAVIOUR BY INDIVIDUAL ECONOMIC AGENTS IF SOCIAL BEHAVIOUR IS UNIMPORTANT – UNBOUNDED RATIONALITY

Theories of the economic behaviour of individuals are normally based on three elements:

1. individuals' preference ordering of their possible outcomes;
2. what they believe or know to be the available set of alternative strategies;
3. a specified relationship between the agent's chosen strategy on the one hand and (1) and (2) on the other.

Whether an individual acts rationally in choosing a strategy will clearly be a function of (1) and (2), which we may call the antecedent conditions. Thus, if individuals do not know the exact relationship between their outcomes and their choice of strategy, they may be unable to choose their best strategy. Ignorance may restrict the ability of individuals to optimize.

However, neoclassical economic theory, which is a major body of current economic theory, specifies a set of antecedent conditions which make unbounded rationality possible. In this state individuals can identify their *optimum optimorum* and choose a correspondingly appropriate strategy. These conditions are:

1. individuals have a complete weak preference ordering[2] of their possible outcomes which is transitive, irreflexive and reflects the true preference of the individual;
2. individuals know of all of their available strategies and relate the outcomes exactly and correctly to their strategies.

Given the further assumption that the process of deciding is itself costless, a rational individual under these conditions will select the optimum strategy from the available set.

The conditions are rarely satisfied, however. When they are not, we are faced with the following questions:

1. To what extent is it rational for economic agents to attempt to satisfy the stated antecedent conditions and put their choice problem into the above form?
2. Is it possible for an individual to choose the strategy that would be optimal under those conditions and to be sure that it is optimal?

Simon stresses[3] that it is not as a rule rational to put one's choice problem in the above form because information gathering and processing involves a cost. So, too, does calculation. Since goal-seeking behaviour involves search and calculation, goal seekers seek a satisfactory outcome rather than an optimal one.

> While economic man maximizes – selects the best alternative from all those available to him; his cousin, whom we shall call administrative man, satisfices – looks for a course of action that is satisfactory or 'good enough'. Examples of satisficing criteria that are familiar enough to businessmen, if unfamiliar to most economists are 'share of market', 'adequate profit', 'fair price'. (Simon, 1961, p. xxv)

Unlike economic man, administrative man uses very crude and undetailed pictures of the world and rules of thumb to reach decisions. They have limited capacities for storing and processing information. Even if decision makers could be given complete knowledge of the relationship between their strategies and outcomes, it might be beyond their ability to store, use and grasp this knowledge. Nor would they have the capacity (as a rule) to order all of their possible strategies completely and transitively.

DISCUSSION OF THE ANTECEDENT CONDITIONS FOR UNBOUNDED RATIONALITY

It is, I think, necessary to concede all of Simon's points. Yet, they do not render neoclassical economic theories irrelevant; for the neoclassical antecedent conditions outlined above are really much stronger than would be required to ensure unbounded rational behaviour.

Individuals may not order their outcomes completely or transitively and may not perceive their outcomes and strategies completely and correctly, and yet their adopted strategy may be the best possible one. They may know from the properties of the objective function and the feasible set, that it is unnecessary to consider all possibilities in order to select an optimal strategy. Yet, they act none the less with unbounded rationality, since they are able to decide on an optimal strategy even though they cannot satisfy all the neoclassical antecedent conditions.

To illustrate some of the possibilities, consider a consumer first. Assume that individuals can always be made better off by a vectorial increase[4] in the quantity of two goods. Let us suppose that a given amount has been budgeted to spend on these two goods and that the problem is to select the most preferred attainable combination. The alternative combinations of the goods (one and two) which the consumer can buy in the budget period might be represented by points on and in ∆*OLM* in Figure 3.1.

Figure 3.1   *The preference ordering assumptions of neoclassical economic theory are stronger than necessary for unbounded rational behaviour by consumers*

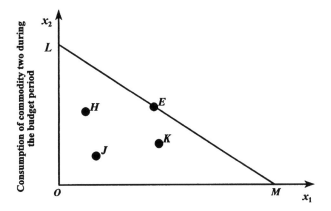

Consumption of commodity one during the budget period

But given their preference ordering of the consumption possibilities and assuming that non-expenditure yields no satisfaction, the optimal attainable outcome for the consumers falls along the closed interval *LM*. Given the general ordering properties, the individual's preference ordering of bundles below and above *LM* is irrelevant. Intransitive orderings in these areas are of no consequence provided they are not inconsistent with the proposition that the most preferred attainable combination is on *LM*. For example, imagine that the consumer ranks *H*, *J* and *K* as follows: *H > J > K*; and *H* and *K* as *H < K*. The second ordering conflicts with the first. But if *E* is ranked higher than *H*, *J* and *K*, this intransitivity is irrelevant since *E* is attainable. Nor is it necessary to order the possibilities below and above *LM* completely. The ordering assumptions (or transitivity and completeness) of the neoclassical theory are stronger than is required to ensure the unbounded rational behaviour which is predicted.

Even along the interval *LM*, it may be unnecessary to order possibilities completely and transitively. The preference ordering of combinations along the budget line *LM* might have a single peak and be strictly unimodal.[5] If the consumer knows this much, complete and consistent evaluation of the possibilities is unnecessary for optimizing behaviour.

Perfect knowledge of the feasible set of strategies or outcomes is also unnecessary for unbounded rational behaviour. If consumers' indifference curves are tilted relative to the budget line, it can be the case that their optimal consumption bundle is the one at *L*. Figure 3.2 indicates a case in which individuals' highest attainable indifference curve I_1 is reached if all of their budgeted expenditure is allocated to commodity two. None of commodity one is consumed. The slope of *LM* shows the rate at which the goods can be exchanged in the market. However, the individual need not know this exact rate in order to choose *L*. The choice of *L* is optimal provided that the absolute slope of the budget line is greater than the absolute slope of the consumer's indifference curve at *L*. Armed only with the information that the exchange rate yields a budget line steeper than the indifference curve at L (that is, without knowing the exact exchange rate), the consumer will be able to make a choice, satisfying the conditions for unbounded rationality, namely, that it is optimal, is known to be so by the agent, and is chosen for that reason.

Figure 3.2   *Perfect knowledge of prices is not required to ensure that a consumer acts with unbounded rationality*

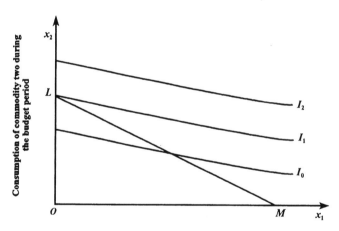

Consumption of commodity one during the budget period

I do not know the exact price of some commodities though I do know the range in which their prices fall. My lack of knowledge about the exact prices of different types of bicycles and of luxury cars need not, given my income (and that I have a preference for comfortable transport), prevent me from acting rationally in my choice of a means of transport. Moreover, intransitivities and incompleteness in my ordering of bicycles and luxury cars may be inconsequential for my choice. In all these cases my choice can be unboundedly rational even though the strong antecedent conditions are not satisfied. But even more significantly, I can know in advance circumstances where these conditions are not satisfied and yet my (rational) choice will be the same as if they happened to be satisfied.

Consider another example. Given the strict unimodality of its profit function, a firm need not know the profitability of all possible levels of output in order to act with unbounded rationality; it need know only about those in the neighbourhood of the output which yields a true maximum. Once an output is discovered such that profit is reduced by any and every set of small deviations from it, this output maximizes profit, and there is no need to evaluate profitability beyond its neighbourhood. However, while this indicates that the strong antecedent conditions specified are not required for unbounded rational behaviour, the problem remains that in most instances the neighbourhood has still to be discovered.

It is apparent, then, that the conditions for preference orderings and states of knowledge postulated by neoclassical theorists are stronger than are necessary for unbounded rational behaviour. The degree to which they can be relaxed has not been fully explored by economists.

CASES WHERE IMMEDIATE UNBOUNDED RATIONAL CHOICE IS IMPOSSIBLE BECAUSE OF INCOMPLETE KNOWLEDGE

None of the above speculation shows that unbounded optimizing behaviour is the rule. In many instances, prior knowledge is insufficient to enable the optimum to be found. It may be possible to improve this knowledge by search and computation but the cost involved in this effort is likely to make the pursuit of unbounded rationality self-defeating.

It is of interest to distinguish three choice situations:

1. where individuals engage in further information gathering and processing before making a choice;
2. where they act on the basis of available information;
3. where they act on the basis of available information, but their choice, besides giving them a direct payoff, yields information which has application to future choices.

The last case may be the most common one. Let us consider each of those cases in turn.

1. *Further activity prior to choice*   Simon concentrates on the case in which individuals can obtain further information prior to their choice of an action. He is dubious of all models of optimizing behaviour, including models based on expected gain and expected utility maximization (1961, p. xxiii).

> Economic man has a complete and consistent system of preferences that allows him always to choose among the alternatives open to him: he is always completely aware of what these alternatives are: there are no limits on the complexity of the computations he can perform in order to determine which alternatives are best; probability calculations are neither frightening nor mysterious to him. Within the past decade, in its extension to competitive game situations and to decision making under uncertainty, this body of theory has reached a state of Thomistic refinement that possesses considerable normative interest, but little discernible relation to the actual or possible behaviour of flesh and blood human beings.

Since optimizing behaviour involves costly search, and payoffs are uncertain, typical individuals do not hold out for maximum rewards but are prepared to settle for a satisfactory reward; they set themselves an aspiration level. Once this level is reached, there is no further search even though the best discovered strategy may well be short of the optimal one. If after a certain amount of search no strategy is discovered which attains it, the aspiration level may be revised downwards or alternatively search effort may increase (Simon, 1961, p. xxii). Beyond this, details are not given.

Yet the type of behaviour which Simon describes is also predicted by some types of optimization theories. If the objective of the individual is maximization of expected net gain or utility and if search is required which involves cost and only probably discoveries, to maximize this value requires a stopping rule, for example, the rule 'if one is selling a used article, as soon as an offer better than $2 is found, accept'. It is usually rational to revise this stopping value as search continues and uncertainty is reduced.   Whether or not individuals know complicated sequential optimizing procedures is beside the point.   Such procedures can approximate and predict their behaviour in the 'as if' rationality sense previously mentioned. If there is permanency in the relationships, the 'as if' rationality concept can be of predictive value even if the behaviour does not fit the restrictive concept of unbounded rationality. However, in stating this I do not rule out the possibility that some search behaviour may exhibit such rationality.

A number of economists have developed models of unbounded rationality in information search and in the decision to cease searching and decide between the options. Thus, Baumol and Quandt (1964) mention a rule for optimally imperfect decisions: 'the appropriate (though not very helpful) marginal condition for what one may call an *optimally imperfect decision* . . . [is] that the marginal cost of additional information gathering or more refined calculation be equal to its marginal (expected) gross yield'. Since there is likely to be uncertainty about the expected values, however, the residual uncertainty would result in a random element in behaviour, that is, random in relation to the objective world. While knowledge puts some limits on it, some randomness remains since it is not profitable (on average) to distinguish finely between the consequences of the available strategies.

2.   *No further information prior to choice and no additional information of future value* Much economic decision making is, of course, based on decision rules – for example, cost plus pricing – which obviate any activities of information search and processing. Such decision making may appear irrational unless the cost of decision making is taken into account. Baumol and Quandt have shown how various rules of thumb when used by management do in fact maximize expected profit. The expected net gains from more refined procedures do not justify their additional cost. Under certain conditions cost plus pricing is optimal even though the decision procedure for each choice separately does not satisfy the antecedent conditions for unbounded rationality required by the neoclassical model. If demand is fluctuating the cost of specifying it closely in any period may exceed the gains from an improved pricing policy. Baumol and Quandt (1964) argue that 'rules of thumb are among the more efficient pieces of equipment of optimal decision making'.

In other choice situations, agents may be interested in assessing the relationships between their options (alternative prices, say) and their end (maximum profits), may have engaged in some information search, but must now decide on the basis of information which does not allow them to identify the optimum optimorum. In such a case, the information may nevertheless be sufficient to rule out some strategies on the grounds that choice of any of them is irrational. Even if individuals' appreciation of the possibilities does not lead to the optimum choice, it may be possible to specify certain conditions that their behaviour would satisfy, if rational.

Take the case of a purely competitive firm which prefers greater profit to less and so wishes to maximize its profit. Its profit can be expressed as

$$\pi = px - (C(x))$$
Profit = Total Revenue − Total Cost

where p represents the price per unit for its product and x the quantity of output of its product during the relevant period. The output for the period must be determined by the firm before the price for the product is known. Output is the controlled variable of the firm and price is uncontrolled. At the time when x must be determined the exact price of its product is unknown by the firm but the total cost function is known. However, imagine that the firm is able to give a lower and an upper limit for the possible price of its product. Letting p_o and p_m represent respectively these limits for price, the firm believes that p must fall in the range $p_o \le p \le p_m$. Then if its marginal cost can be represented by the curve MC in Figure 3.3, it is irrational for the firm to produce an output outside the range $x_1 \le x \le x_m$. Given the prior limit on p, profit is certain to be greater by producing an output in this range, than by producing any output outside of it. Profit for x_m is certain to be greater than for $x > x_m$ and profit for x_1 is certain to be greater than for $x < x_1$. The smaller the band of values of prices believed to be possible, the more closely does the band of possible rational action accord with neoclassical unbounded action provided that the actual p is included in the predicted range. If the band tends to shift in the same direction as p, many of the neoclassical predictions about variations of supply are approximated. However, as cobweb theories of markets[6] indicate, the band of predictions does not always vary in the direction of the actual price.

Figure 3.3   Even under conditions of uncertainty a set of choices can be excluded as being irrational

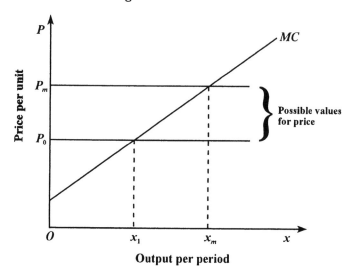

In order to predict market changes, economic theories require data on how economic agents form their predictions. A number of dynamic market theories, for example, cobweb models, incorporate rather mechanistic theories about this, for example, that firms predict that the price of the next period is the same as the last and act accordingly, or that it is a weighted average of the prices of the last *n* periods and so on. In an economic world of perpetual disequilibrium, models of this type seem more relevant than neoclassical general equilibrium models.

3. *No further information prior to choice but additional information of future value* Possibly the most common economic situation is one in which the individual must make an immediate choice on the basis of information too limited to satisfy the requirements of unbounded rationality, but in which the choice not only yields an immediate payoff to the agent but also additional information which may be of future value in decision making.

Consider the case of a firm which wishes to maximize its profit. The firm is assumed to know that its profit function is strictly unimodal[7] and stationary in time. Suppose that the firm can improve its knowledge of the profit function only by trial and error in production, that is, by trying different levels of production and observing their effect on profit. It cannot, for example, purchase information or conduct market surveys and so on which might yield greater information. In each period, the firm produces and sells a particular quantity of output and observes its profit. In the light of these observations it is able to adjust its output in future periods. Assuming that the firm always desires increased profit, some adjustments of output are irrational. This can be illustrated from Figures 3.4 and 3.5. The firm's profit and output per period are indicated in these figures. The height of the bars in the figures indicate the observed profit at the corresponding outputs.

Consider the case of Figure 3.4. The firm first produces the output corresponding to point 1 and then the output corresponding to point 2, and observes that profit is the same in both instances. To produce an output subsequently in the banded interval, that is at 1 or to its left and at 2 or to its right, would be irrational, since greater profit must be achieved by producing an output between 1 and 2. As the search proceeds, the area of possible rational behaviour is liable to become smaller and smaller.

This is indicated in the example of Figure 3.5. On the basis of the first trial (the output corresponding to 1) no levels of output can be ruled out as being worthy of a trial. If 2 is subsequently tried, levels of output at and to the left of 1 can be ruled out as optimal (but no others). However, if the level of output corresponding to 3 is then tried, levels of output at or above 2 can be ruled out as suboptimal. Thus the area of rational search is reduced to the levels of output between 1 and 2.[8]

Figure 3.4   Search narrows the range of rational behaviour

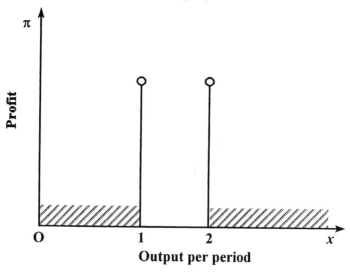

*Figure 3.5   Another example of search reducing the range of rational
behaviour*

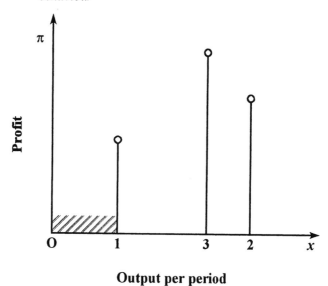

If a decision maker's objective function satisfies appropriate general mathematical properties, then, under stationary conditions, use of a number of search and response procedures ensures that behaviour tends to the unbounded optimum.[9] In circumstances like this, unbounded rational behaviour is approached as the number of trials is increased provided that the function which is to be maximized remains stationary. In general, the convexity properties of neoclassical economic models are such that in a stationary world convergence to unbounded rational behaviour is assured by the use of sensible trial and error procedures.[10]

The above analysis indicates that search or experimentation in some particular directions would be irrational under these conditions. However, we may also ask ourselves whether search or experiment would be rational at all. If an agent is unwilling to take the chance that profit on a new trial is lower than the highest profit already known to be attainable, search is irrational even if it is not irrationally directed. On the other hand, search or experimentation in a direction which is not irrational holds out the chance of greater profit not only in the trial period but in the future as well. Nevertheless, as in the above case, it may be impossible to assign a probability to the chance of finding a more profitable strategy and to estimate the magnitude of increased profitability which is involved. Within certain bounds, faith rather than rationality becomes the spring of human action.

Using the prior information about the nature of the profit function, the area of rational search can be narrowed as search takes place. Different sets of prior information enable the rational search area to be reduced in different ways.

For several circumstances in which the general nature of the objective function is known, mathematicians have suggested effective methods of search. These include Fibonacci search, search by the golden section and various gradient methods.[11] In some problems, a number of these methods can be applied and each has different properties and uncertainty characteristics. None is irrational but neither does one method dominate the others in all characteristics which the decision maker might feel to be important. It might be difficult or impossible to decide rationally which method should be used. Taking into account the extra costs of thinking about this and the very improbable gains, it might not be irrational to choose a search method by chance or faith once the field of possible rational methods has been narrowed down.

RATIONALITY AND EQUILIBRIUM AGAIN

In neoclassical economic models, unbounded rational behaviour occurs only if the equilibrium conditions of the models are satisfied. Equilibrium and unbounded rationality are inseparable in this context. Hicks (1946, p. 132) makes this quite clear: 'The degree of disequilibrium marks the extent to which expectations are cheated, and plans go astray'. When the economy is in perfect equilibrium, the expectations of economic agents are fully realized and their plans are ideal; for then no one is inclined to upset the balance, since no one believes they could improve their position by a change of policy. If equilibrium is the rule, unbounded rationality is the rule. To attack the value of the concept of unbounded rationality is to attack the value of neoclassical equilibrium analysis. We live, however, in a world of disequilibrium and constant change. Conditions do not remain stationary enough to permit any substantial movements to equilibrium or unbounded rationality and important economic decisions must be made in those circumstances. By studying only equilibrium conditions and changes of equilibria (the approach of comparative statics) we can fail to make useful economic predictions and policy decisions.

However, one can see a number of ways in which the neoclassical position can be defended. Comparative statics is of greatest value for policy and analytical purposes when the convergence to an equilibrium is extremely rapid. A neoclassical economist might hold that convergence to unbounded rational behaviour is extremely rapid because on average economic agents are well supplied with prior information. Though the world is not stationary it changes at a rate which enables unbounded rationality to be approached.

Nevertheless, a number of economists have speculated that randomness of decision making is increasing in communities where wealth is increasing. Rational decision making requires deliberation and other actions which take time. Time is a scarce resource. Linder (1970), building on an earlier suggestion of Harrod, suggests that time for decision making is become comparatively more costly in terms of the alternatives forgone. As a result of economic progress, the value of time for consumption activities has increased and with increasing wealth the marginal disutility of a given error decreases. Hence, decisions are given less time and made on the basis of reduced evidence. In consequence, the consumer more often engages in impulse buying, and is more subject to influences by advertising, persuasion and so on. The neoclassical model of unbounded rationality becomes increasingly inapplicable to consumers. Even if the time devoted to decision making does not fall with economic progress, but even rises slightly, increases in the range of strategies, possibilities and outcomes as a result of technical progress may result in a relative decrease of knowledge by individuals (even if their absolute knowledge increases) so that the randomness of their behaviour increases. Increases in the shortage of time have many interesting social consequences, some of which are mentioned by Linder.

INCOMPLETE PREFERENCE ORDERINGS

Although incompleteness in an individual's preference ordering need not rule out the possibility of immediate unbounded rationality and although where it does, unbounded rationality may eventually be achieved by search, there are circumstances in which incomplete preferences make unbounded rationality impossible.   Neoclassical economists did not consider the possibility of incompleteness in preference orderings. Yet there are clearly circumstances in which rational individuals need to search and explore because of gaps in their preference orderings.   I do not know my preference for whale and seal meat, not having tested either, and there are some very fundamental matters (concerned with alternative organizations of society) about which I cannot decide my preference and so on. I cannot accept Wicksteed's (1933, pp. 122–3) view:

> Any alternatives, however constituted, which could conceivably be offered to the man would find him either decisively preferring one to the other or unable to decide between them; that is to say, every conceivable alternative stands either above or below any other that you may select, or on a level with it. And the things so valued constitute the man's relative scale of preferences, the basis upon which his life is built. This scale of preferences is the register of the man's ideals, of the relative weight and value that he attaches to this or that alternative under every variety of condition.

If A and B are two attainable alternatives, it is conceivable that individuals do not know their preference ordering of A and B. They may, however, try A and then B or vice versa and develop an ordering on the basis of this experience. But is it not conceivable in some circumstances that their final ordering depends upon the sequence in which A and B are tried? Trying A first, then B, individuals might conclude that they prefer B to A; had the sequence been B then A, they might have preferred A to B.   Thus, they reach contradictory conclusions depending upon the sequence of the trials. Individuals are mistaken in cases like this if they believe that experience will enable them to decide what they really prefer, since what they prefer will depend on the order of trial.

Choices of alternative occupations, choice of exposure to cultural experiences, choice of a partner and choice of different forms of social organization run foul of the above possibility. One reason why this is so is that individuals are changed by their experiences; their values, aspirations and expectations are altered by their experiences and observations.[12] Attempts by individuals to map out their preferences exactly may lead to their deflection. The problem is analogous to the problem of deflection of particles by observation which is discussed in quantum mechanics. Clearly, deflection is not significant in all types of search but it seems highly probable that this phenomenon is important in areas where our feelings are most strongly influenced, for example, feelings bordering on the spiritual. A searcher can conceivably be deceived into believing that search is efficacious in discovering the optimal strategy even though it is the search itself that generates the preferences by which the strategy is judged best.

AGGREGATIVE AND SELECTIVE THEORIES

Rational behaviour is sometimes claimed by economists, as mentioned earlier, to be characteristic of individuals in aggregate but not of any particular individual. It is an 'average' concept. For example, Hicks says that the theory of demand does study human beings but only as entities having certain patterns of market behaviour (1956, p. 6), and postulates an ideal consumer who acts according to a scale of preferences and 'chooses that alternative, out of the various alternatives open to him which he most prefers, or ranks most highly' (1956, p. 18). This preference hypothesis is basic to the traditional economic theory of demand.

Hicks (1956, p. 55) claims that:

> the preference hypothesis only acquires a *prima facie* plausibility when it is applied to a statistical average. To assume that the representative consumer acts like an ideal consumer is a hypothesis worth testing: to assume that an actual person, the Mr Brown or Mr Jones who lives round the corner, does in fact act in such a way does not deserve a moment's consideration.

However, the predictions of theories based on the average may be markedly wrong if there are considerable deviations around average behaviour in a group. It is also conceivable that all or most members of a group may be so ill-informed that the preference hypothesis is not typically satisfied.

Again, it is sometimes said that forces of selection ensure that the more rational decision makers in society obtain expanded roles at the expense of the irrational. Thus economic decisions, especially on the production side, tend to be made by rational individuals, but rational in the very limited sense of maximizing on the basis of defined objectives. Alchian (1950), for example, suggests that only firms and managers that maximize profit are likely to survive in the long run and he therefore expects the bulk of managers and firms to be profit maximizers. But this supposes intense competition. If competition is not intense, management may pursue other goals such as maximizing sales subject to a satisfactory level of profit and do so in an optimal way. It may still be acting rationally in the sense that it selects the best strategy for its scale of preferences. However, it is not under external (competitive) pressure to optimize and may in fact fail to do so; thus, for example, so-called managerial slack or inefficiency may creep into the administration of the firm. On the consumption side of the economy, the concept of rationality by selection is less relevant; even here, however, more irrational individuals may tend to obtain lower incomes and so have a smaller impact on aggregate consumption.

Nevertheless, as pointed out in Chapter 14, selection does not necessarily ensure the survival of the fittest, efficient or of optimizers. Furthermore, survival may depend to some extent upon a suitable degree of group diversity and symbiosis rather than on individual optimizing efforts. Indeed, it can be irrational for a group as a whole for all members to try to engage in unbounded rational behaviour – it may, for example, be optimal for some to be followers and rely to a considerable extent on the search effort of others. It is also conceivable that in a few cases phenomena like the 'butterfly effect' discussed in chaos theory are present (Gleick, 1987) and as a result the fittest do not necessarily survive (Gould, 1987). Thus, one needs to be sceptical of the view that 'natural' selection will lead only to the survival of rational man and woman in the economy or place them in its top positions.

CONCLUDING COMMENTS

While the concept of unbounded rationality has more possibilities for application in an uncertain world than seems to be the case at first sight, it fails to capture the full range of economic decision-making problems which individuals face. It is, therefore, an insufficient basis for general economic theories because the cases it fails to cover are far from trivial and infrequent. The problems involved for economic theory and applied economics will become ever more apparent when group behaviour and social situations are discussed later in this book.

Given the rich variety of behaviour possible under conditions of bounded rationality (for example, because different individuals possess different degrees of knowledge, may adopt divergent search procedures or experience non-uniform costs of search) and the possibility of other types of behaviour of a less than rational sort, economic theories which insist on the use of 'representation' or 'average' economic agents impoverish economic theory and are limited in their practical applications. There is an increasing need to capture diversity of behaviour of individuals in economic theorizing. Such diversity, among other things, has implications for the evolution of economic systems and their institutions.

Furthermore, one needs to consider whether the traditional reductionist approach to economic theorizing always gives the best view of the economic world. Such an approach tends to overlook symbiotic and competitive relationships within and between groups which are not related to individuals *per se* but are dependent upon the overall structure of social relationships; they involve social externality or spillover phenomena. Such issues will be explored later in this book.

NOTES

1. For examples of this see Tisdell (1976), also Georgescu-Roegen (1966, p. 275).
2. A preference ordering is a weak one if in addition to allowing the possibility of decided preference it allows indifference. If preferences involve a complete weak ordering then all possible alternatives are ordered, and taking any two alternatives, one is either preferred to the other or the individual is indifferent about them. This rules out circumstances in which the individual does not know whether he or she prefers one alternative to another.
3. Simon (1957, 1961). Simon's view has much in common with those of Baumol and Quandt (1964).
4. A vectorial increase occurs if there is an increase in the quantity of at least one product and no fall in the quantity of the other.
5. A function which is strictly unimodal has a single peak and continually falls away from that peak.
6. So called because the price quantity observations trace out patterns on supply and demand curves which look like a cobweb. Cobweb patterns occur in the supply of agricultural produce. Farmers may react to a high price for their produce by overproducing. The overproduction depresses price and they may react by unduly reducing their output. Price then rises above equilibrium and the underproduction is followed by overproduction and so the process repeats itself with farmers being out in their predictions. Equilibrium may, but need not, be attained in the long run.
7. Profit is a single peaked function of output and falls away continually from its peak.
8. For further analysis of the way in which search results reduce the rational direction of further search see Wilde and Beightler (1967, Section 6.03).
9. Arrow and Hurwicz (1960), Wilde and Beightler (1967).
10. Arrow and Hurwicz (1960), pp. 49, 84.
11. See for example Box, Davies and Swann (1969), and Wilde and Beightler (1967).
12. If search takes time, and some types of search inevitably require a considerable amount of time, decision makers' preferences may alter independently of their experience, for example, due to the fact that they are maturing or growing older. Past information and experience might then only be of limited value as a guide to future rational choice and search need not culminate in unbounded rational behaviour.

REFERENCES

Alchian, A.A. (1950), 'Uncertainty, Evolution and Economic Theory', *Journal of Political Economy*, 58, 211–21.

Arrow, K.J. and Hurwicz, L. (1960), 'Decentralization and Computation in Resource Allocation', in Pfouts, R. (ed.), *Essays in Economics and Econometrics*, Chapel Hill: University of North Carolina, 34–104.

Baumol, W.J. and Quandt, R.E. (1964), 'Rules of Thumb and Optimally Imperfect Decisions', *American Economic Review*, 54, 23–46.

Box, M.J., Davies D. and Swann, W.H. (1969), *Non-Linear Optimization Techniques*, Edinburgh: Oliver & Boyd.

Georgescu-Roegen, N. (1966), *Analytical Economics: Issues and Problems*, Cambridge, Mass.: Harvard University Press.

Gleick, J. (1987), *Chaos*, New York: Viking.

Gould, J.G. (1987), *Wonderful Life: The Burgess Shale and the Nature of History*, New York: Norton.

Hicks, J.R. (1946), *Value and Capital*, 2nd edn, Oxford: Oxford University Press.

Hicks, J.R. (1956), *A Revision of Demand Theory*, Oxford: Oxford University Press.

Lange, O. (1945), 'The Scope and Method of Economics', *Review of Economic Studies*, 13, 19–32.

Linder, S.B. (1970), *The Harried Leisure Class*, New York: Columbia University Press.

Simon, H.A. (1957), *Models of Man*, New York: Wiley.

Simon, H.A. (1961), *Administrative Behaviour*, 2nd edn, New York: The Macmillan Company.

Tisdell, C. (1976), 'Rational Behaviour as a Basis for Economic Theories', in Benn, S.I. and Mortimore, G.W. (eds), *Rationality and the Social Sciences*, London: Routledge.

Wicksteed, P.H. (1933), *The Common Sense of Political Economy*, London: Routledge & Kegan Paul.

Wilde, D.J. and Beightler, C.S. (1967), *Foundations of Optimization*, Englewood Cliffs, New Jersey: Prentice Hall.

4. Rules Versus Discretion in Decision Making: Micro and Macro Applications

INTRODUCTION

Decision makers who would like to engage in perfectly unbounded rational behaviour are often prevented from doing so because of their lack of knowledge, and ultimately when a decision must be made face residual uncertainty. The question arises of whether they should then determine their controlled variables (for example, supply of a product in the case of a firm, government expenditure or money supply in the case of a government) on the basis of their 'best' estimates of what values the uncontrolled variables will assume. It seems that advocates of rational expectation theories, such as Muth (1961), believe that they should. I present a dissenting view to that incorporated in most rational expectation theories. Rational expectation theories are now well entrenched in macroeconomics (see, for example, Sargent, 1986; Lucas, 1987; Leslie, 1993). This chapter is designed to show that even when there is some positive correlation between predicted and actual values of the uncontrolled variable, it may not pay to fine tune the controlled variables to such predictions.

Although it is not the main purpose of this chapter to discredit theories of rational expectations as explanations of the behaviour of economic agents, I have serious reservations about such theories as predictors of human behaviour. Human behaviour is much more diverse. The theory, therefore, appears to be a special case. Furthermore, we cannot suppose that economic forces of selection (see the previous chapter and Chapter 14) involving evolutionary processes result in the survival only of those who act in accordance with the theory of rational expectations.

Both for macroeconomic and microeconomic policy decisions, the question of whether it is optimal to pursue a sensitive zigzag policy based upon one's changing forecasts or a steady course based on long-term forecasts is one of perennial importance. This chapter shows that even if policy makers have some (positive) ability to predict, it may nevertheless be optimal for them to follow an inflexible policy. Indeed, it shows that, ignoring the increased decision costs which 'fine tuning' policies may involve and the unfavourable secondary uncertainty effects which they may generate in a group,[1] deficiencies in the ability to predict may, even if there is (considerable) ability to predict, make flexible or zigzag policies undesirable. In doing so, it investigates the relative merits of alternative inflexible policies and compares them with randomized ones and others.

While the theoretical framework of the chapter is comparatively crude and while the argument is only developed for cases in which the objective function is quadratic after restrictions are taken into account, patterns emerge which are helpful from a prescriptive point of view and which also explain the rationality of actual behaviour which might otherwise appear to be irrational: for example, the decision maker who has predictive ability but does not adjust to his or her short-term predictions may well be acting rationally.

The analysis is first developed in abstract and then applied to microeconomic and macroeconomic decision problems. In the microeconomic section, the optimal type of policy is considered for both purely competitive and monopoly-type firms faced by demand uncertainty for their product, and it is shown that even though the firm has ability to predict changing price or demand conditions, nevertheless it may be optimal for it to produce an unvarying level of output. In the macroeconomic section, objective functions are introduced which depend upon inflation, employment and growth. Optimal policies are sought on the basis of three different types of models. The first type relies on the Phillips curve, the second is a simple Keynesian one and the final one is based on the quantity theory of money. For all the situations which are depicted, it turns out that inflexible policies or steady ones may be preferable to stop-go ones even if the policy maker has (positive) ability to predict.

THE SPECIAL STATUS OF INFLEXIBLE MANAGEMENT POLICIES: A GENERAL MODEL

In order to analyse abstractly the merits of adopting inflexible rather than zigzag policies, suppose that time is a discrete variable, that all relevant functions are stationary in time and that after restrictions are taken into account the objective function for any period *t* reduces to a function in an uncontrolled variable and a controlled variable only. Assume that for any period, t, the restricted objective function may be written as

$$V_t = V(p_t, x_t) \tag{4.1}$$

where p_t is the value of a non-controlled variable and x_t is the value of a controlled variable for t. However, the value of x_t is assumed to be rigidly determined prior to t and before p_t is known. Yet, it is assumed to be freely variable at the time when it is determined and to be determined by maximizing V_t on the basis of the predicted value of p_t, $\hat{p}_t$. Thus, in many cases, for example those in which the maximizing value of x_t is a linear function of $\hat{p}_t$, the objective function can be expressed as a function of the actual value of the non-controlled variable and its predicted value, namely, as

$$W_t = W(p_t, \hat{p}_t) \tag{4.2}$$

after maximizing behaviour is taken into account.

Since the decision maker is unlikely to be able to predict p_t exactly, it is necessary to have a decision rule which takes this into account. While a number of complicated decision rules are imaginable, the essence of the situation might be distilled by assuming that the planner has a fixed and finite planning horizon and prefers any policy which increases the sum of the W-values for the planning interval which stretches to this horizon.[2] For example, if the decision maker's planning interval is $1 \leq t \leq N$, then the decision maker prefers any strategy which

increases $\sum_{t=1}^{N} W_t$. This condition is satisfied by any strategy which

increases $\frac{1}{N}\sum_{t=1}^{N} W_t = E[W]$ where $E[W]$ represents the average per-period

value of W. While it is the *ex post* value of the sum of the W-values which the planner wishes to maximize, I shall assume that the *ex ante* values, which allow for prediction errors, do not materially differ from *ex post* values and this will simplify the exposition.[3]

While other types of objective functions might be explored, it is worthwhile to concentrate on a simple one which seems to have a number of economic applications[4] (Theil, 1961, pp. 412, 413). Imagine that after restrictions are taken into account, the objective function is of the following form which is quadratic in x:

$$\begin{aligned} V_t &= f(p_t) + \gamma_1 p_t x_t + \gamma_3 x_t - \gamma_2 x_t^2 \\ &= f(p_t) + (\gamma_1 p_t + \gamma_3) x_t - \gamma_2 x_t^2 \end{aligned} \tag{4.3}$$

where $\gamma_1 \lessgtr 0$, $\gamma_3 \lessgtr 0$ and $\gamma_2 < 0$. Given the previous assumptions, the decision maker acts upon the basis of a predicted value[5] of p_t, $\hat{p}_t$, and therefore maximizes

$$\hat{V}_t = f(\hat{p}_t) + (\gamma_1 \hat{p}_t + \gamma_3) x_t - \gamma_2 x_1^2. \tag{4.4}$$

Because this is at a maximum for

$$\frac{d\hat{V}_1}{dx_t} = \gamma_1 \hat{p}_t + \gamma_3 - 2\gamma_2 x_t = 0 \tag{4.5}$$

$$x_t = \frac{\gamma_1 \hat{p}_t + \gamma_3}{2\gamma_2}. \tag{4.6}$$

Substituting for x_t in (4.3) in order to determine the expression W_t which depends only on p_t and $\hat{p}_t$,

$$W_t = f(p_t) + \frac{(\gamma_t P_t + \gamma_3)(\gamma_1 \hat{p}_t + \gamma_3)}{2\gamma_2} - \frac{\gamma_2(\gamma_1 \hat{p}_t + \gamma_3)^2}{4\gamma_2^2} \tag{4.7}$$

$$= f(p_t) + \frac{(\gamma_1 \hat{p}_t + \gamma_3)}{4\gamma_2} [2(\gamma_1 P_t + \gamma_3) - (\gamma_1 \hat{p}_t + \gamma_3)]$$

$$= f(p_t) + \frac{\gamma_1 \hat{p}_t + \gamma_3}{4\gamma_2} [2\gamma_1 P_t + \gamma_3 - \gamma_1 \hat{p}_t]$$

$$= f(p_t) + \frac{1}{4\gamma_2} [\gamma_1^2 (2p_t \hat{p}_t - \hat{p}_t^2) + 2\gamma_1\gamma_3 P_t + \gamma_3^2]. \tag{4.8}$$

While this is a cumbersome expression, a simple expression follows from it which is the pivot of the argument.

However, before deriving this pivotal expression, note that from (4.8), where the moments refer to values of the planning interval,

$$E[W] = E\{f(p)\} + \frac{1}{4\gamma_2} [\gamma_1^2 (2E[p]E[\hat{p}] + 2\,\text{Cov}\,(p, \hat{p})$$
$$- E[\hat{p}]^2 - \text{var}\,\hat{p}) + 2\gamma_1\gamma_3\,E[p] + \gamma_3^2]. \tag{4.9}$$

A number of conclusions follow from equation (4.9). If

$$2\,\text{Cov}\,(p, \hat{p}) - \text{var}\,\hat{p} < 0, \tag{4.10}$$

it is better to follow an inflexible policy based on the prediction that $p = E[\hat{p}]$ throughout the planning interval than to adjust to one's imperfect short-term forecasts. If one effectively predicts that p is equal to the average of forecasted values of p for the planning interval, $2\,\text{Cov}\,(p, \hat{p}) - \text{var}\,\hat{p}$ necessarily falls to zero and the other terms of (4.9) remain unchanged so that $E[W]$ is increased if originally (4.10) is negative. If one is following an inflexible policy, it is best to set the effective unvarying estimate of p equal to $E[p]$, the average actual value of p for the planning interval. This is so, since if inflexibility exists,

$$\frac{\partial E[W]}{\partial E[\hat{p}]} = \frac{\gamma_1^2}{4\gamma_2} [2E(p) - 2E(\hat{p})] = 0 \qquad (4.11)$$

for $E[\hat{p}] = E[p]$.

In order to determine the desirability of alternative policies and to obtain a simple pivotal expression, compare the payoff from the optimal inflexible policy with that of the j-th alternative policy. The $E[W]$ value for the optimal inflexible policy is found by substituting $E[p]$ for $E[\hat{p}]$ in (4.9). Representing this value as $E[W]^*$ and that for the j-th policy as $E[W]_j$, the difference between their $E[W]$-values is

$$D_j = E[W]^* - E[W]_j. \qquad (4.12)$$

Depending upon whether D_j is positive, zero or negative, the j-th policy is respectively inferior, equal to or better than the inflexible policy which is based on the unvarying estimate that $p = E[p]$. Also comparing any two alternative policies in a set $j = 1, ..., m$ the one is to be preferred which has the lowest D-value.

Since from (4.9)

$$E[W]^* = E(f\{p\}) + \frac{1}{4\gamma_2} [\gamma_1^2 E[p]^2 + 2\gamma_1\gamma_3 E[p] + \gamma_3^2] \quad (4.13)$$

and since, indicating moments which depend upon the j-th policy by a j subscript, $E[W]_j$ is similar to (4.9) with relevant j subscripts added to the moments,

$$D_j = \frac{\gamma_1^2}{4\gamma_2} [E[p]^2 - 2 E[p]E[\hat{p}]_j - 2 \text{ Cov } (p, \hat{p})_j + E[\hat{p}]_j^2 + \text{var } \hat{p}_j]$$

$$= \frac{\gamma_1^2}{4\gamma_2} [(E[p] - E[\hat{p}]_j)^2 - 2 \text{ Cov } (p, \hat{p})_j + \text{var } \hat{p}_j]. \qquad (4.14)$$

Considerable simplification of the problem has been achieved. D_j and hence, its sign, depends only on the first and second moments of p and $\hat{p}$. Further simplification is possible. Since the coefficient outside the brackets of (4.14) is positive, D_j is of the same sign as and varies in the same direction as

$$J_j = (E[p] - E[\hat{p}]_j)^2 - 2 \text{ Cov } (p, \hat{p})_j + \text{var } \hat{p}_j. \qquad (4.15)$$

Both equations (4.14) and (4.15) are of central importance.

Some of the consequences of expressions (4.14) and (4.15) are as follows:

1. If the *j*-th policy is a flexible one, in which case

$$\text{var } \hat{p}_j \neq 0, \text{ and if}$$
$$\text{var } \hat{p}_j > 2 \text{ Cov } (p, \hat{p})_j, \tag{4.16}$$

   there is at least one inflexible policy which is preferable to the flexible one, for example, one in which *p* is continually predicted as equal to $E[p]$.

2. But if (4.16) is satisfied, there are a number of inflexible policies which are preferable to the *j*-th. Letting $\xi = |E[p] - E[\hat{p}]_j|$, any effective unvarying prediction of *p*, Θ, the range $E[p] - \xi \leq \Theta \leq E[p] + \xi$ leads to an improvement because it causes the squared term in the function *J* either to fall in value or remain unchanged while the sum of other terms falls (to zero). Furthermore, continuity assumptions imply if (4.16) is satisfied, that $E[W]$ is raised[6] for some effective unvarying estimates of *p* which differ from $E[p]$ by (just) more than ξ.

3. Even if the policy maker has ability to predict as indicated by a positive value for Cov $(p, \hat{p})_j$, inequality (4.16) may be satisfied, which means that a number of inflexible policies are superior to following a zigzag one based on these predictions of *p*. Alternatively, if *R* represents the linear correlation coefficient of *p* and $\hat{p}_j$ and if σ_p and $\sigma_{\hat{p}}$ represent the standard deviations of *p* and $\hat{p}_j$ respectively, then

$$\text{Cov}(p, \hat{p}_j) = R\sigma_p\sigma_{\hat{p}} \tag{4.17}$$

   and inequality (4.16) may be expressed as

$$\tfrac{1}{2} \sigma_{\hat{p}}^2 > 2R\sigma_p\sigma_{\hat{p}}. \tag{4.18}$$

   Thus inequality (4.16) holds if

$$\tfrac{1}{2} \sigma_{\hat{p}} > R\sigma_p \tag{4.19}$$

   and can clearly hold if there is some ability to predict as indicated by a positive value of the correlation coefficient,[7] *R*. For example, (4.19) is satisfied if $\sigma_{\hat{p}} = \sigma_p$ and if $R < 0.5$.

4. The smaller is the value of J_j the better is the *j*-th alternative. Thus if the *j*-th alternative is an inflexible one, (Cov $(p, \hat{p})_j = 0$, var $\hat{p}_j = 0$), then the closer the effective unvarying estimate of *p*, in this case $E[\hat{p}]_j$, approaches to $E[p]$ the

better is the *j*-th alternative. Given an inflexible policy and letting Θ represent the unvarying estimate of *p*, and letting λ be a constant, it follows also from (4.15) that inflexible policies for $\Theta = E[p] + \lambda$ and for $\Theta = E[p] - \lambda$ are equally as good. It makes no difference if the effective estimate, Θ, overestimates the average value of the non-controlled variable or underestimates it by the same fraction.

5. If J_j is non-zero, D_j increases with $\gamma_1^2 / 4\gamma_2$. The coefficient $\gamma_1^2 / 4\gamma_2$ will be referred to as the *coefficient of discrimination*. The larger is this coefficient the greater is the basis for discriminating between alternative policies; the greater is the difference in the payoff from them and the more clearly should any alternative either be adopted or rejected. It might be observed that the coefficient of discrimination is larger the smaller is the second derivative of V_t with respect to x_t and increases with the cross partial derivative of V_t.

Thus, among other things, it is clear that even if one has ability to predict but not perfect ability it may be better to follow an inflexible policy rather than adjust to one's changing estimates. If an inflexible policy is adopted, it is best to set the effective unvarying estimate of *p* equal to *E[p]*. Furthermore, if the payoff from a flexible policy is less than for the optimal inflexible policy, there are a number of inflexible policies which are superior to the flexible one. In practice, this means that if one only approximately knows the value of *E[p]*, it might be (and can be) better to base an inflexible policy on this estimate rather than adjust to one's short-term forecasts for *p*. This is so even if one has predictive ability.

This discussion raises an interesting side issue. If one has imperfect predictive ability, can a randomization policy of some sort be optimal? The question is particularly interesting because in some game theory situations randomized strategies are optimal (von Neumann and Morgenstern, 1964). The answer is that, given our previous assumptions, a randomized selection of effective predicted *p*-values can never be optimal because there is at least one, indeed, there are several inflexible policies which are superior to any such randomized one. This follows from points (1) and (2) above since in any randomized selection of the $\hat{p}$-values Cov $(p, \hat{p}) = 0$ but var $\hat{p} > 0$ and consequently inequality (4.16) holds.

Nevertheless, this does not imply that a randomization policy cannot be better than some alternative policies. For example, a randomization policy will be better than following one's imperfect estimates if one's estimates are such that Cov $(p, \hat{p}) < 0$ and if the randomization of policy leaves $E[\hat{p}]$ and var $\hat{p}$ unchanged. Of course, there are also circumstances in which Cov $(p, \hat{p}) > 0$ for a flexible policy (there is predictive ability) and a randomization policy by moving $E[\hat{p}]$ closer to $E[p]$ and either leaving var $\hat{p}$ unchanged or reducing it can bring about an improvement. But even if the randomization policy does mark an improvement, there will be at least one inflexible policy which is better than randomizing. Thus inflexible policies have a special status.

THE RATIONALITY OF INFLEXIBLE MICROECONOMIC MANAGERIAL DECISIONS

The results of the previous section have important microeconomic applications. Indeed, it was in this field that many of the previous hypotheses first occurred to me.[8] They were stimulated by discussions with vegetable growers, some of whom indicated to me that they found it to be their optimal policy, in view of the price uncertainty for their products, to plant rather constant acreages of various vegetable crops and to only vary these as long-term average prices changed. Consider, then, the applicability of the previous results to a purely competitive firm and to a monopoly-type firm.

Assume that the firm wishes to decide on its optimal output strategy and that as in Knight's case, 'entrepreneurs contract for productive services in advance at fixed rates, and realize upon their use by the sale of the product in the market after it is made' (Knight, 1921, p. 197). At the time factors of production are hired, costs of production are assumed to be known but the price of the final product is unknown. In terms of the basic model of the previous section, the price of the purely competitive firm's product, p, is its non-controlled variable and output, x, is its controlled variable and the firm wishes to maximize profit for its planning interval. Prior to t, x_t is freely variable but once determined in some prior period is rigidly determined.

Now, for any period t assume that the purely competitive firm's revenue is

$$r_t = p_t x_t \qquad (4.20)$$

and that its cost is

$$C_t = \alpha_0 - \alpha_1 x_t + \alpha_2 x_t^2. \qquad (4.21)$$

The output and sales quantities of one period have no influence on the costs and revenues of a later period. After taking market and technological restrictions into account, the objective function, in this case the profit function, for period t is

$$II_t = p_t x_t - \alpha_0 + \alpha_1 x_t - \alpha_2 x_t^2 \qquad (4.22)$$

which rearranging gives an expression of the same form as (4.3), namely,

$$II_t = V_t = -\alpha_0 + (p_t + \alpha_1) x_t - \alpha_2 x_t^2 \qquad (4.23)$$

and thus $\gamma_1 = 1$, $\gamma_3 = \alpha_1$ and $\gamma_2 = \alpha_2$, and the results of the previous section apply. In this case, the coefficient of discrimination of (4.14), $\gamma_1^2/4\gamma_2$, reduces to $1/4\alpha_2$ and, therefore, varies inversely with the second derivative of the profit function with respect to output. Hence, it is larger the more slowly marginal cost increases with increases of output, that is, the flatter is the marginal cost curve.

The discussion of the previous section implies that even if the purely competitive firm has some ability to predict the price of its product it may pay it, nevertheless, to follow an inflexible policy, and that an inflexible policy of some type will always be better than any randomized selection of effective predicted price values. All the sidelights of the previous section hold and the inferences drawn from equations (4.14) and (4.15) are applicable. For example, the best inflexible policy for the firm to follow is to predict the average price $E[p]$ for p over the planning interval and thus produce in every period an output of

$$x = \frac{E[p] + \alpha_1}{2\alpha_2}. \qquad (4.24)$$

There may be other values of output in this neighbourhood for which it is better for the firm to produce inflexibly in every period rather than to adjust to its imperfect per-period forecasts of price. The theory indicates that behaviour of this inflexible type may be entirely rational.

The results are not confined to pure competition but apply also to monopoly-type firms. To show this, assume the previous conditions with the exception now that

$$p_t = a_t - b x_t \qquad (4.25)$$

and the monopolist is not certain of the value of a_t when he or she chooses x_t, that is, the monopolist is not certain of the level of demand for his or her product. The variable a_t is uncontrolled.

Taking technological and market restrictions into account, the monopolist's profit for period t is

$$\begin{aligned}
II_t &= (a_t - b x_t) x_t - \alpha_0 + \alpha_1 x_t - \alpha_2 x_t^2 \\
&= a_t x_t - b x_t^2 - x_0 + \alpha_1 x_t - \alpha_2 x_t^2
\end{aligned} \qquad (4.26)$$

which is of the same form as (4.3), namely,

$$\Pi_t = V_t = -\alpha_0 + (a_t + \alpha_1) \, x_t - (b + \alpha_2) \, x_t^2 \qquad (4.27)$$

where, remembering that a_t is the uncontrolled variable, $\gamma_1 = 1$, $\gamma_3 = \alpha_1$ and $\gamma_2 = b + \alpha_2$. Hence, the results of the previous section also apply.

Thus even if monopolists have ability to predict the level of demand for their product, it may be better for them to adopt an inflexible policy rather than adjust to their period-to-period predictions of demand. It may be better for a monopolist to produce and market an unvarying quantity of output. This depends on the sign of

$$J_j = (E[a] - E[\hat{a}]_j)^2 - 2 \, \text{Cov} \, (a, \hat{a})_j + \text{var} \, \hat{a}_j \qquad (4.28)$$

where j indicates a monopolist's alternative policy. The monopolist's coefficient of discrimination is $\gamma_1^2/4\gamma_2 = 1/4(b + \alpha_2)$. The greater is this coefficient, the more important is it for the monopolist to choose between alternative policies. The coefficient varies inversely with the absolute rate of change of marginal revenue and marginal cost. The flatter is the marginal revenue curve and the marginal cost curve, the greater is the coefficient of discrimination and the more important is it for the firm to choose between alternative policies.

Given the discussion of the previous section, the firm's optimal inflexible policy is to produce an output of

$$x = \frac{E[a] + \alpha_1}{2(b + \alpha_2)} \qquad (4.29)$$

in every period. If this inflexible policy is better than an alternative policy, a number of other inflexible policies are also better than this alternative. Returns are the same if the effective unchanging prediction of a overestimates $E[a]$ or underestimates it by the same fraction, and the other conclusions of the previous section apply, *mutatis mutandis*.

RULES VERSUS DISCRETION IN MACROECONOMIC POLICY

The analysis has been shown to have definite application to microeconomics. It helps to explain microeconomic behaviour which might otherwise appear irrational and it gives prescriptive leads. It has similar applications to macroeconomic policy. To illustrate this, three types of macro models are examined. One type depends upon the Phillips hypothesis, another is a simple Keynesian one, and the other relies on the quantity theory of money. These models have limitations.

However, the relevance of this analysis neither stands nor falls on the basis of the particular types of models discussed here. The models considered are but a rough beginning.

First, consider a macro model which rests on the Phillips hypothesis (Phillips, 1958) and in which the unrestricted objective function[9] of the policy maker depends on the rate of inflation and the level of unemployment and is of the particularly simple type

$$\Phi_t = - \alpha_2 \, p_t^2 - \beta_2 \, U_t^2 \qquad (4.30)$$

where p_t represents the proportionate rise of prices in period t and U_t represents the percentage level of unemployment. The policy maker's ideal is no inflation and no unemployment. However, taking the Phillips curve into account, this may be unattainable. While it is probably closer to reality to suppose that the Phillips curve is of a hyperbolic form,[10] as an approximation assume that it is of the linear form and

$$p_t = a_t - bU_t. \qquad (4.31)$$

The assumptions of the second section are supposed to apply, *mutatis mutandis*. U_t is a controlled variable whose value must be determined prior to t at a time when a_t's value is not known but b's is. The variable a is uncontrolled. Thus when U_t is determined the level of cost push inflation and of productivity change for t is not exactly known.

By substituting (4.31) into (4.30), an expression of similar form to (4.3) is obtained, namely,

$$\begin{aligned} V_t &= - \alpha_2 (a_t - bU_t)^2 - \beta_2 U_t^2 \\ &= - \alpha_2 (a_t^2 - 2a_t bU_t + b^2 U_t^2) - \beta_2 U_t^2 \\ &= - \alpha_2 a_t^2 + 2\alpha_2 a_t bU_t - (\alpha_2 b^2 + \beta_2) U_t^2. \end{aligned} \qquad (4.32)$$

Hence, remembering that a_t is the relevant non-controlled variable, $-\alpha_2 \, a_t^2$ corresponds to $f(p_t)$ in (4.3), and the γ-values are $\gamma_1 = 2\alpha_2 b$, $\gamma_3 = 0$ and $\gamma_2 = \alpha_2 b^2 + \beta_2$. The coefficient of discrimination is

$$\frac{\gamma_1^2}{4\gamma_2} + \frac{(2\alpha_2 b)^2}{4(\alpha_2 b^2 + \beta_2)} = \frac{(\alpha_2 b)^2}{\alpha_2 b^2 + \beta_2}.$$

It increases with the policy maker's aversion to inflation and it declines as the policy maker's aversion to unemployment rises. Further, other things equal, it increases with b, that is, with the steepness of the Phillips curve.

Once again the results of the earlier section apply. The optimal inflexible policy for the planning interval is to hold the unemployment level at

$$U = \frac{2\alpha b E[a]}{2(b^2 + \beta)} = \frac{\alpha b}{b^2 + \beta} E[a] \qquad (4.33)$$

in every period and to let prices fluctuate given this restraint. Even if policy makers have some ability to predict it may be better for them to follow an inflexible policy rather than adjust to their short-term predictions. To determine whether any inflexible policy is better than the j-th alternative, the sign of

$$J_j = (E[a] - E[\hat{a}]_j)^2 - 2 \text{ Cov } (a, \hat{a})_j + \text{var } \hat{a}_j \qquad (4.34)$$

is examined. If it is positive, a number of inflexible policies are better than the j-th.

The results are essentially the same if the unrestricted objective function is generalized to

$$\Phi_t = \alpha_0 + \alpha_1 p_t - \alpha_2 p_t^2 + \beta_0 + \beta_1 U_t - U_t^2 \qquad (4.35)$$

and a linear Phillips curve is assumed. The only difference is that $x_3 \neq 0$. The results for the general case set out in an earlier section apply.

The fact that growth is not explicitly contained in the previous objective functions might be regarded as a serious oversight since it is an important objective of many countries today. Yet, if we do not regard it as already being implicitly introduced, it may be explicitly introduced by adding a term ηG_t to (4.30) or (4.35), where G_t represents the growth of real output. Furthermore, assume that to some extent growth depends on the rate of inflation and the level of unemployment. If

$$G_t = i_0 + i_1 U_t - i_2 U_t^2 + \xi_0 + \xi_1 p_t - \xi_2 p_t^2 \qquad (4.36)$$

then G_t can be eliminated from the unrestricted objective function. If, further, p_t is a linear function of U_t, that is, the Phillips curve is linear, p_t can also be eliminated, and a restricted objective function of the type of (4.3) is obtained which depends only on U_t. Making a_t the uncontrolled variable, the mathematical results of the general introductory section then apply, *mutatis mutandis*.

Turn now to a Keynesian model. Assume that the unrestricted objective function is

$$\Phi_t = \lambda_0 + \lambda_1 Y_t - \lambda_2 Y_t^2 \tag{4.37}$$

where Y_t represents the level aggregate demand. The ideal level of aggregate demand in any period of the planning interval is

$$\bar{Y} = \frac{\lambda_1}{2\lambda_2}.$$

However, this may not be attainable with certainty because of uncontrolled variation. For example, imagine that because of a multiplier process,[11]

$$Y_t = \frac{1}{k}(G_t + Z_t) \tag{4.38}$$

where $Z_t = I_t + x_t$ and I_t represents the level of net investment in period t, x_t specifies the level of exports and G_t indicates the level of government expenditure. Furthermore, suppose that G_t is a controlled variable and Z_t is not. G_t is determined before Z_t is known and the general assumptions of the introductory mathematical section are assumed to apply. Should the government adjust its spending to its period-to-period estimates of Z or follow an inflexible policy?

To answer this, substitute restriction (4.38) into (4.37). This gives

$$V_t = \lambda_0 + \frac{\lambda_1}{k}(G_t + Z_t) - \frac{\lambda_2}{k^2}(G_t^2 + 2Z_t G_t + Z_t^2) \tag{4.39}$$

which, rearranging and remembering that Z_t is the uncontrolled variable, is of the same form as (4.3), namely,

$$V_t = \lambda_0 + \frac{\lambda_1}{k}Z_t - \frac{\lambda_2}{K^2}Z_T^2 - \frac{2\lambda_2}{k^2}Z_t G_t + \frac{\lambda_1}{k}G_t - \frac{\lambda_2}{k^2}G_t^2. \tag{4.40}$$

Consequently, $\gamma_1 = -2\lambda_2/k^2$, $\gamma_3 = \lambda_1/k$ and $\gamma_2 = \lambda_2/k^2$ so that the coefficient of discrimination is

$$\frac{\gamma_1^2}{4\gamma_2} = \frac{\dfrac{4\lambda_2^2}{k^4}}{\dfrac{4\lambda_2}{k^2}} = \frac{\lambda_2}{k^2} \tag{4.41}$$

$$= \lambda_2 m^2 \tag{4.42}$$

where $m = 1/k$ is the multiplier. The greater is the multiplier and the greater is the diminishing marginal utility of increased income (effective demand), the larger is the coefficient of discrimination. All the results of the introductory mathematical section apply.

For example, it may be better to follow an inflexible policy rather than adjust to one's predictions of Z (the uncontrolled macroeconomic

variable) even if one has ability to predict the period-to-period values of
Z. An inflexible policy will be better than the *j*-th alternative policy if

$$J_j = (E[Z] - E[\hat{Z}]_j)^2 - 2 \text{ Cov } (Z, \hat{Z})_j + \text{var } \hat{Z}_j, \qquad (4.43)$$

where $\hat{Z}$ indicates the predicted value of Z, is positive. If for any
feasible alternative *j*, (4.43) is positive then it is better for the
government to follow an inflexible policy and its optimal inflexible
policy is set to its expenditure in each period of the planning horizon at

$$G^* = \frac{\lambda_1}{2\lambda_2} m^{-1} - E[Z] \qquad (4.44)$$

$$= \bar{Y} m^{-1} - E[Z] \qquad (4.45)$$

$$= \bar{Y} k - E[Z]. $$

Given an inflexible policy, the optimal level of government spending in
each period is equal to the ideal level of income (aggregate demand)
times the inverse of the multiplier less $E[Z]$. If J_j is positive, there are a
number of unvarying estimates in the neighbourhood of G^* which give
a greater payoff than the *j*-th policy.   The other results of the
introductory mathematical section also apply.

This rudimentary model makes no allowance for growth.   Further,
none of the models considered so far introduce money explicitly.
Especially in view of the recent debate, this is a shortcoming.   It is
worthwhile to introduce it explicitly even if by means of a crude
quantity theory.

Imagine (given, for example, that the growth of net output varies in a
particular manner) the policy maker's objective function to be

$$\Phi_t = \alpha_0 + \alpha_1 p_t - \alpha_2 p_t^2 \qquad (4.46)$$

where p_t represents the rate of inflation in *t*.   It follows that the ideal
rate of inflation is

$$\bar{p}_t = \frac{\alpha_1}{2\alpha_2}. \qquad (4.47)$$

Where *P* represents the price level, *M* the quantity of money, *X* the
level of real income (output), and *k* is a constant, in equilibrium[12]

$$P_t = \frac{M_t}{kX_t}. \qquad (4.48)$$

Thus letting m_t represent the proportionate rise in the quantity of money
in period *t* and x_t represent the proportionate rise in real output in *t*,

$$P_t = m_t - x_t. \tag{4.49}$$

In equilibrium, the rate of inflation is equal to the proportionate increase in the money supply less the proportionate increase in real output.

Imagine that the general assumptions of the introductory mathematical section apply and that m_t is a controlled variable whereas x_t is 'non-controlled'. By substituting (4.49) into (4.46) an expression of the same form as (4.3) is obtained. It is

$$
\begin{aligned}
\Phi_t = V_t &= \alpha_0 + \alpha_1 (m_t - x_t) - \alpha_2 (m_t^2 - 2 x_t m_t + x_t^2) \\
&= \alpha_0 - \alpha_1 x_t - \alpha_2 x_t^2 + 2\alpha_2 x_t m_t + \alpha_1 m_t - \alpha_2 m_t^2,
\end{aligned} \tag{4.50}
$$

and thus the results of the introductory mathematical section apply. In this case $\gamma_1 = 2\alpha_2$, $x_3 = -\alpha_1$ and $\gamma_2 = \alpha_2$. Therefore, the coefficient of discrimination is $\gamma_1^2 / 4\gamma_2 = 4\alpha_2^2 / 4\alpha_2 = \alpha_2$ and so increases with the policy maker's aversion to inflation.

For convenience, take a year as the length of a period. Then it follows that even if the policy maker has ability to predict yearly increases of real output, it may nevertheless be better for him or her to expand the money supply at a constant percentage rate. A policy of steadily expanding the money supply is better than the j-th alternative policy if

$$J_j = (E[x] - E[\hat{x}]_j)^2 - 2 \, \text{Cov} \, (x, \hat{x})_j + \text{var} \, \hat{x}_j \tag{4.51}$$

is positive. The predicted percentage growth of real output is represented by $\hat{x}$. If J_j is positive then a number of steady rates of expansion of money are preferable to the j-th policy. However, the optimal steady percentage rate of expansion of the money supply is

$$m = \frac{2\alpha_2 E[x] + \alpha_1}{2\alpha_2} \tag{4.52}$$

$$= E[x] + \frac{\alpha_1}{2\alpha_2} \tag{4.53}$$

$$= E[x] + \bar{p}. \tag{4.54}$$

Money supply ought to be expanded at a steady percentage rate equal to the average percentage rate of growth of real output per year plus the ideal (percentage) rate of inflation. The other results of the introductory mathematical section also apply.

Imagine that the above model is applicable and, for example, that the United States growth of real output over the planning interval, given general fiscal policy, is estimated to be 4 per cent on average. Further assume that the ideal rate of inflation is 2 per cent. Now, if for all (feasible) discretionary policies for money supply (4.51) is positive, then none should be adopted because expansion of the money supply at a steady rate of 6 per cent per year will mark an improvement. Also, some steady rates of expansion in the neighbourhood of 6 per cent will be better than following a discretionary policy. (See proposition 4 in the introductory mathematical section.) Even if policy makers have some ability to predict period-to-period growth of real output, a discretionary monetary policy may be inferior to a non-discretionary one. Using (4.51), the exact conditions for this can be stated if we accept the above model. Despite the model's limitations,[13] the argument supports the notion that it can be a folly to follow a discretionary monetary policy.

This notion is not new in academic circles. For example, Shaw (1958) used the above monetary model to argue for a trend expansion of the money supply in line with the growth of real national income. On the basis of probable errors in predicting year-to-year growth in real national income, he argued in favour of an automatic monetary pilot and a Demand Standard of monetary control but did not analyse the crucial elements of the error pattern. 'By the rule of the Demand Standard, the nominal supply of money would be increased at a constant rate compounded annually' (Shaw, 1958, p. 64). His views are shared by other economists, but not all.

Samuelson (1969) is one of the dissenters. There are at least two grounds for dissent. One is a disbelief in 'The ancient Quantity Theory of Money'. The second is a rejection of the view that prediction errors are empirically significant. In any case, Samuelson (1969) in his testimony before the *Canadian Royal Commission on Banking and Finance* (1962) suggested that it is a folly to aim for a stipulated steady growth in the money supply.

My discussion weighs neither in favour of nor against the Quantity Theory of Money. However, this rudimentary discussion indicates that, if this theory is accepted, Shaw's policy recommendation has merit if the ability to predict the year-to-year growth of real national income is low, whereas if one's ability to predict is perfect or great a discretionary policy is wisest. This surprises no one. But ability to predict does not imply that discretionary policies are best. To decide whether they are best, the sign of the appropriate J_j term must be considered.

CONCLUDING COMMENTS AND OBSERVATIONS

Even if the policy maker has ability to predict, the structure of the restricted objective function may be such that it is better for him or her to follow an inflexible (steady) policy rather than adjust to his or her period-to-period estimates of a non-controlled variable. For the crude conditions investigated, the question of whether it is better to follow a zigzag policy or an inflexible one was shown to revolve on the sign of a simple expression, namely (4.15). The results of the investigation were shown to have important applications to both microeconomics and macroeconomics. Firms which have ability, but less than perfect ability, to predict prices or the level of demand for their product may be acting quite rationally by not adjusting to their period-to-period predictions and following a fairly inflexible policy on output. This is true, *a fortiori*, if the extra calculation and information costs involved in frequent marginal adjustments are taken into account. Thus the theory strongly suggests that period-to-period *marginal* or fine adjustments are suboptimal. In the area of macroeconomics, stop-go monetary and fiscal policies may be less satisfactory than steady ones even if policy makers have ability to predict.

Professor Muth (1974) in 'A Note on Economic Policy, Forecasting and Flexibility' shows that flexible policies are as a rule superior to inflexible policies provided that predictions are *optimally* formed after taking account of one's propensity to be incorrect. This is a self-evident proposition. Furthermore, while the note is critical of my essay (Tisdell, 1971), I can find no fault with the logic of Muth's illustrative model although the assumptions are restrictive. Whereas Muth makes objective rationality the central point of his analysis, my models treat objective rationality as a special case. In reality, Muth's model, and also Nelson's (1961), which is mentioned at the end of Muth's note, are not inconsistent with my model but are special cases of it.

The disagreement arises from our different hypotheses about the behaviour of economic agents. For instance, Muth objects to 'Tisdell's presumed behaviour for the decision maker'. However, Muth appears to be confused about presumption because, contrary to his statement, I do not wish to rule out the predictive possibility which he sets out in his equation (7). On the other hand, I am rather sceptical about the objective rationality which it assumes.

The $\hat{p}_t$ value which I used above can be regarded as a maximum equivalent value (Tisdell, 1971, p. 37; Tisdell, 1968). It is the value of the non-controlled variable such that if the economic agent did maximize his or her objective function on the basis of it, his or her observed behaviour would result. In some circumstances, $\hat{p}_t$ can be a certainty equivalent value in Theil's (1954) sense.

To illustrate this point, assume as Muth does that the economic agents always maximize the conditional value of their objective function V. Then taking the quadratic case and letting $\bar{p}_t$ represent the anticipated value of the non-controlled variable (because Muth has used $\hat{p}_t$ in an unintended way) my approach gives in this special case, where E represents an expected value,

$$\hat{p}_t = Ep_t \mid \bar{p}_t = Ep + \frac{\text{cov}(p, \bar{p})}{\text{var } \bar{p}} \ (\bar{p}_t - \bar{Ep}). \qquad (4.55)$$

Except for the slight change of symbols, this is the same as Muth's equation (7). However, my approach is more general than Muth's and only reduces to Muth's special case when the above behavioural assumptions are satisfied.

Muth's model has the disadvantage that it assumes optimal or objectively rational behaviour. Uncertainties are likely to be such in practice that decision makers are forced to choose between flexible and inflexible policies which may both be sub-optimal. Thus, it is most important not to constrain our theories by the assumptions which Muth makes. There is no reason to believe that objectively rational expectations or objectively rational behaviour prevails universally. Behaviour is much more diverse and predictions are liable in many cases to be less perfect than suggested by Muth's theory of rational expectations, a theme developed further in this book.

NOTES

1. Uncertainty may cause firms and households to hold divergent expectations and this divergency may have undesirable efficiency or welfare effects. See for example, Hicks (1946, p. 133).
2. The planning interval is taken as datum and the difficult task of deciding on an optimum planning interval has not been tackled.
3. The analysis can certainly be used for comparing past policies, and, with caution, can also be used for planning future policy.
4. The objective function considered is of the same type as Henri Theil's certainty equivalence one. But the problem treated in this chapter is quite different to his. See Theil, (1961, pp. 412, 423).
5. For any actual value of x_t one can imagine that there is a unique corresponding predicted value of p_t because (6) in Muth (1974) is a linear function, and so is monotonic.
6. For (4.16) to be satisfied there must be some zigzagging. Otherwise,
   Cov $(p, \hat{p})_j = 0$ and var $\hat{p}_j = 0$.

7. Note, however, that expression (4.16) cannot hold if $R = 1$ and is less likely to hold the greater is R.
8. Hints at these ideas are to be found in Tisdell (1963, 1968, Chapter 6).
9. The objective functions in this section may be quantified in terms of the von Neumann and Morgenstern utility index.
10. The general assumptions of Archibald and Lipsey (1967) are employed here.
11. For further details of the model assumed here, see Archibald and Lipsey (1967).
12. The model assumed here is also outlined by Archibald and Lipsey (1967).
13. This and the previous macro models are based on static equilibria.

REFERENCES

Archibald, G.C. and Lipsey R.G. (1967), *An Introduction to a Mathematical Treatment of Economics*, London: Weidenfield & Nicholson.

Hicks, J.R. (1946), *Value and Capital: An Inquiry Into Some Fundamental Principles of Economic Theory*, 2nd edn, Oxford: Clarendon Press.

Knight, F.H. (1921), *Risk, Uncertainty and Profit*, Boston and New York: Houghton Mifflin.

Leslie, D. (1993), *Advanced Macroeconomics*, New York: McGraw-Hill.

Lucas, R.E. (1987), *Models of Business Cycles*, London: Blackwell.

Muth, J.F. (1961), 'Rational Expectations and the Theory of Price Movements', *Econometrica*, 29, 315–35.

Muth, J.F. (1974), 'A Note on Economic Policy, Forecasting and Flexibility', *Weltwirtshaftliches Archiv*, 110, 173–5.

Nelson, R.R. (1961), 'Uncertainty, Prediction, and Competitive Equilibrium', *Quarterly Journal of Economics*, 75, 41–62.

Phillips, A.W. (1958), 'The Relation Between Unemployment and the Rate of Change of Money Wage Rates in the United Kingdom, 1861–1957', *Economica*, 25, 283–99.

Samuelson, P.A. (1969), 'The Folly of Monetary Rules', in Kohler H. (ed.), *Readings in Economics*, 2nd edn, New York: Holt, Rinehart & Winston.

Sargent, T.J. (1986), *Rational Expectations and Inflation*, New York: Harper & Row.

Shaw, E.S. (1958), 'Money Supply and Stable Economic Growth', in Jacoby, Neil H. (ed.), *United States Monetary Policy: Its Contribution to Prosperity Without Inflation*, New York: s.n.

Theil, H. (1954), 'Econometric Models and Welfare Maximisation', *Weltwirtschaftliches Archiv*, 72, 60–81.

Theil, H. (1961), *Economic Forecasts and Policy*, 2nd rev. edn, Amsterdam: North-Holland.

Tisdell, C.A. (1963), 'Uncertainty, Instability, Expected Profit', *Econometrica*, 31, 243–7.

Tisdell, C.A. (1968), *The Theory of Price Uncertainty, Production, and Profit*, Princeton, New Jersey: Princeton University Press.

Tisdell, C.A. (1971), 'Economic Policy, Forecasting and Flexibility', *Weltwirtschaftliches Archiv*, 106(1), 34–54.

von Neumann, J. and Morgenstern, O. (1964), *The Theory of Games and Economic Behaviour*, New York: John Wiley.

5. Planning, Learning and Decisions: Flexibility and Retention of Options

INTRODUCTION

In the previous chapter it was argued that inflexible or non-discretionary decisions can be optimal even when an economic agent has some positive ability to predict uncontrolled variables. In that case the penalty of errors outweighed the advantages of fine tuning of decisions, given the structure of the problem. While learning is possible within that model, it is not substantial enough in a range of circumstances to warrant adjustment to the short-run predictions of the economic decision maker.

This chapter explores some of the consequences for planning and decision making given that effective learning takes place with the passage of time, that is, effective learning about the values of uncontrolled variables occurs.[1] First, the optimality of delaying decisions is considered given that with delay learning about the values of uncontrolled variables occurs, and assuming that an earlier decision eliminates the option of a delayed decision. The more general question is then taken up of learning and independence between controlled variables in time. Specifically, how do learning possibilities affect the optimal determination of controlled variables in an earlier period when the values of some variables affect the options for varying controlled variables in later periods? Given possibilities of learning, what decisions ought be made in an earlier period to retain options in a later one?

The appropriateness of an economic plan is altered by the scope which decision makers have for learning. Plans need to be adjusted depending upon how much policy makers are likely to learn with the passage of time. Some of the necessary adjustments are discussed in this chapter. Since learning is important in economic life and since the necessary allowances for it are not negligible, it is surprising that they have been given so little attention in the literature (prior to the 1960s).

75

However, at the outset it is necessary to make a distinction between 'learning' as it will be used here and learning by doing. The Lundberg–Arrow phenomenon of learning by doing (Arrow, 1962) refers to rises of productivity as a result of greater dexterity, improvements of skill and perfection of optimal habits with the passage of time. Here 'learning' refers to the growing knowledge or information of decision makers which renders better decisions possible and which may be obtained with little or no action on the part of the decision maker. It might be considered to be a gift which accrues as time passes. For example, the extent of demand for a product in a particular period is likely to be more nearly known the nearer the decision maker is to that period. As the period is approached, the predictability of price improves and learning therefore takes place even though no new skills are being perfected. For brevity, we might call this learning without doing or learning by waiting.

Possibilities for learning depend upon the degree of uncertainty of the policy makers (compare Arrow, 1969, p. 30). The greater is the uncertainty of the policy makers the less is their information, and thus the greater is the scope of the policy makers for learning. The potential increase of information may be difficult or impossible to realize fully although one normally expects that some of the potential is realized as time passes.

Plans which are optimal if learning is absent are unlikely to be optimal if learning is present. As a rule, if learning is significant, it pays to make economic plans more flexible or to provide economic conditions which permit increased flexibility or retain options even if this involves additional cost. The optimality of flexibility or keeping options open arises from the presence of learning, not the mere existence of uncertainty. Indeed, if non-resolvable uncertainty increases and thus, other things unchanged, learning is reduced, inflexible plans are increasingly favoured (compare Tisdell, 1968, Chapter 6). Although this view is at variance with the traditional one, once learning and uncertainty are connected in the above manner it is not hard to see intuitively that it holds. An increase in uncertainty involves less learning and less scope for varying controlled variables. Hence less advantage stems from flexibility.

If the degree of uncertainty about a relevant non-controlled variable which affects payoff does not change with time, multiperiod actions can be rigidly decided today without forgoing any potential payoff since there is no learning and therefore no possibility of effective readjustment of actions. But learning is rarely absent. Decisions about controlled variables (the value of instruments) can sometimes be postponed in order to gain extra information. The optimality of delaying economic decisions so as to take advantage of learning possibilities is discussed below. Furthermore, if learning is important in a multiperiod decision problem and if earlier values of the controlled variables limit the possibility of varying later values of the controlled variables, adjustments need to be made to the values of earlier instruments if learning is significant. Earlier decisions provide a setting for later ones, and learning possibilities influence the optimality of the earlier decisions. To allow for learning, it may be optimal to bias values of earlier controlled variables in a systematic direction, and examples of this are given below.

Learning factors were given little attention in traditional neoclassical economics. Although Hicks (1946) makes some allowance for learning in the multiperiod theory which he outlines in *Value and Capital*, the theory has a number of shortcomings, some of which are discussed below. Possibly the earliest significant contribution on this subject is that by Hart (1942), in 'Risk, Uncertainty, and the Unprofitability of Compounding Probabilities'. More recently, important contributions have been made by Simon (1956) and Theil (1961) on the question of certainty equivalence.

OPTIMALITY OF DELAYING A DECISION: MICROECONOMIC EXAMPLE – PRODUCTION DECISION OF A BUSINESS FIRM

To illustrate some of the elements which influence the optimality of delaying decisions, consider a simple example. Imagine that decision makers wish to maximize the expected value of an objective function of the form

$$\pi \ (p, \ x) = px - ax^2 \tag{5.1}$$

where they control x but not p. The policy makers have the option of determining the value of x at the point in time $t - n$ or of delaying this until a later point t. (The general conclusions below are not changed if the term ax^2 of (5.1) is replaced by a more general quadratic.) What factors will influence their decision to procrastinate?

To make the problem more concrete let us relate it to a microeconomic situation and then consider a macroeconomic example. Let π represent the profit obtained by a firm in period $t + 1$ from the sale of its output, x, of that period at a price per unit of p. The first term of equation (5.1) is then the firm's revenue from this output and the second one is its cost of the output. The firm can rigidly determine its output for $t +$ 1 at either $t - n$ or at t. The optimality of delaying the decision until t and bearing an extra cost, if necessary, depends upon the value to the firm of the extra information which is gained by the delay. The expected value of this extra information is easily assessed.

At $t - n$ the firm is unlikely to know the price per unit which x will fetch in $t + 1$ but we shall imagine that it at least assigns a probability weighting to different values of p and that these enable an expected value and variance for p to be estimated. Given the inadequacy of the decision maker's information, p is a random variable at $t - n$ and might have a subjective probability distribution like that shown in Figure 5.1. On the other hand, imagine that p is known at t so that all uncertainty about the price of the product can be eliminated by waiting.

Figure 5.1   *Probability distribution about price* p *at* t $- $ n *indicating uncertainty but this can be eliminated by waiting*

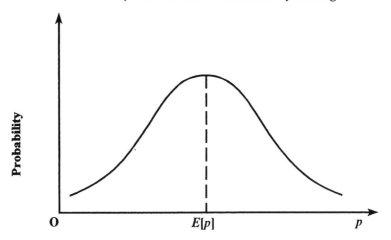

Compare the expected (gross) profit from determining x in $t - n$ with that from delaying the decision until t. If x is determined at $t - n$, the firm's expected profit is

$$E[\pi] = E[px - ax^2] \qquad (5.2)$$
$$= E[p]x - ax^2 \qquad (5.3)$$

since π is linear in the random variable p. In order for this expression to be at a maximum, it is necessary for x to be determined in $t - n$ so that marginal expected price equals marginal cost, that is so that

$$E[p] - 2ax = 0. \tag{5.4}$$

Hence, the optimal value of x is

$$x = E[p]/2a. \tag{5.5}$$

Substituting the optimal value of x into equation (5.3), maximum expected profit from determining output at $t - n$ is

$$E[\pi] = E[p]^2 \ (\frac{1}{2a} - \frac{a}{4a^2}) \tag{5.6}$$

$$= E[p]^2 \ (\frac{2}{4a} - \frac{1}{4a}) \tag{5.7}$$

$$= \frac{1}{4a} \ E[p]^2. \tag{5.8}$$

The expected profit if the decision about x is delayed until t, can be calculated in the following way: if x is determined in t, price is known and so profit is maximized by producing an output which equates price and marginal cost. Consequently,

$$x = p/2a. \tag{5.9}$$

Hence, substituting for x in equation (5.1),

$$\pi = p\frac{p}{2a} - a(\frac{p}{2a})^2 \tag{5.10}$$

$$= \frac{1}{4a}p^2. \tag{5.11}$$

This is profit if p is known. But at $t - n$, p is not known though its expected value and variance can be calculated from the decision maker's subjective probability distribution. Given the delay and optimal adjustment to the price which actually occurs, maximum expected profit by delaying is equal to the expectation of function (5.11), that is,

$$E[\frac{1}{4a}p^2] = \frac{1}{4a} \ (E[p]^2 + \text{var } p). \tag{5.12}$$

Consequently, the extra (gross) gain from delaying the decision about x until t is the difference between expression (5.12) and (5.8) which amounts to

$$V = \frac{1}{4a} \text{ var } p. \qquad (5.13)$$

Two propositions follow from this:

1. If the slope of the marginal cost curve $(2a)$ is positive but not infinite, the greater is variable p the larger is the gain from waiting. The expression variable p is a measure of the decision maker's ignorance at $t - n$ about p and also measures the amount of information which is gained between $t - n$ and t. Other things constant, the value of waiting rises with the amount which can be learned by procrastinating.
2. Given that something can be learned by delaying (var $p > 0$), waiting is more valuable the less is the slope of the marginal cost curve, that is, the more flexible is x.

Thus learning is necessary if there is to be a gain from waiting but increased information becomes of smaller value as inflexibility increases, that is, as $4a \rightarrow \infty$ and in the limit is of no value. Furthermore, flexibility is more valuable the greater is learning, and learning or information is more valuable if the scope for adjustment or flexibility is substantial. This is illustrated in Figure 5.2.

The marginal cost curve for a particular technique is shown there by MC. At $t - n$, the firm believes that there is a 50 per cent chance of the price of x being p_1 and 50 per cent chance that it is p_2. Thus, if x is determined at $t - n$, maximum expected profit is equivalent to the area of $\triangle ABG$ (except for the constant). If on the other hand x is determined at t, expected profit is equivalent to 0.5 [area $\triangle AJH$ + area $\triangle ACF$] which can be shown[2] to be equal the area of ($\triangle ABG + \triangle BDE$) where EB is of equal but opposite slope to MC. Thus the area of $\triangle BDE$ measures the gain from waiting. This triangle is larger the further apart are p_1 and p_2 and thus the greater is the initial ignorance and the subsequent information. Also, the smaller is the slope of MC through B the larger is the area of the relevant triangle, possible prices given. Thus learning favours flexible techniques whereas increased non-resolvable uncertainty favours inflexible techniques. A firm is prepared to pay a greater fixed cost for a flexible technique if learning is important.

Figure 5.2   Illustration that flexibility is more valuable the greater is learning and learning or information is more valuable if the scope for adjustment or flexibility is substantial

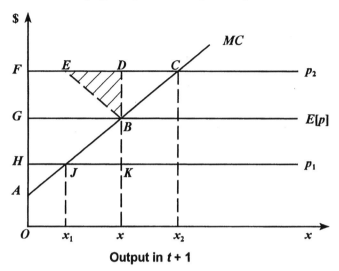

Output in *t* + 1

LEARNING, DELAY AND MACROECONOMIC POLICY MAKING

The importance of learning for macroeconomic policy making should not be overlooked either. By postponing decisions about controlled macro variables, such as the level of government expenditure and the quantity of money, governments may gain knowledge which increases the net expected value of their actions and this may be so even though the lag between the delayed decision and its effects has to be reduced at considerable additional cost. Taking a macroeconomic example, let us consider some of the elements which influence the value of delaying a decision. The example has formal similarities with the previous micro example and is selected because of its simplicity.

Imagine that the rate of price inflation, p, is of considerable concern to the government and that its preference for different rates of inflation can be represented by a von Neumann and Morgenstern utility index. In fact, suppose that the government's objectives can be represented by a utility function

$$U = - ap^2 \tag{5.14}$$

where p represents the proportionate rise of prices in period $t + 1$. The government's ideal is to avoid inflation and deflation in $t + 1$. Deviations from this ideal cause its dissatisfaction to increase at an accelerating rate.

Suppose that the government is able to influence the rate of inflation by varying the quantity of money. Furthermore, suppose that p is governed by the proportionate rise in the quantity of money, m, and the proportionate increase of aggregate real output, x, in $t + 1$, and that the particular relationship

$$p = \lambda(m - x) \tag{5.15}$$

prevails where λ is a positive constant. For example, $\lambda = 1$, if the crude Quantity Theory holds. (Archibald and Lipsey, 1967, p. 360.)

If the government controls m but not x and has the option of determining m at $t - n$ or at t, how much does it gain by delaying the decision about m? Supposing that x is not perfectly predictable at $t - n$ but is perfectly predictable at t, the increase in expected utility as a result of the delay can easily be computed and the factors which increase the value of waiting can be isolated.

At $t - n$, x is a random variable. Let $E[x]$ represent its average value and var x represent its variance. The expected utility from deciding in $t - n$ optimally (but irrevocably) upon the value of m can be determined as follows. Substituting (5.15) into (5.14)

$$U = - a\lambda^2 (m^2 - 2mx + x^2). \tag{5.16}$$

Hence, since x is a random variable and m is controlled,

$$E[U] = - a\lambda^2 (m^2 - 2mE[x] + E[x]^2 + \text{var } x). \tag{5.17}$$

Expected utility, $E[U]$ is at a maximum with respect to m if

$$\frac{dE[U]}{dm} = - a\lambda^2 (2m - 2E[x]) = 0. \tag{5.18}$$

This is satisfied when

$$m = E[x]. \tag{5.19}$$

Thus expected utility is maximized by varying the quantity of money at the same percentage rate as the expected (or average) percentage variation of real output. If m is determined by this rule, (5.19) can be substituted into (5.17) to express the (maximum) level of expected utility which can be achieved by deciding on m at $t - n$. It is

$$E[U] = -a\lambda^2 \text{ var } x. \tag{5.20}$$

On the other hand if the decision about m is deferred until t, x is then known and the optimal value of m can be found by maximizing (5.16). It is

$$m = x \tag{5.21}$$

and thus expected utility is zero if the decision about m is made in t. Hence, the gain in expected utility from delaying the decision is

$$V = a\lambda^2 \text{ var } x. \tag{5.22}$$

Therefore the value of a delay rises as the possibilities for learning (as indicated by the size of var x) increase, is higher the more responsive are price variations to differences between x and m, and is larger the greater is the acceleration of dissatisfaction if price inflation deviates from the ideal. The value of the information received by delaying is larger in these circumstances and the government ought to be prepared to bear a larger cost in order to postpone its decision.

A simple Keynesian type of model (Archibald and Lipsey, 1967, pp. 91–2) also yields analogous conclusions. Imagine that government expenditure is controlled but that private investment expenditure and the value of exports are not, that their predictability improves with time and that the government has the option of delaying its decision about the level of government expenditure. If its utility is a suitable quadratic function of the level of aggregate demand, the value of delaying the decision is greater the faster the acceleration of dissatisfaction for deviations from the ideal level of aggregate demand, is higher the greater is the information which is obtained about the value of private investments and exports, and is larger the greater is the multiplier.

CERTAINTY BIAS, EQUIVALENCE AND LEARNING

Decision-making situations are much more complicated in practice than in the cases discussed. In the most general case, the problem is not so much a question of delaying decisions but of making a decision today so as to provide the best setting for tomorrow's decisions, given that learning takes place and that today's decision affects tomorrow's possibilities. Traditional neoclassical economic theory has failed to stress that the range of learning possibilities has implications for today's decisions.

For example, take the multiperiod theory of production and consumption as outlined by Hicks in *Value and Capital*. Hicks proposes that production and consumption plans be adjusted in a special way to allow for uncertainty about prices. He says: 'If we are to allow for uncertainty of expectations in these problems of the determination of plans, we must not take the most probable price ± an allowance for uncertainty of the expectation, that is to say, an allowance for risk' (Hicks, 1946, p. 196). Unfortunately, Hicks gives us no guide for calculating the appropriate allowances.

Nevertheless, Hicks suggests the following procedure: from the vector of most probable discounted prices, R, a specific adjusted vector, $\check{R}$, is obtained. R is used to calculate the optimal multiperiod quantities of commodities and this plan is acted upon. As the plan is carried out, expectations about prices may change and the original plan is adjusted to allow for the new expectations.

Consider a firm, for example, planning its production for the interval of time $1 \leq t \leq T$ which consists of T subintervals. According to Hicks, the firm devises its production plan so as to maximize its present discounted adjusted value

$$K = \check{R}X \qquad (5.23)$$

subject to its production function

$$f(X) = 0 \qquad (5.24)$$

where X is a vector whose elements consist of the dated quantities of commodities. The maximum value of K occurs for a unique value of X if $f(X)$ is strictly concave.

Representing the solution by $\bar{X}$, $\bar{X}$ specifies unique quantities of the commodities for each of the periods within the planning interval, for example, $[\bar{x}_{11}, \bar{x}_{21}, ..., \bar{x}_{q1}]$ for the initial period if there are q commodities, $[\bar{x}_{12}, \bar{x}_{22}, ..., \bar{x}_{q2}]$ for period two and so on. Hicks contends that the vector $\bar{x}$ indicates the optimal quantities of input and output in the initial period but not necessarily the optimal quantities for subsequent periods. If learning occurs in later periods, plans for these periods may need to be altered. While Hicks allows that plans may need to be modified to allow for learning as they are being performed, he does not explore the consequence of this for the optimal determination of early decisions.

Present production sets limits to the future flexibility of production and the dispersion of future learning possibilities does make a difference to optimal production in the initial period and subsequently. This has been obscured by the Hicksian analysis. (Cohen and Cyert, 1965; and Tisdell, 1968, Chapter 10.)

In order to deal directly with this matter, it is necessary to specify the aim of the policy makers under conditions of uncertainty. It will be assumed that they wish to maximize the expected value of some objective function. In the case of the firm, this might be the expected utility associated with the probable capitalized or present value of the firm. Given a function of the form $U(P, X)$ where P is a vector of dated uncontrolled variables and X a vector of dated controlled variables, the problem is to choose X so as to maximize $E[U(P, X)]$ if new predictions of the non-controlled variables are likely to arise as the initial plan is acted upon.

One possible procedure for determining the earlier values of the controlled variables is to replace all the non-controlled variables in the payoff function $U(P, X)$ by their expectations and maximize the resultant expression. The earlier values of the non-controlled variable are then set as targets, but the policy maker will deviate from the later values as new information comes to hand. However, Hart (1942) has shown that this procedure is often not optimal. If learning or changed predictions are likely, he points out that it may be a fallacy to compound probabilities and use expectational values of the non-controlled variables because the optimal values of the controlled variables are often influenced by higher moments of the non-controlled variables than the first. In cases where the higher moments do have an influence, the above procedure is said to involve certainty bias. If they have no influence, certainty equivalence is said to exist, the above procedure maximizes expected profit and point predictions suffice to determine optimal policy.

Theil (1961, p. 424) has shown that if the objective function is a suitable quadratic, first-period certainty equivalence occurs. If the non-controlled variables are replaced by their expectations and the maximum of the resulting surrogate function is found, it specifies the optimal values of the controlled variables for the first period, even if values of the controlled variables for later periods are redetermined as additional information comes to hand. The surrogate function can be shown to differ from the expected value of the payoff function by a constant (in this case, a variance term) and thus both functions reach their maximum for the same values of the non-controlled variables. But certainty equivalence only occurs under special conditions. It might be interesting to consider a simple example in which it is absent.

This is most easily introduced by first considering a case in which effective learning does not occur but the presence of uncertainty leads to certainty bias. This is followed by a case in which effective learning occurs but this learning is a random variable at the initial decision date. The common thread in both the problems is the random variable in the payoff function. The random variable is controlled in the learning situation but not in the other. However, mathematically the difference is of no importance.

MICROECONOMIC MANAGERIAL EXAMPLE OF CERTAINTY BIAS

In the first example, imagine that a purely competitive firm produces one product, x, by means of a single variable factor, l. The factor l might be a composite, for example, in the case of a farm, land and wheat grain in fixed proportions. The firm's profit for any period might be expressed as

$$\pi = px - wl \qquad (5.25)$$

where x is the output for that period, p is the price per unit of the product, w is the price per unit of the factor and l is the quantity of the factor applied to yield x. Suppose that the firm's production function is

$$x = -al^2 + bl - \beta l\epsilon^2 \qquad (5.26)$$

where ϵ is a random element, for example, in the case of a farm, it might be precipitation during a growing period in inches. Note that ϵ may be expressed as $(\bar{\eta} - \eta)$ where $\bar{\eta}$ is a constant (other than zero), for example, the deviation of rainfall from a particular level, $\bar{\eta}$. Assume that at the time when l must be determined, p and w are known but not ϵ and that the firm wishes to maximize its expected profit and choose l accordingly.

The optimal value of l is then determined in the following way: substituting expression (5.26) into (5.25), profit can be expressed as

$$\pi = p(-al^2 + bl - \beta l\epsilon^2 - wl. \qquad (5.27)$$

Hence,

$$E[\pi] = p(-al^2 + bl - \beta l\{E[\epsilon]^2) + \text{var } \epsilon\}) - wl. \qquad (5.28)$$

Consequently, if expected profit is to be at a maximum, l must be chosen so that

$$\frac{dE[\pi]}{dl} = p(-2al + b - \beta\{E[\epsilon]^2 + \text{var } \epsilon\}) - w = 0. \quad (5.29)$$

The equality is satisfied if

$$1 = \frac{1}{2a} (- \frac{w}{p} + b - \beta\{E[\epsilon]_2 + \text{var } \epsilon\}). \quad (5.30)$$

Hence, other things equal, the optimal value of l is lower the greater is var ϵ, for example, the greater is the variance of the non-controlled and uncertain element in production. In the farming illustration, plantings of wheat tend to be smaller the greater is the variance of precipitation. Also note that uncertainty leads to a downward bias in l. Certainty equivalence is absent if var $\epsilon > 0$.

MACROECONOMIC EXAMPLE OF CERTAINTY BIAS

Consider another example of certainty bias which is relevant to public planning. Imagine that the benefits, B, from government investment depend not only on the aggregate level of government investment, G, but also on the level of private investment, I. Suppose that the particular relationship

$$B = aG^2 + bG + \beta GI^2 \quad (5.31)$$

prevails, G is controlled but I is supposed to be not controlled by the government and G must be determined at a time when I is not perfectly known. Where $E[I]$ is the expected value of I at that time and var I is its variance, the expected benefits from any level of G are

$$E[B] = - aG^2 + bG + \beta GE[I^2] \quad (5.32)$$
$$= - aG^2 + bG + \beta GE[I]^2 + \beta G \text{ var } I. \quad (5.33)$$

Thus if the government wishes to maximize the expected benefit from its investment, it ought to select G so that

$$\frac{\delta E[B]}{\delta G} = - 2aG + b + \beta E[I]^2 + \beta \text{ var } I = 0. \quad (5.34)$$

This equality is satisfied if

$$G = \frac{1}{2a} [b + \beta E[I]^2 + \beta \text{ var } I]. \quad (5.35)$$

Thus if $\beta < 0$, the benefits from public investment are greater the higher is private investment and the optimal value of G should be biased above the certainty equivalent value if var $I > 0$. The bias ought to be greater the larger is var I and β. On the other hand, if $\beta < 0$, the bias of G should be downwards. Rational economic action may require the incorporation of biases in decisions to allow for uncertainty even if the decision maker has a neutral attitude towards risk bearing.

MODIFYING THE ABOVE EXAMPLES TO ALLOW FOR LEARNING

These examples can be modified so as to allow for learning. For example, let us modify the micro example considered above. In production function (5.26), replace l by l_1, a factor applied in the initial period, and ϵ by l_2, a factor which is applied in a later period and change the production function slightly so that it is more appropriate to the problem. For example, let the production function be

$$x = - al_1^2 + bl_1 - \beta l_1^{-1} l_2^2 + al_2. \qquad (5.36)$$

In both periods diminishing marginal productivity arises for application of the factors, but in the second period the rate of marginal decline of output is slower the larger is l_1. The firm's profit function is

$$\pi = p(- al_1^2 + bl_1 - \beta l_1^{-1} l_2^2 + al_2) - w_1 l_1 - w_2 l_2 \qquad (5.37)$$

where w_1 and w_2 represent the price per unit of l_1 and l_2 respectively.

Imagine that when the value of l_1 must be determined, all elements in the above profit function are known except w_2. The value of w_2 is discovered, however, at the time that l_2 is determined. Consequently, learning occurs during the planning interval. The initial problem of the firm is to find a value of l_1 which, allowing for learning possibilities and subsequent possible variations of l_2, maximizes expected profit by creating the best setting for the later decision. The problem is akin to the last one. Although l_2 is a controlled variable, its optimal value is random at the initial period since it is a function of a random variable, w_2.

The optimal value of l_1 can be found in the following way: whatever value of l_1 is adopted, l_2 must be subsequently determined to maximize profit given whatever freedom exists to do so. In this case, optimality requires that

$$\frac{\delta \pi}{\delta l_2} = 0, \qquad (5.38)$$

for example, $-2\beta l_1^{-1}l_2p + ap - w_2 = 0$. (5.39)

This is satisfied if (rearranging (5.39))

$$l_2 = \frac{-w_2+ap}{2\beta p}\ l_1.$$ (5.40)

Substitute for l_2 in equation (5.37) using (5.40) and call the new equation (5.41).

On taking the expectation of (5.41), a term in $E[w_2^2] = E[w_2]^2 +$ variable w_2 arises, and on maximizsing the expectation of (5.41) with respect to l_1 it is found that, other things equal, the optimal value of l_1 is an increasing function of variable w_2. Given the expected value of w_2 and other things, the optimal value of l_1 is greater the greater is the degree of information, variable w_2, which one expects to obtain about w_2. In other words, the greater is the resolvable uncertainty the larger is the optimal value of l_1.

Compared to the 'certainty equivalent' value of l_1, the optimal value of l_1 is biased upwards if resolvable uncertainty exists and is biased further upwards the greater is the resolvable uncertainty about w_2. The 'certainty equivalence procedure' leads to bias of l_1 below its optimal value if variable $w_2 > 0$. Increases of irresolvable uncertainty also work towards lower initial commitment of the factor.

The main conclusion here is that the scope for learning about w_2 is greater, the greater is the initial optimal commitment of the factor l_1. In view of the finding of the last section this is not surprising because the greater is l_1, the less rapid is the diminishing marginal productivity of l_2 (in the second period) because

$$\frac{\delta x}{\delta l_2} = -2\beta l_1^{-1}l_2$$

and the second partial derivative is $-2\beta l_1^{-1}$. In standard terminology, the flexibility of output in the second period is greater the greater is l_1. The more information which is likely to come to hand, the more likely it is that flexibility is profitable and that measures to achieve it (such as an increase of l_1 in this case) are also optimal. (Note that if l is interpreted to be the quantity of a resource conserved in period 1, this model would imply that the optimal level of conservation of l would be higher, the larger is the variance of learning possibilities.)[3] However, if irresolvable uncertainty increases, flexibility commands a smaller premium and decisions are more likely to incorporate inflexibility. Learning possibilities do lead to biases in earlier decisions.

Similar circumstances to those discussed may also arise in public economic planning. This is readily appreciated if the previous case is modified so that it yields the costs and benefits of the supply of a publicly produced commodity. Let x represent the quantity of the commodity supplied by the public sector, π indicate the present discounted net (social) benefit of its supply, p denote the present discounted (social) value of each unit of the commodity, w_1 indicate the per unit (social) value of the factor applied initially and w_2 the present discounted (social) per unit value of the factor applied subsequently. Of course, the factor which is used in the later period may be of the same type as the one which is initially utilized. Assuming that the relationships of the previous example hold and that the government aims to maximize the expected present discounted net benefit of its productive activity, the application of the factor initially should be of a larger quantity the greater is the expected amount of learning about the social value (price) of the factor to be applied in the subsequent period. The initial application should be higher, the greater is resolvable uncertainty as indicated by variable w_2. An increase in the employment of the factor in the initial period increases flexibility in the subsequent period and allows greater advantage to be taken of improved information. In general, in models of this nature if flexibility (inflexibility) rises with increased initial application of factor so also does the optimal upward (downward) bias of its initial employment increase as the scope for learning widens.

The above discussion sketches only a few influences of learning on economic planning. The illustrations have been chosen so as to indicate in a simple way the types of bias which learning can impart to optimal decision making. It is a fundamental weakness of parts of economic theory that these influences have been ignored.

In macroeconomic theory and policy, the neglect is marked. For example, explanations of liquidity preference as behaviour towards risk, such as Tobin's (1958), which are based on portfolio diversification, seem to be inadequate for they concentrate merely on the probability distribution of returns from various assets and ignore the ease with which assets can be realized which in turn limits an asset holder's ability to adjust to changing information. This appears to be a shortcoming of many portfolio diversification theories, including that of Markowitz (1959). Furthermore, there seems to be scope for taking greater account of learning in macro policy decisions. Should the government delay a measure until further information comes to hand, should it bias a controlled monetary or fiscal variable in a particular direction to provide a setting for a future uncertain decision and so on? There has been less neglect of learning in microeconomic theory and indeed the value of additional information has been given considerable stress in managerial economics, for example, by Schlaifer (1959). Frequently, however, underlying economic principles have been neglected in managerial economics in favour of emphasis upon statistical particulars. The need now is to develop general principles which will find application to both microeconomic and macroeconomic planning.

CONCLUDING COMMENTS

This contribution illustrates the significance of learning possibilities for the optimal timing and nature of decisions. However, the type of learning considered here is essentially of a passive type, that is, learning with the passing of time. Learning of an active type by experimentation is not dealt with here although a case of this type is considered in Chapter 3 and the economics of research and development is discussed later in this book. Learning of the experimental type is difficult to analyse but is important in real life as, for example, is pointed out by Nelson (1987) and by Nelson and Winter (1982).

NOTES

1. I wish to thank Professor R.C. Jensen of the University of Queensland for a valuable comment on an earlier draft of this contribution.
2. Proof: if $p = p_1$, profit is area $\triangle AJH$. If $p = p_2$, profit is area $\triangle ACF$. Hence, in this case, expected profit is 0.5 times the sum of these areas. This expression for expected profit can be shown to be equal to the area of $\triangle ABG + 0.5$ area $\triangle BCE$ since by construction the area of $HJBG$ = area $GBEF$. The area of $\triangle BDE$ is half that of $\triangle BCE$. Hence, the above proposition holds.
3. As is well known, Arrow and Fisher (1974) showed that if development is irreversible and the benefits of development uncertain, maximization of expected benefits may favour conservation even when decision makers are risk neutral. Henry (1974) showed that the use of certainty equivalence by a risk-neutral decision maker could lead to development being chosen when conservation is optimal as evaluated by stochastic dynamic programming or by using the principle rather than the surrogate function (see Chapter 5). Conrad and Clark (1987, p. 210) comment that 'this seemingly subtle point
   has significant policy implications because many resource managers are mandated to substitute expected values for random variables when performing cost benefit analysis', thus leading to a bias for initial development'.

REFERENCES

Archibald, C. and Lipsey, R.G. (1967), *An Introduction to A Mathematical Treatment of Economics*, London: Weidenfeld & Nicolson.

Arrow, K.J. (1962), 'The Economic Implications of Learning by Doing', *Review of Economic Studies*, 29, 155–73.

Arrow, K.J. (1969), 'Classificatory Notes on the Production and Transmission of Technological Knowledge', *The American Economic Review*, 59, 29–35.

Arrow, K.J. and Fisher, A.C. (1974), 'Environmental Preservation, Uncertainty and Irreversibility', *Quarterly Journal of Economics*, 87, 312–19.

Cohen, K.J. and Cyert, R.M. (1965), *Theory of the Firm*, Englewood Cliffs: Prentice-Hall.

Conrad, J.M. and Clark, C.W. (1987), *Natural Resource Economics: Notes and Problems*, Cambridge: Cambridge University Press.

Hart, A.G. (1942), 'Risk, Uncertainty, and the Unprofitability of Compounding Probabilities', in Lange, O., McIntyre, F. and Yntema, F. (eds), *Studies in Mathematical Economics and Econometrics*, 110–18, Chicago: University of Chicago Press.

Henry, C. (1974), 'Investment Decisions under Uncertainty: The Irreversibility Effect', *American Economic Review*, 64, 1006–12.

Hicks, J.R. (1946), *Value and Capital*, 2nd edn, Oxford: Clarendon Press.

Markowitz, H. (1959), *Portfolio Selection: Efficient Diversification of Investments*, New York: John Wiley.

Nelson, R. (1987), *Understanding Technical Change as an Evolutionary Process*, Amsterdam: North-Holland.

Nelson, R. and Winter, S. (1982), *An Evolutionary Theory of Economic Change*, Cambridge, Mass.: Harvard University Press.

Schlaifer, R. (1959), *Probability and Statistics for Business Decisions: An Introduction to Managerial Economics under Uncertainty*, New York: McGraw-Hill.

Simon, H. A. (1956), 'A Note on Certainty Equivalence in Dynamic Programming', *Econometrica*, 24, 74–81.

Theil, H. (1961), *Economic Forecasts and Policy*, 2nd edn, Amsterdam: North-Holland.

Tisdell, C.A. (1968), *Theory of Price Uncertainty, Production and Profit*, Princeton, New Jersey: Princeton University Press.

Tobin, J. (1958), 'Liquidity Preference as Behaviour Towards Risk', *Review of Economic Studies*, 25, 65–86. Reprinted in Mueller, M.G. (1966), *Readings in Macroeconomics*, New York: Holt, Rinehart & Winston.

6. Certainty Equivalence and Bias in the Management of Production

BACKGROUND

Optimal current economic decisions are frequently altered by random elements even when decision makers have preferences which are risk neutral. The best values for the controlled variables often depend not just on the expected values of the non-controlled variables but also on characteristics of the spread of the probability distribution of the non-controlled variables, as shown in the previous chapter. As early as 1942, Hart stressed that where a firm's actual profit depends on some uncontrolled random elements and the firm wishes to maximize expected profit, the procedure of replacing the non-controlled variables in the profit function by their expectations and selecting the values of the controlled variables by maximizing the resultant expression does not as a rule lead to optimality.

Hart's warning (Hart, 1942) about the likely illegitimacy of compounding probabilities is of importance in agricultural management, for example. According to the type of product which they supply, farmers' profits, or more generally their utilities, depend upon random prices and random inputs such as the volume of rainfall and temperature levels, degree and type of pest infestation and disease and fertility of plants and of animals. As a rule a farmer's maximum expected profits, and more obviously maximum expected utilities, depend upon the mean values of such random variables as well as higher moments of these variables, and this must be allowed for in decision making. The theory of certainty equivalence and bias enables us to determine the type of allowance, if any, which needs to be made.

Simon (1956), Theil (1961) and Malinvaud (1969) identified some conditions under which optimal values of the controlled variables can be obtained by the above procedure and other conditions under which they cannot. Theil in particular has generalized and extended this subject and has applied his results to macroeconomic and microeconomic management.   The concepts of certainty equivalence and certainty bias are used extensively by Theil in his work.

Certainty equivalence has two meanings in the economic literature but in this chapter I shall be concerned only with certainty equivalence and bias in Theil's sense.[1] Theil states that certainty equivalence occurs if the procedure mentioned above results in optimal values for the controlled variables; otherwise certainty bias exists. To outline this concept more generally, consider a decision the aim of which is to maximize the expected value of an objective function which depends on controlled and (some random) non-controlled variables.   Certainty equivalence exists if by replacing the non-controlled variables in the objective function by their expectations and maximizing the resultant expression, the values obtained for the controlled variables are the same as those which maximize the expected value of the objective function. If these values for the controlled variables do not maximize the expected value of the objective function, certainty bias occurs and then the shortcut of replacing the random variables by their expected values and maximizing the surrogate function does not achieve the main aim.

In a multiperiod model, first-period certainty equivalence arises when the above procedure (the surrogate procedure) results in values of the controlled variables for the first period which are the same as those required to maximize the principle function.[2] However, if first-period certainty equivalence occurs, the values of the controlled variables for later periods derived by the surrogate procedure may not maximize the principle function and may need to be freshly determined as new information comes to hand.

Because a firm's principle function may depend on many characteristics of the probability distribution of the uncontrolled variables, the firm may find it costly to specify this function.   In comparison to the alternative of using the surrogate function, the extra gain from specifying and using the principle function may fail to cover the extra cost.[3] It is important from a managerial point of view to determine when this is so.

Clearly, if certainty equivalence exists, the surrogate function is just as efficient as the principle function for determining the optimal values of the controlled variables. If the firm's sole aim is to determine the optimal value of its controlled variables, nothing is gained by specifying the principle function and indeed there may be an extra cost. If there is an extra cost, the surrogate procedure is preferable. However, the surrogate procedure may still be optimal even when it leads to bias in the controlled variables, that is, to values which differ from those which maximize the principle function. The extra gain from specifying and using the principle function may not compensate for the extra cost.   In various circumstances, the surrogate procedure is an optimal rule of thumb in the same way as Baumol and Quandt (1964) show various other rules of thumb to be optimal.   The conditions under which the surrogate procedure is optimal, is likely to be optimal, or would be optimal if slightly modified, affect the best way of reaching managerial decisions.

Besides applications to managerial economics, the analysis has prescriptive social application.   For example, let us suppose that most firms do use the surrogate procedure.   This can result in a consistent collective (industry-wide) bias in production which might be corrected to social advantage by either taxing or subsidizing production, depending upon the circumstances.

In order to make these points concrete and to examine circumstances which make the surrogate procedure optimal, I shall concentrate on the production decisions of a purely competitive firm which aims to maximize its expected profit.   In the next section a simple model is analysed and in the subsequent section some generalizations are considered in order to isolate the crucial factors which influence bias when the surrogate procedure is utilized.

A SIMPLE ILLUSTRATION FROM PRODUCTION THEORY OF CERTAINTY EQUIVALENCE AND BIAS

Consider a purely competitive firm which wishes to maximize its expected profit and suppose that its profit depends upon a controlled variable, L, and a non-controlled variable, ε.   The uncontrolled variable may enter into the profit function directly through the production function or it may come in indirectly.   In the direct case, the random factor influencing production may, for example in agriculture, be the amount of rainfall, sunlight, warmth or the degree of infestation of a crop by pests.

The firm's output in any period is assumed to depend on its chosen value of L and the value of an uncontrolled variable ε.   Thus the firm's production function is

$$x = H(L,\varepsilon) \tag{6.1}$$

and its profit is

$$\pi = px - wL, \tag{6.2}$$

where p is the price per unit of the product and w the price per unit of the factor. Hence, the firm's profit function (its objective function according to the above usage) is

$$\pi = pH(L,\varepsilon) - wL. \tag{6.3}$$

Assume that the firm knows p and w when L must be determined, but not ε. The firm's expected profit function, its principle function, is then

$$E\,[\pi] = pE[H(L,\varepsilon)] - wL. \tag{6.4}$$

When does the value of L which maximizes the surrogate function,

$$R = pH(L, E[\varepsilon]) - wL \tag{6.5}$$

also maximize the value of the principle function? If the contributions of L and ε to output are independent, certainty equivalence clearly occurs. For example, if the firm's production function is

$$H(L,\varepsilon) = f\,(L) + T(\varepsilon), \tag{6.6}$$

then $E[\pi] - R = p\{E[T(\varepsilon)] - T(E[\varepsilon])\}$, so that the difference is constant and independent of L. But if the contributions of the controlled variable, L, and the non-controlled variable ε to output are interdependent, certainty equivalence also occurs if their joint interdependent contribution to output depends linearly on ε. Thus, for example, certainty equivalence occurs if

$$H(L,\varepsilon) = f\,(L) + \psi(L)(\beta_1 + \beta_2\varepsilon) + T(\varepsilon). \tag{6.7}$$

The second term on the right-hand side of (6.7) shows that output is jointly influenced by L and ε, but ε enters only linearly in this term. Thus the functions $E[\pi]$ and R once again only differ by the constant $p\{E[T(\varepsilon)] - T(E[\varepsilon])\}$ and certainty equivalence is maintained.

Function (6.7) allows for a wide variety of production relationships. For example ψ' and ψ'' might be of any sign, and consequently the cross-marginal physical productivity of L can be of any sign and may be a diminishing, increasing or constant function of L. Furthermore, $T(\varepsilon)$ can be of any nature. Nevertheless the linearity in ε of the cross-production relationship might well be regarded as restrictive. The cross-contribution to output might in reality be a diminishing marginal value of ε or an increasing one, rather than a constant marginal value. In these circumstances, certainty bias is likely because the optimal value of L will depend upon characteristics of the distribution of ε besides its mean.

Take a very simple example. Assume that the firm's production function is

$$x = -aL^2 + bL - \lambda L \varepsilon^2. \tag{6.8}$$

The firm's profit function is

$$\pi = p(-aL^2 + bL - \lambda L \varepsilon^2) - wL \tag{6.9}$$

and ε enters non-linearly into the cross-production term involving L and ε. To evaluate the bias introduced by the surrogate procedure, consider the principle function and then the surrogate function. Noting that the expectation of ε^2, that is $E[\varepsilon^2]$, equals $[E[\varepsilon]]^2 + $ var ε, the principle function is

$$E[\pi] = p(-aL^2 + bL - \lambda LE[\varepsilon^2]) - wL \tag{6.10}$$

$$= p(-aL^2 + bL - \lambda L\{[E[\varepsilon]]^2 + \text{var } \varepsilon\}) - wL. \tag{6.11}$$

The necessary condition for a maximum of this function is that

$$\frac{dE[\pi]}{dL} = p(-2aL + b - \lambda\{[E[\varepsilon]]^2 + \text{var } \varepsilon\}) - w = 0, \tag{6.12}$$

and this is satisfied if

$$\bar{L} = \frac{1}{2a}\left[-\frac{w}{p} + b - \lambda\{[E[\varepsilon]]^2 + \text{var}\,\varepsilon\}\right]. \tag{6.13}$$

Hence, the optimal value of L varies inversely with the variance of the non-controlled variable, ε. For example, ε may be the amount of precipitation or the deviation of annual rainfall from some ideal amount for the growing of a crop. The surrogate function is

$$R = p(-aL^2 + bL - \lambda L[E[\varepsilon]]^2) - wL. \tag{6.14}$$

The requirement for a maximum of this function is that

$$\hat{L} = \frac{1}{2a}\left(-\frac{w}{p} + b - \lambda[E[\varepsilon]]^2\right). \tag{6.15}$$

Thus the surrogate procedure leads to a value for $\hat{L}$ which is in excess of $\bar{L}$. In fact, it leads to the selection of a value for L which is biased above the optimal value by $1/2a$ var ε.

Figure 6.1 illustrates the type of relationship which exists between functions (6.11) and (6.14) if a given probability distribution for ε is assumed. The difference between the two functions equals $p\lambda L$ var ε. The surrogate procedure overestimates expected gains and involves a loss (in terms of the alternative expected profit forgone) of AB.

Other things equal, the expected profit forgone by adopting the surrogate procedure is less the greater is $2a$. Expected profit forgone varies inversely with the rate of decline in the marginal productivity of

L in producing x. This can be shown algebraically but is also easy to illustrate diagrammatically.

Figure 6.1 Principle and surrogate profit functions

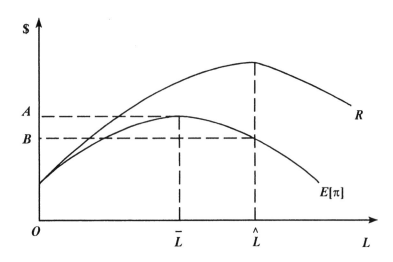

In Figure 6.2 the surrogate marginal expected productivity of L is shown by curve BD. The surrogate production function, as can be seen from equation (6.8) is

$$x = -aL^2 + bL - \lambda L[E[\varepsilon]]^2, \qquad (6.16)$$

so that the surrogate marginal expected productivity of L is

$$\frac{dx}{dL} = -2aL + b - \lambda[E[\varepsilon]]^2. \qquad (6.17)$$

However, the true expected production is

$$x = -aL^2 + bL - \lambda L[E[\varepsilon]]^2 - \lambda L \text{ var } \varepsilon \qquad (6.18)$$

and thus the true marginal expected productivity of L is

$$\frac{dx}{DL} = -2aL + b - \lambda[E[\varepsilon]]^2 - \lambda \text{ var } \varepsilon. \qquad (6.19)$$

This function differs from (6.17) by the constant $-\lambda$ var ε and for the hypothetical case illustrated in Figure 6.2 might be represented by curve CK, given that the surrogate marginal expected productivity curve of L is BD.

If expected profit is to be at a maximum as can be seen from rearranging (6.12), L must be such that the true marginal expected productivity of L equals w/p. As is apparent from the first-order condition for a maximum of (6.14), the maximum of the surrogate profit function requires that the surrogate marginal expected productivity of L be equated to w/p. This occurs in Figure 6.2 for the value of L at which CK intersects the line w/p. Thus, given that CK is the true marginal expected productivity of L and BD the surrogate, real expected profit equivalent to the hatched triangle is forgone by using the surrogate procedure.

Figure 6.2 Principle and surrogate marginal product functions

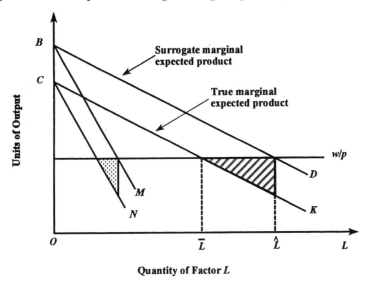

The profit forgone by using the surrogate procedure becomes smaller (other things unchanged) as output becomes less responsive to changes in L, that is, the greater is the rate of decline of dx/dL. As $2a$ becomes greater, both the surrogate and true marginal expected productivity curves become steeper about their respective fixed points C and B, but the difference between the curves remains a constant. In the case shown in Figure 6.2, $2a$ may increase so that the surrogate marginal expected productivity curve is BM and the true one is CN. As $2a$ increases, other things equal, the intercept of the true marginal and corresponding surrogate curve with the line w/p becomes smaller. Hence, the base of the triangle representing expected profit forgone becomes smaller. However, the difference between the curves remains constant (that is equal to λ var ε) so that the height of these triangles remains constant.   Thus, by the rule for finding the area of triangles, the area of the relevant triangles becomes smaller as $2a$ increases and the real expected profit forgone by adopting the surrogate procedure becomes less.   Given steeply diminishing marginal productivity of the controlled variable, the extra information contained in the principle procedure adds little to expected profit and may not cover the extra cost of collecting and using it.   This situation parallels similar ones which have been considered by Nelson (1961) and Tisdell (1970; also Chapter 5).

This example has indicated some of the managerial implications of certainty bias and can illustrate some of its consequences for economic welfare.   Let us assume that all firms use the surrogate procedure to determine   their   production.   Consequently,   output   of   particular commodities may be above or below a socially optimal level.   I shall take it that Paretian optimality requires the value of the true marginal expected output from each factor of production to be equal to its price (cost) per unit.   If the random elements influencing the production of each firm tend to be independent between firms, then by the law of large numbers, industry output will show little random variation and the above condition seems necessary for Paretian optimality.

For simplicity, assume within the economy that only the production of product x involves any uncertainty.[4]   Suppose that a given number of firms produce x and that they all adopt the surrogate procedure and have the same (or similar) production function as in (6.8) with ε entering as the only random element.   The result is that a greater than optimal amount of L is allocated to the production of product x.   Each firm employs $\hat{L}$ of L so that, as Figure 6.2 indicates, the value of true marginal expected output of L in producing x is below the price or cost per unit of L.   This price also measures the value of output forgone elsewhere.   There is overproduction of product x from an efficiency point of view.   This could be corrected by suitably taxing the use of L in producing x, or in this case by taxing the output of x.   The required per-unit real tax on the employment of L is λ var ε which is equivalent to BC in Figure 6.2.

The larger is the variance of ε, other things equal, the greater is the overallocation of L to producing x and the higher the required per-unit tax.   Firms operating in districts in which, for example (assuming that ε is an indicator of rainfall) rainfall is very variable, may overexpand their use of L by a much greater amount than those in districts with less variable rainfall.   In order to achieve the necessary condition for Paretian optimality, a higher per-unit tax would be required on producers in areas subject to more variability of rainfall.

Of course, this does assume that all firms use the surrogate procedure. It is a matter for empirical investigation to find out how widely it is used. But if it is widely used, social implications follow, some of which may be of particular relevance to agricultural districts that have variable weather patterns which affect production.

If the sign of the term $\lambda L \varepsilon^2$ in the production function, (6.8), is changed from negative to positive the direction of the bias introduced by the surrogate procedure is altered. Thus, from the point of view of the firm's management the surrogate procedure leads to a less than optimal employment of factor L. However, it is still true that, other things equal, the extent of this error and the expected profit forgone varies inversely with the steepness with which the marginal productivity of L declines. On the social plane, and assuming the collective conditions mentioned above, too little of resource L is devoted to the production of product x if the surrogate procedure is widely used. This could be corrected by a per-unit subsidy on the employment of L in the industry. The real per-unit subsidy to each firm needs to be λ var ε per unit of L employed in producing x. Thus firms experiencing the greatest variance in ε would need to be paid the greatest per-unit subsidy. The policy conclusions are therefore reversed in this case. It is, of course, an empirical matter to find out the type of interrelationships in production which are really relevant.

In order to facilitate applications of the analysis, it is helpful to generalize it. To generalize it to cases involving quadratics in ε in the interdependent production terms is straightforward but cumbersome. Rather than do this, let us proceed more generally for the type of production function considered above.

GENERALIZATION OF THE DIRECTION OF BIAS INTRODUCED BY THE SURROGATE PROCEDURE

While the direction of bias introduced into the controlled variable by use of the surrogate procedure is obvious in the previous case, the direction of the bias is not immediately apparent in the more general case. Nevertheless, we can set out the factors which determine this bias. By knowing these, we can predict the qualitative correction to the value of the controlled variable which will increase expected profit. Furthermore, we can determine (given certain conditions and the use of the surrogate procedure by firms in the industry) whether taxation or subsidization of the employment of the controlled variable in the industry will promote economic efficiency and whether greater or smaller marginal fiscal payments are required when the value of the non-controlled elements is more variable.

Assume that the firm's production function is of the form

$$x = f(L) + h(L)g(\varepsilon) + T(\varepsilon). \tag{6.20}$$

The middle term on the right-hand side of (6.20) indicates that the interdependence between L and ε in production involves separability and could, for example, be of the Cobb–Douglas type. Since only optimal values for L are to be considered, nothing is lost in generality if the last term on the right-hand side of (6.20) is dropped. Thus the relevant production function becomes

$$x = f(L) + h(L)g(\varepsilon). \tag{6.21}$$

In view of this, the firm's profit function is

$$\pi = p(f(L) + h(L)g(\varepsilon)) - wL, \tag{6.22}$$

and hence the firm's principle function is

$$E[\pi] = p(f(L) + h(L)E[g(\varepsilon)]) - wL, \tag{6.23}$$

and its surrogate function is

$$R = p(f(L) + h(L)g(E[\varepsilon])) - wL. \tag{6.24}$$

The principle and surrogate functions are distinguished by the difference between the terms $E[g(\varepsilon)]$ and $g(E[\varepsilon])$.

If $E[\pi]$ is to be at a maximum with respect to L, L must be such that

$$f'(L) + h'(L)E[g(\varepsilon)] = \frac{w}{p}. \tag{6.25}$$

The true marginal expected productivity of L must be equal to the real price of L. By contrast, the necessary condition for a maximum R with respect to L should be such that

$$f'(L) + h'(L)g(E[\varepsilon]) = \frac{w}{p}. \tag{6.26}$$

Let $\bar{L}$ and $\hat{L}$ represent the values of L which respectively satisfy equations (6.25) and (6.26) and also meet the second-order conditions for a maximum of $E[\pi]$ and R respectively. These results follow: the difference between $\hat{L}$ and $\bar{L}$, the direction of the bias if any, depends upon the sign of $h'(L)g(\varepsilon)$ and on whether $g(\varepsilon)$ is strictly concave, strictly convex or linear. If either $h'(L)g(\varepsilon)$ is zero or $g(\varepsilon)$ is linear, then certainty equivalence occurs. In the latter case, $E[g(\varepsilon)] = g(E[\varepsilon])$.

Consider cases in which ε has a cross-effect on production and $g(\varepsilon)$ is not linear.

1. Take the case where $h'(L)g(\varepsilon) > 0$ for all ε which are probable and assume that $g(\varepsilon)$ is strictly concave, that is, $g'' < 0$. Two

possibilities can be distinguished. If $g(\varepsilon) > 0$ for all ε which are probable, then $h'(L) > 0$ and $\hat{L} > \bar{L}$. The surrogate value of L exceeds the optimal value. On the other hand, if $g(\varepsilon) < 0$ for all ε which are probable, then $h'(L) < 0$ and $\hat{L} > \bar{L}$. The surrogate result is less than the optimal value for L.

Proof: in the possibility where $g(\varepsilon) > 0$ for all probable ε, $h'(L)$ is positive. In view of the strict concavity of $g(\varepsilon)$, it follows from Polya's theorem (Hardy, *et al.*, 1934, p. 74) that $g(E[\varepsilon]) > E[g(\varepsilon)]$ and so $h'(L)g(E[\varepsilon]) > h'(L)E[g(\varepsilon)]$. Thus the curve representing the surrogate marginal expected productivity of L is higher than the curve representing the true marginal expected productivity of L. With w/p constant, it follows that $\hat{L} > \bar{L}$. This is illustrated by the example in Figure 6.2. In the possibility where $g(\varepsilon) < 0$ for all probable ε, $h'(L)$ is negative. Since $g'' < 0$, it is still true that $g(E[\varepsilon]) > E[g(\varepsilon)]$. However, the inequality of the absolute values of these negative quantities is reversed. If $g(\varepsilon) < 0, |g(E[\varepsilon])| < |E[g(\varepsilon)]|$. Thus given the double negative in the cross-expression for the marginal product of L, $h'(L)g(E[\varepsilon]) < h'(L)E[g(\varepsilon)]$. Hence, in this case the surrogate marginal expected product curve for L lies below the true marginal expected product curve of L. Therefore, $\hat{L} < \bar{L}$. The surrogate value of L is biased downwards so an upward correction would be called for if the decision maker wished to get closer to optimality.

2. Take the case where $h'(L)g(\varepsilon) < 0$ for all ε which are probable and assume that $g(\varepsilon)$ is strictly concave, that is, $g'' < 0$. Then if $g(\varepsilon) > 0$ for all probable ε, $\hat{L} < L$ and the surrogate procedure biases the value of L downwards. Corrective subsidies can improve economic efficiency. On the other hand, if $g(\varepsilon) < 0$, $\hat{L} > L$, the surrogate procedure leads to upward bias in L and corrective taxes can increase economic efficiency. The proof follows in a similar way to that stated in (1) above.

3. If $g(\varepsilon)$ is strictly convex, that is, $g'' > 0$, each of the above propositions is reversed, for if $g(\varepsilon)$ is strictly convex rather than strictly concave $g(E[\varepsilon]) < E[g(\varepsilon)]$. Thus the relative positions of the surrogate and true marginal expected productivity curves are reversed and the policy conclusions correspondingly changed.

It is impossible to summarize the full range of these relationships briefly in a non-technical fashion. However, note that when the cross-marginal physical product of L is positive and the random non-controlled input adds positively to output through the cross-production relationship, the surrogate procedure causes the value of L to be biased downwards if $g(\varepsilon)$ is strictly convex, and to be biased upward if $g(\varepsilon)$ is strictly concave. When $g(\varepsilon)$ is strictly convex the marginal variation in *g* for a change in *ε* (and also the consequent change of output) is at a decreasing rate, whereas the opposite is so when $g(\varepsilon)$ is strictly concave.

CONCLUDING DISCUSSION

The above production functions involve only one controlled variable (a variable input) and one random non-controlled variable (another input). Because of the multiplicative term in the production function the cross-contributions of the two factors to production are separable.   The discussion can be extended to include a number of variable controlled factors and non-controlled factors in the production function.   For example, this is easy if, say, *K* is a vector of factors and the production function in

$$x = f(K,L) + h(L)g(\varepsilon) + T(\varepsilon). \qquad (6.27)$$

More complicated relationships could be cited.   However, unless a particular problem needs to be solved, there seems little point in outlining these possibilities.   The simple case of one controlled and one non-controlled factor indicates the type of relationships (such as convexity or otherwise of particular functions) which are liable to have an influence in the more general case and the variety of results which are possible.

It is also apparent that the degree of flexibility which is optimal to incorporate into the productive process can easily be analysed by using production functions with separable cross-terms.   To decide between alternative techniques if the firm wishes to maximize expected profit, it is necessary (given one controlled and one non-controlled factor) to examine the size of the area between the line *w/p* and the alternative true marginal expected productivity curves of *L* which correspond to the different techniques.   The analysis is relevant whether *ε* enters in a direct way into production or indirectly through its adjustment to another random variable, such as a price, the value of which becomes known or less uncertain with the passage of time.   Because it specifically identifies the source of the possible alteration of output, this approach to considering flexibility has an advantage over those which merely concentrate on the cost of changing planned output (Theil, 1961; Turnovsky, 1972).

In the above analysis, it is supposed that utility is a linear function of profit.   The extent to which this is a restrictive assumption in practice is debatable.   Nevertheless, there is evidence that farmers' utility functions are on the whole non-linear.   For example, Officer, Halter and Dillon (1967) found from their early study in the Armidale region that farmers tend to be risk averse. Yet this aversion is surprisingly small if one judges by the coefficients which they give in their Table 1 (Officer et al., 1967, p. 173). Stronger evidence of non-linearity of utility functions comes from a study by Francisco and Anderson (1972) of pastoralists' decisions in the West Darling region of New South Wales. In further extension of the present analysis it does seem desirable to relax the non-linearity assumption. Even when the assumption is relaxed, the surrogate procedure can be shown to be an optimal rule of thumb under a range of conditions, and important managerial implications still follow.

Yet analysis in terms of expected profit remains significant. It sometimes can be used to indicate optimal choices from a social welfare point of view. Second, the analysis demonstrates that uncertainty may rationally cause a firm which is maximizing its expected profit to bias its controlled variables away from those values which are optimal when the non-controlled variables are equal to their certainty equivalents. Thus bias of the controlled variables away from values which are optimal in the absence of uncertainty (or when certainty equivalents are used), such as conservative stocking rates which McArthur and Dillon (1971) explain on the basis of risk aversion, can also arise in risk-neutral situations if production functions are of a particular nature. In practice, both risk preferences and 'real' factors are likely to cause systematic bias in decisions made under uncertainty. So also are the rules of thumb and surrogate procedures which are adopted by farmers.

Theoretical and empirical work on decision making must take account of these three factors.

NOTES

1. For an outline of the other concept of certainty equivalence see, for example, Mishan (1971, Chapter 38) and Dillon (1971).

2. The function representing the expected value of the objective function will be called the principle function. The objective function in which the non–controlled variables are merely replaced by their expected values will be called the surrogate function. Thus if $U = U(x,y)$ is the objective function after all constraints are taken into account and x is a controlled variable and y is non-controlled, the principle function is $E[U] = E[U(x,y)]$ and the surrogate function is $U(x, E[y])$.

3. Where π' represents the firm's profit after deducting decision cost D_c, $\pi' = \pi - D_c$. Hence, where $\bar{L}$ represents the optimal value of the controlled variable obtained from the principle procedure and $\hat{L}$ that from the surrogate procedure, the principle procedure is only preferable if

$$\pi(\bar{L}) - D_c(\bar{L}) > \pi(\hat{L}) - D_c(\hat{L}).$$

As a rule, D_c is larger for the principle procedure. In practice, values of the variables in the above inequality are not likely to be perfectly known by the decision maker and thus expected values may need to be used.

4. We could also suppose that there is uncertainty elsewhere but that the optimal rule is applied in producing products other than x. The results below would then apply. However, a difficulty can arise if uncertainty occurs elsewhere and the surrogate procedure is used universally. The uncertainty can then become Paretian irrelevant in the same way as Kahn (1935) indicates that universal monopoly or universal externalities *can* become Paretian irrelevant.

REFERENCES

Baumol, W.J. and Quandt, R.E. (1964), 'Rules of Thumb and Optimally Imperfect Decisions', *American Economic Review*, 54(1), 23–46.

Dillon, J.L. (1971), 'An Expository Review of Bernoullian Decision Theory in Agriculture: Is Utility Futility?', *Review of Marketing and Agricultural Economics*, 39(1), 3–80.

Francisco, E.M. and Anderson, J.R. (1972), 'Chance and Choice West of the Darling', *Australian Journal of Agricultural Economics*, 16(2), 82–93.

Hardy, G.H., Littlewood, J.E. and Polya, G. (1934), *Inequalities*, Cambridge: Cambridge University Press.

Hart, A.G. (1942), 'Risk, Uncertainty and the Unprofitability of Compounding Probabilities', in Lange, O. McIntyre, F. and Yntema, F. (eds), *Studies in Mathematical Economics and Econometrics*, Chicago: University of Chicago Press, 110–18.

Kahn, R.F. (1935), 'Some Notes on Ideal Output', *Economic Journal*, 45(177), 1–35.

Malinvaud, E. (1969), 'First Order Certainty Equivalence', *Econometrica*, 37(4), 706–18.

McArthur, I.D. and Dillon J.L. (1971), 'Risk, Utility and Stocking Rate', *Australian Journal of Agricultural Economics*, 15(1), 20–35.

Mishan, E.J. (1971), *Cost-Benefit Analysis*, London: George Allen & Unwin.

Nelson, R.R. (1961), 'Uncertainty Prediction and Competitive Equilibrium', *Quarterly Journal of Economics*, 75(1), 41–62.

Officer, R.R., Halter, A.N. and Dillon, J.L. (1967), 'Risk, Utility and the Palatability of Extension Advice to Farmer Groups', *Australian Journal of Agricultural Economics*, 11(2), 171–83.

Simon, H.A. (1956), 'Dynamic Programming under Uncertainty with a Quadratic Criterion Function', *Econometrica*, 24(1), 74–81.

Theil, H. (1961), *Economic Forecasts and Policy*, 2nd edn, Amsterdam: North-Holland.

Tisdell, C.A. (1970), 'Implications of Learning for Economic Planning', *Economics of Planning*, 10(3), 177–92.

Turnovsky, S.J. (1972), 'Production Flexibility, Price Uncertainty and the Behaviour of the Competitive Firm', Faculty of Economics, Australian National University, Canberra.

7. Learning by Doing and Productivity Progress

INTRODUCTION

The discussion of learning so far has been confined to using it to mean accretion of information or reduction in uncertainty. The consequences of this for economic decision making including the production decisions of business firms have been explored. However, in addition to this, learning is sometimes considered in the economics and managerial literature in a different way, often described as learning by doing or productivity progress. This refers to increases in productivity that occur with the passage of time after a business firm embarks on the production of a new product or installs a new production process.

Productivity progress may reflect improved dexterity of workers and ability of workers and managers to solve production problems as they become more familiar with new production processes. A part of productivity progress may be due to increasing dexterity in work practices (some people may not regard this as learning in any deep sense), increases in knowledge of how best to deal with technical or engineering problems in the production process (genuine learning) and improvements in organization of the business firm as it learns how to best adjust to innovation and change in its production processes. The latter may be an extremely important factor. In addition, the physical properties of new machinery, if new machinery is involved, may result in productivity increases up to a point as this machinery is run in. Eventually, of course, as machinery ages, this factor may become a drag on productivity. As far as I am aware no empirical studies have been completed which decompose productivity progress into all of these elements. Furthermore, for business firms where marketing is important, learning by doing and productivity progress can be important in relation to marketing activities, but this appears to have been given little attention in economics so far.

This chapter is designed to illustrate the importance of productivity progress in the start-up phase of manufacturing industry, taking Bangladesh jute mills as a case study. As suggested above, productivity progress in manufacturing involves evolutionary elements, for example, often adaptation of organizational structures in response to new or changed conditions of production.[1]

Productivity progress and learning in manufacturing have been widely discussed in the literature (Conway and Schultz, 1959; Hay and Morris, 1979; Yelle, 1979). Typically manufacturing productivity starting from the installation of a new manufacturing process shows a period of continuous increase before it eventually levels off. The rising phase is popularly known as the 'start-up' phase (Baloff, 1966a, 1967; Baloff and Kenelly, 1967; Harvey, 1976; Pegels, 1976). It is generally believed that learning is the principal contributor to productivity increase in this phase and is likely to be confined to this phase. For this reason, the terms 'start-up' and 'learning' are often used interchangeably in the literature on this subject (for example, Pegels, 1976). It is widely believed that learning is a finite process and once it stops, the level of productivity stabilizes and remains roughly stationary thereafter (Baloff, 1966a; Hartley, 1965). The purpose of this chapter is to estimate learning or productivity parameters for the start-up phase of jute manufacturing plants in Bangladesh. While such parameters have been estimated for several manufacturing industries in developed countries, there are no such studies available for manufacturing in less-developed countries (LDCs).

Jute manufacturing consists of two basic processes: (a) spinning of jute and (b) weaving of jute yarn. Spinning includes the processes from batching to winding and weaving from beaming to finishing. Some jute mills concentrate on spinning alone whereas others are involved only in weaving. This is the common practice in advanced countries such as the UK and Belgium. But Bangladesh mills engaged in spinning are mostly involved in weaving as well. Nevertheless, weaving operations in Bangladesh mills are completely separated from spinning operations (Kibria and Tisdell, 1984). Spinning results in the production of yarn and weaving (using yarn as an input) results in the output of fabric. Both yarn and fabric are marketable products.

To estimate the parameters of learning and productivity progress in the start-up phase of Bangladesh mills, spinning and weaving processes were examined separately. Again, within each process, the productivity progress for the major products will be examined separately. For spinning, this involves considering heavy yarn and light yarn and for weaving, sacking and hessian. To do this, we concentrate on the ten oldest spinning mills (out of a sample of 40) and 12 oldest weaving mills (out of 39) in Bangladesh. Observations for the start-up phase of these mills are sufficiently numerous for us to have some confidence in the statistical results obtained.

The most common assumption about productivity progress in the start-up phase of a manufacturing process is that it depends on the level of cumulative output using this process. Increases in productivity are ascribed chiefly to learning by doing (Arrow, 1962). Baloff (1966a, 1966b) suggests that manufacturing productivity in the start-up phase is well characterized by the exponential function:

$$Y = aX^b \qquad (7.1)$$

where Y is an index of manufacturing productivity, X measures cumulative output and a and b are parameters. In this 'learning model', empirically derived estimates of b have tended to fall in the range of zero to one.

While the fitting of this function to the cumulative output of spinning mills in Bangladesh since their commencement gives acceptable statistical results, time-dependent functions as discussed later give a superior fit to the data. This may be because the production of jute yarn principally occurs in a factory on a number of independent spindles in the case of spinning mills and on independent looms in weaving mills. Production of neither jute yarns nor fabric is of an assembly-line type and therefore does not include a single flow line within the factory as is common for many of the other manufacturing processes which have been studied using relationship (7.1) or modifications of it.

Learning and productivity progress might depend upon the elapsed time since the installation of a new manufacturing process as suggested by Fellner (1969) and Zevin (1975). Empirical support is reported by David (1970) and by others. The spirit of this hypothesis, which it shares with the cumulative output approach, is that even in the absence of new investments, the production process itself stimulates and generates additional learning. More specifically, 'economies of learning' are experienced even though production techniques remain unchanged (Lundberg, reported in Arrow, 1962). Our results below also support this view. In the case of jute spinning and weaving in Bangladesh, mills have been given an initial endowment and vintage of machinery which has not been altered during their lifetime. Nevertheless, as will be seen, productivity in these mills increased substantially over a long period. Note that because there is a positive correlation between the age of a mill and the cumulative level of output produced by a mill, one would expect the time-dependent approach and Baloff's approach to give qualitatively similar results.

TYPES OF FUNCTIONS FITTED TO THE DATA

Two types of time-dependent functions are fitted to the data for each jute-spinning and -weaving mill in our sample. One is a time-dependent exponential function and the other is a time-dependent linear function based on ratios of each mill's annual productivity compared to productivity of the mill in the initial year of its operation.

An exponential function is first fitted to the data and is of the form

$$P = AT^\beta \qquad (7.2)$$

where P is the labour productivity (defined below), and T the age of the mill measured in finite years since its inception. This function is similar to that of Baloff, (1966a, 1966b, 1967), Baloff and Kennelly (1967), and Liao (1982) in which cumulative output rather than elapsed time is the independent variable. The available data series were truncated so that they include only the segment up to and including the year of observed peak productivity attainment. Coefficients A and β are the parameters of the model that determine the specific shape and location of the learning or productivity progress curve for a particular start-up. Parameter A represents the productivity experienced during the first year of operation of a mill while B is an index of the rate of productivity gain during a particular start-up – it is the elasticity of productivity with respect to the age of a mill. The larger the value of β the greater is the relative rate of productivity improvement. The parameters of (7.2) are estimated by ordinary least squares method using the logarithmic transformation of this function.

A different and to some extent simpler method of considering productivity progress during the start-up phase was also considered. For each mill, productivity during each year was expressed as a percentage of productivity during its initial year of operation and the linear equation

$$Z = a + bT \qquad (7.3)$$

was fitted by ordinary least squares regression. In this equation Z represents labour productivity (defined below) as a percentage of initial year productivity of a mill, T is the age of the mill and a and b are parameters. One would expect a to be close to 100 when this equation is estimated. The parameter b represents the annual increase in the percentage of productivity *compared to the initial productivity*. Given the ratio nature of the equation, b-values permit straightforward comparisons between mills, in a similar way to the β-values in equation (7.2). Equation (7.3) compared to equation (7.2) is slightly simpler and its estimation does not require logarithmic transformation. Equation (7.3) implies that initial productivity is to be made the base of the ratios used. The greater simplicity of relationship (7.3) compared to equation (7.2) favours it if it gives a satisfactory fit to the data.

NATURE OF THE DATA

The investigation is based on data collected directly by Dr M.G. Kibria from 40 jute-spinning mills and 39 jute-weaving mills in Bangladesh in 1981, but only data for the oldest ten spinning mills and the oldest 12 weaving mills are used here. The original survey of jute-spinning mills includes 18 in Dacca, 18 in Chittagong and 14 in Khulna zones (Bangladesh). For weaving, the distribution is: 19 in Dacca, 12 in Chittagong and 20 in Khulna zones. Care was taken to ensure that the sample, which is a relatively large one, was representative. Mills of all sizes and from all zones were represented in it. These mills account for more than half of the total spindles in the Bangladesh jute-spinning industry, and just under two-thirds of all the looms in the Bangladesh jute-weaving industry. Note that the mills in the subsample of oldest mills are also of varying sizes and drawn from different parts of the country.

For spinning mills the data collected included up-to-date information on capital used (number of spindles), employment (number of spinners) and production (in grams) of all these mills, on an annual basis, since their inception. These data were collected and compiled separately for each of the two products, heavy and light yarns. Data collected for all weaving mills included up-to-date information on capital used (number of looms), employment of labour (number of weavers) and output (in grams), also on an annual basis since their inception. This information was assembled separately for each of the two products, sacking and hessian.

Physical data are used exclusively in this study. Relative homogeneity (in terms of physical capital equipment, that is, spindles) within the jute-spinning industry (Kibria and Tisdell, 1984), and also almost identical capital equipment (physical characteristics of the machines, that is, looms) in the jute-weaving industry (Kibria and Tisdell, 1983), makes this a reasonable approach.

For the current investigation, the most important single item of data is an indicator of productivity. Total volume of output cannot be used because of the variation in the size of the mills (and consequently capital use, employment and output), as well as intramill variations of these factors from year to year. By taking productivity per unit of labour directly used in the production process (which, incidentally, is the approach used by most other studies in this field) we can overcome this problem. However, some operational problems remain to be resolved.

Who is employed directly in the jute manufacturing process? In the jute-spinning process, spinners account for about 60 per cent of the total labour requirements and in jute weaving, weavers account for 80 per cent of total labour requirements. For each of the processes, the number of ancillary workers varies proportionately or almost so with the number of spinners in spinning and weavers in weaving. Consequently, output per direct labourer might be translated in these cases into the simple form of 'production per year per spinner' for spinning and 'production per year per weaver' for weaving without significant distortion. However, this is too simplistic. The amount of time mills actually work is found to vary between individual mills as well as from year to year. A simple measurement of annual per-spinner or per-weaver production thus ceases to be applicable. This difficulty can be overcome by adjusting the labour figure for the number of hours the mill actually works. This yields the productivity per hour per spinner or weaver as the case may be. Thus a series for annual labour productivity per hour can be obtained for each mill since its commencement of operations and used to estimate productivity progress parameters.

It is pertinent to note that spinning frames for heavy yarn and light yarn in the subsample of mills considered here are all of the old slip draft type and belong to the same vintage. Looms also belong to the same vintage.

EMPIRICAL RESULTS

An examination of the crude data reveals that the extent of productivity increase at peak productivity (for example, actual maximum productivity) compared to initial productivity of each mill is considerable for all jute-spinning and -weaving mills considered in our sample of older mills. The percentage increase in productivity compared to its initial value averages 18.82 per cent for heavy yarn and 34.17 per cent for light yarn (these are unweighted averages per mill) and ranges between the mills from 7.82 to 45.49 per cent for heavy yarn and from 4.59 to 57.76 per cent for light yarn. The corresponding percentage increase for weaving mills averages 18.15 per cent (excluding mill seven, it comes to 13.36) for sacking and 21.33 per cent for hessian and ranges between the mills from 11.25 to 16.74 per cent (excluding mill seven, and to 70.89 if it is included) for sacking and from 12.95 to 51.12 per cent for hessian. The maximum level of labour productivity is reached after mills have been in operation for just over 12 years on average for spinning and just over 11 years for weaving. Evidence however indicates that for more recently established spinning and weaving mills the start-up phase has become shorter.[2]

In order to specify productivity progress in the start-up phase, equations (7.2) and (7.3) were fitted to the data. The results for heavy-yarn production are set out in Table 7.1 and those for light yarn are given in Table 7.2. High R^2-values have been obtained for both equations for nearly all mills and parameter estimates are significant at the one per cent level for most mills.

Table 7.1   Heavy-yarn productivity per spinner hour as a function of mill age in the start-up phase in Bangladesh

		Coefficients of Eq. (7.2)			Coefficients of Eq. (7.3)		
Mill	Number of Observations	A	β	R^2	a	b	R^2
1	15	9.189	0.046**	0.893	98.966	0.713**	0.916
2	13	9.185	0.062**	0.924	101.661	1.313**	0.902
3	15	9.323	0.052**	0.827	100.288	1.001**	0.881
4	12	9.409	0.095	0.842	98.527	2.414**	0.941
5	11	9.390	0.040**	0.895	101.008	0.933**	0.880
6	10	9.800	0.024*	0.536	102.324	0.513	0.387
7	13	9.283	0.054**	0.974	100.978	1.289**	0.956
8	11	9.221	0.049**	0.929	101.219	1.138**	0.859
9	12	9.331	0.162**	0.943	107.745	3.428**	0.879
10	11	9.323	0.056**	0.945	102.224	1.230**	0.793

Notes
** 1% level of significance.
* 5% level of significance.

Parameter β as noted before, indicates the rate of productivity gain experienced during the start-up of a mill. Differences in its magnitude provide a means of direct comparison of intermill performance in productivity gains. Values of the β parameter show considerable variation from case to case, thus indicating that relative rates of productivity gain do vary greatly between different mills. The estimated values of β are in most cases in the range 0.040 to 0.062 for heavy yarn: and for light yarn are about 0.105 to 0.136. All estimated β-values are positive and less than unity.

Table 7.2 Light-yarn productivity per spinner hour as a function of mill age in the start-up phase in Bangladesh

Mill	Number of Observations	Coefficients of Eq. (7.2)			Coefficients of Eq. (7.3)		
		A	β	R^2	a	b	R^2
1	11	8.405	0.130**	0.829	91.437	2.811**	0.929
2	13	8.431	0.135**	0.915	99.181	3.326**	0.975
3	15	8.408	0.136**	0.936	101.218	2.861**	0.928
4	12	8.228	0.105**	0.966	98.778	2.018**	0.964
5	13	8.479	0.107**	0.945	100.102	2.415**	0.944
6	11	8.623	0.178**	0.853	93.958	4.255**	0.956
7	14	8.431	0.128**	0.733	96.708	3.032**	0.857
8	10	8.371	0.232**	0.972	99.818	6.071**	0.975
9	10	8.836	0.028**	0.843	99.789	0.516**	0.716
10	11	8.437	0.150**	0.953	98.707	4.077**	0.967

Notes
** 1% level of significance.
* 5% level of significance.

In nearly all cases, the observed β-values are higher for light yarn than those for heavy yarn. Light yarn is produced in a relatively lengthier and presumably more complex spinning process. The very nature of this process requires greater skill, which is acquired through the performance of a more varied task, than that required in the spinning process of heavy yarn. The greater experience obtained thereby may be a contributing factor to the relatively higher growth of productivity in the light-yarn mills.

Note that the values of A are very similar for all firms but that there is a greater relative variation in the β-values. Estimated productivity in the initial year is similar for all mills but the rate of growth of productivity in the start-up phase shows considerable variation between mills. The coefficient of variation of A for heavy yarn is 1.80 per cent and for light yarn 1.82 per cent, whereas the coefficient of variation of the β-values for heavy yarn is 57.63 per cent and 37.92 for light yarn.

Turning to the linear relationship specified in (7.3), the a coefficients for the spinning mills, as expected, are close to 100 in all cases. The coefficient b ranges from about 0.5 to 3.5 for heavy yarn and from about 0.5 to 6.0 for light yarn. This indicates an addition of 0.5 per cent to 3.5 per cent annually on the base (initial productivity) for heavy yarn and 0.5 to 6.0 per cent for light yarn. The average value of b for heavy yarn is 1.40 and for light yarn is 3.14. The rate of increase in productivity in the start-up phase is on the whole greater for light jute yarn than for heavy yarn. The coefficient of variation of the b-values for light yarn is also greater than for heavy yarn. The coefficient of variation of b for heavy yarn is 59.43 per cent compared to 45.69 per cent for light yarn. In practically all cases, the estimated coefficients are statistically significant either at the one per cent or five per cent level.

Equations (7.2) and (7.3) also provide good fits to the data for weaving mills as far as sacking and hessian production are concerned. Most R^2-values are high (0.8 or greater), and estimates of β and b are statistically significant at the five per cent level as can be seen from Tables 7.3 and 7.4.

The estimated values of β for the majority of the cases are between 0.050 and 0.088 for sacking, and between 0.063 to 0.091 for hessian. All of the β-values are positive and are less than unity. There is little difference in the values of A between mills. Hence, like spinning mills, the estimated productivity in the initial year is very similar for weaving mills. Also, the variation in the β-values is not marked. This indicates that the rate of growth of productivity in the start-up phase between the weaving mills sampled is surprisingly similar.

The coefficient of variation of A for sacking is 6.65 per cent (4.12 per cent excluding mill seven) and for hessian 2.90 per cent, whereas the coefficient of variation of the β-values for sacking is 81.23 per cent (32.29 per cent, if mill seven is excluded) and 49.76 per cent for hessian.

Turning to linear equation (7.3), Tables 7.3 and 7.4 indicate that for the weaving of sacking and for the weaving of hessian, a coefficients are close to 100, except for unusual mill seven. The b-values range from about 0.8 to 2 (to 8.5 if mill seven is included) for sacking and

Table 7.3 Sacking productivity per weaver hour as a function of mill age in the start-up phase in Bangladesh

Mill	Number of Observations	Coefficients of Eq. (7.2)			Coefficients of Eq. (7.3)		
		A	β	R^2	a	b	R^2
1	11	8.139	0.070**	0.953	101.14	1.31**	0.861
2	11	8.403	0.074**	0.968	100.52	1.39**	0.874
3	11	8.293	0.066**	0.891	102.39	1.18**	0.755
4	10	8.260	0.085**	0.958	99.12	1.69**	0.862
5	11	8.159	0.057**	0.913	101.74	1.01**	0.772
6	10	8.180	0.063**	0.964	100.22	1.25**	0.882
7	11	6.591	0.352**	0.956	82.56	8.48**	0.956
8	11	8.112	0.145**	0.981	91.99	2.23**	0.970
9	11	8.233	0.065**	0.915	98.55	1.64**	0.996
10	11	8.279	0.050**	0.709	104.00	0.83**	0.523
11	10	8.225	0.067**	0.955	98.19	1.41**	0.968
12	10	7.095	0.088**	0.898	95.01	1.63**	0.948

Notes
** 1% level of significance.
* 5% level of significance.

from about one to five for hessian. This indicates an addition of 0.8 per cent to 2.0 per cent annually on the base (initial productivity) for sacking and 1.0 and 5.0 per cent for hessian. The average value of b for sacking is 1.42 (2.00, if mill seven is included) and for hessian is 2.10. The rate of increase in productivity in the start-up phase is on the whole slightly greater for hessian than for sacking. The coefficient of variation of the b-values for hessian is also greater than for sacking, if, of course, mill seven is ignored. The coefficient of variation of b for sacking is 25.5 per cent excluding mill seven) compared to 55.49 per cent for hessian.

Table 7.4 Hessian productivity per weaver hour as a function of mill age in the start-up phase in Bangladesh

		Coefficients of Eq. (7.2)			Coefficients of Eq. (7.3)		
Mill	Number of Observations	A	β	R^2	a	b	R^2
1	10	7.214	0.091**	0.979	98.82	1.86**	0.903
2	12	7.239	0.079**	0.984	98.46	1.46**	0.980
3	13	6.912	0.236**	0.950	90.55	4.88**	0.984
4	13	7.491	0.175**	0.884	93.12	4.44**	0.985
5	11	7.158	0.085**	0.955	96.51	1.70**	0.993
6	12	7.004	0.075**	0.972	98.30	1.38**	0.959
7	12	7.598	0.064**	0.943	98.88	1.18**	0.944
8	12	7.144	0.080**	0.966	98.73	1.48**	0.946
9	12	7.119	0.065**	0.919	99.10	1.53**	0.982
10	11	7.131	0.063**	0.921	100.47	1.56**	0.944
11	11	7.333	0.123**	0.935	97.30	2.08**	0.880
12	10	7.594	0.082**	0.994	98.16	1.70**	0.969

Notes
** 1% level of significance.
* 5% level of significance.

CONCLUSION

There is definite evidence that labour productivity in both Bangladeshi jute-spinning and -weaving mills increases for a considerable number of years after the commencement of their operation. This occurs in the absence of new investment and using machinery of the originally installed vintage. While the percentage annual increases in productivity observed in the older mills are low, they nevertheless amount over the whole start-up phase to a considerable percentage rise in productivity compared to initial productivity of mills. While such increases have been attributed in the literature primarily to learning by doing, other factors such as rising rates of utilization of installed machinery and the mechanical running in of newly installed machines also play a part in increasing productivity in the start-up phase of jute spinning and weaving (compare Evenson and Binswanger, 1978). It should be noted that learning by doing is not confined to operators on the shop floor but also may extend to managers and engineers.

In this study it was found that initial predicted productivities are similar for all mills for each of the products obtained from spinning and weaving. However, major differences arise in the productivity of mills after a period of operation because of differences in their rate of gain in productivity during the start-up phase. Such differences are especially important for jute-spinning mills. Differences in these rates may reflect variations in the quality of management between mills, for example divergent attitudes of management towards organizational slack. However, further study is required to pinpoint the main reasons for the intermill variations in β and b values.

The limited variation in the values of β and b for jute-weaving mills indicates relative uniformity in productivity progress functions for the start-ups of such mills. Given the high values of R^2, rates of growth of productivity experienced in the earlier phases of weaving operations can be extrapolated without risk of undue error for the whole of their start-up phase (compare Billon, 1966). This is true both for the exponential approximations to weaving processes and for the simpler linear ratio approach. The uniformity of productivity coefficients between mills and high R^2 values are especially evident in the case of hessian production.

NOTES

1. The remainder of Chapter 7 is a slightly modified version of Kibria and Tisdell (1985).
2. This may be because some skilled labourers or managers are recruited from existing mills.

REFERENCES

Arrow, K.J. (1962), 'The Economic Implications of Learning by Doing', *Review of Economic Studies*, 29, 155–73.
Baloff, N. (1966a), 'Start-ups in Machine-Intensive Production Systems', *Journal of Industrial Engineering*, 17, 25–32.
Baloff, N. (1966b), 'The Learning Curve: Some Controversial Issues', *Journal of Industrial Economics*, 14, 275–82.
Baloff, N. (1967), 'Estimating Parameters of the Start-up', *Journal of Industrial Engineering*, 8, 248–53.
Baloff, N. and Kennelly J.W. (1967), 'Accounting Implications of Product and Process Start-ups', *Journal of Accounting Research*, 5, 131–43.
Billon, S.A. (1966), 'Industrial Learning Curves and Forecasting', *Management International Review*, 6, 65–79.

Conway, R.W. and Schultz, Jr., A. (1959), 'The Manufacturing Progress Function', *Journal of Industrial Engineering*, 10, 39–54.

David, P.A. (1970), 'Learning by Doing and Tariff Protection: A Reconsideration of the Ante-Bellum United States Cotton Textile Industry', *Journal of Economic History*, 30, 521–601.

Evenson, R.E. and Binswanger, H.P. (1978), 'Technology Transfer and Research Resource Allocation', in Binswanger, H.P. and Ruttan, V.W., *Induced Innovation: Technology, Institution and Development*, Baltimore and London: Johns Hopkins University Press.

Fellner, W. (1969), 'Specific Interpretations of Learning by Doing', *Journal of Economic Theory*, 1, 119–40.

Hartley, K. (1965), 'The Learning Curve and Its Application to the Aircraft Industry', *Journal of Industrial Economics*, 13, 122–8.

Harvey, D.W. (1976), 'Financial Planning Information for Production Start-ups', *Accounting Review*, 51, 838–45.

Hay, D.A. and Morris D.J. (1979), *Industrial Economics: Theory and Evidence*, Oxford: Oxford University Press.

Hirsch, W.Z. (1952), 'Manufacturing Progress, Functions', *The Review of Economics and Statistics*, 34, 143–55.

Hirsch, W.Z. (1956), 'Firm-Progress Ratios', *Econometrica*, 24, 136–43.

Kibria, M.G. and Tisdell, C.A. (1983), 'An Analysis of Technological Change in Jute Weaving in Bangladesh, 1954–55 to 1979–80', *The Developing Economies*, 21, 149–59.

Kibria, M.G. and Tisdell, C.A. (1984), 'Jute Spinning in Bangladesh: Technological Change in Light and Heavy Yarn Production', *Industry and Development*, 9, 35–49.

Kibria, M.G. and Tisdell, C.A. (1985), 'Productivity Progress Parameters for Manufacturing in a LDC: The State of Learning Phase in Bangladesh Jute Mills', *Australian Economic Papers*, 24, 370–79.

Liao, W.M. (1982), 'Emulating Learning Curve Parameters for Managerial Planning and Control', *Accounting and Business Research*, 12, 141–7.

Pegels, C.C. (1976), 'Start-up or Learning Curves – Some New Approaches', *Decision Sciences*, 7, 705–13.

Yelle, L.E. (1979), 'The Learning Curve: Historical Review and Comprehensive Survey', *Decision Sciences*, 10, 302–28.

Zevin, R. (1975), 'The Use of Long-Run Learning Function: With Application to a Massachusetts Cotton Textile Firm, 1823–1860', in *Growth of Manufacturing in 19th Century New England*, New York: ARNO Press, New York Times Company.

PART III

Group Decisions, Organizations and Information

8. Group Rationality and Behaviour

This portion of the book focuses on concepts of group rationality and on how group rationality can be best achieved, taking into account impediments to cooperation within groups. Such impediments include possible conflicts between the objectives of members of a group and other problems involved in coordinating and directing the actions of members of a group in response to changing environments. Such problems may even occur when the group is a team, a body with a commonly agreed objective. These problems include the optimal communication of information in a group (given that different group members may possess different information and transmission and storage of information is costly) and how best to respond to the information transmitted in a group. Within a group asymmetry of information often exists and costs are involved in transmitting and storing it. Furthermore, the ability of individuals in a group usually differs and all are subject to bounded rationality. Such factors are of fundamental importance for the behaviour of groups and for the creation of economically optimal organizations.

Because of such factors, rational solutions for group behaviour considered to be optimal in a perfect world without friction, are unachievable or not optimal in a world of imperfections. This in particular restricts the scope for applying the traditional Paretian optimality criterion for group rationality. Because of impediments within groups, slack within organizations can be optimal, as will be shown later, and also it may pay to introduce biases into the transmittal of some information. Given the complexity of economic organizations, decentralization of decision making is often optimal. The use and limitations of transfer pricing for this purpose in a business firm are explored. The theory of games plays a central role in the analysis of group rationality involving conflict. Some of the general limitations of this analysis are discussed later in this chapter but a more detailed discussion occurs in Chapter 12. This leads on to a discussion of the role of symbiosis rather than competition in a group's survival and in its collective gains, especially of a business group.

123

CONCEPTS OF GROUP RATIONALITY

Analogous concepts for group rationality exist to those for the rationality of individuals. A group can be considered to act with unbounded rationality when its behaviour is such as to achieve Paretian optimality for its members, that is, a situation in which it is impossible to make any of its members better off without making other members worse off. Unbounded group rationality underlies much of the theory of games. It implies perfect knowledge of the strategies available to the group (at least, in essential respects), that the payoffs are well known and that coordination of strategies, if required, is costless. An extremely high degree of knowledge is assumed. Transaction costs and institutional constraints are assumed to be absent. While perfect knowledge is not required for unbounded rationality of a group (as is the case for rational behaviour of an individual, as pointed out in Chapters 2 and 3 and will be further elaborated in Chapter 12), knowledge requirements for unbounded group rationality are liable to be high. These, together with transaction costs, problems of organization and institutional constraints, undoubtedly limit the relevance of this concept of unbounded group rationality.

Various concepts of bounded group rationality are possible. Bounded group rationality takes account of the transaction costs involved in communicating information in groups and in coordinating the actions of members of a group. In principle, Baumol and Quandt's (1964) concept of optimally imperfect decisions can be extended to a group, if its members are prepared to act as a team and have a common objective. The presence of slack in organizations or the transmittal of information may, for instance, be assessed in some organizations (on the basis that it is a team) by considering its impact on the expected value of the objective function for the group. This is done, for example, in Chapters 9 and 10.

Apart, however, from transaction costs involved in managing and organizing groups, problems can arise from uncertainty and from conflict between members in their objectives. The uncertainty problem may arise from differences of opinion about what is possible or likely to occur in a particular situation. These differences may create problems for group rationality even when there is no conflict between objectives of the members. Such factors seriously limit group rationality.

In considering group rationality and behaviour, economists as a whole have tended to rely on static analysis. Equilibria, for example, play an important role in solutions based upon the theory of games and in many descriptions or predictions about how groups of economic agents are liable to act.

Concentration on such factors may result in important evolutionary aspects of groups being ignored. The difficulties of organizations in altering administrative or other structures may, for instance, be overlooked; that is, inertia or irreversibility effects of organizational change may be ignored. Furthermore, the value of diversity of behaviours in organizations can be overlooked, as can the inherent capacity of an organization or group to adapt or transform itself to cope with changing environments.

The need to build flexibility into organizational structures of groups in an imperfectly predictable world can easily be lost sight of in the static analysis of group behaviour.

We need to use more than one concept of group rationality, to better understand group behaviour and, of course, all group behaviour may not be rational. In this book, various concepts of group rationality of the type outlined above are used for analytical purposes. The remainder of this chapter provides a general outline and simple discussion of limitations to unbounded rationality as a guide to group behaviour and group rationality.

INTRODUCING SOME BOUNDS UPON THE PARETO OPTIMALITY OF GROUP BEHAVIOUR

The Pareto optimality concept has been extensively used in economics and a number of related disciplines.[1] The assumption of the Pareto optimality of group behaviour has been widely employed in game theory constructs, some related theories of group behaviour and, at least implicitly, in a number of economic models which are designed to explain the behaviour of a collection of economic agents. It has also been suggested that the whole society should strive to attain Pareto optimality in order 'to maximize its welfare'. There is no doubt that the concept has and does exert considerable influence in the positive and normative areas of economic thought, despite the fact that many writers have noted its serious limitations.[2]

Here, the limitations of the Pareto optimality hypothesis of group behaviour are considered. Arguments in general terms are given in the hope that these might help with the conceptualization of some of the basic problems associated with the Pareto optimality hypothesis of group behaviour.[3] To begin to clarify some of the factors which may determine whether group behaviour is Pareto optimal or not, it is of assistance to classify groups according to differences in the 'extent' of the interdependence of their members.

Taking any group of individuals, the following possibilities exist:

1. No (possible) action of any member can influence the satisfaction of any other member (complete independence).

2. Every (possible) action of at least one member affects the satisfaction of another member or other members but no other member can affect this satisfaction (one-way dependence). Obviously, this condition cannot apply to every member of the group.
3. Every (possible) action of any member affects the satisfaction of every other member (complete interdependence).
4. This leaves cases which are a mixture. They may involve independence or one-way dependence for some acts and interdependence for others.

INDIVIDUALS IN AN INDEPENDENT GROUP SITUATION

If the following assumptions are satisfied, a group's behaviour is certain to be Pareto optimal:

a. Group possibility (1) is the only one for the society.
b. All members of the group have perfect knowledge of all the alternative courses of action which can be taken.
c. All members have perfect foresight of the different outcomes (payoffs) which would stem from alternative courses of action and which would affect their satisfaction.
d. No members change their preference ordering of the courses of action as time elapses.
e. All members have a complete preference ordering over possible courses of action which meets the usual consistency requirements and is also consistent with their ordering of the outcome which attach to the acts.
f. All members choose their most preferred course of action.

If the preceding assumptions are satisfied, then members of the group will never feel disappointed with the course of action they have taken, nor will they ever have occasion to diverge from their planned course. There hardly seems to be the remotest probability that a group has or will ever fulfil these conditions. We note that if condition (f) is violated and all the others hold, then Pareto non-optimality follows by logical necessity. However, if condition (a) continues to hold, violations of any other combination of conditions do not necessarily result in Pareto non-optimality. Pareto non-optimality may arise from inadequate knowledge of possible courses of action, from imperfect knowledge of outcomes, from a change in preference orderings with time,[4] or from inconsistencies or gaps in preference orderings,[5] but none of these factors is by necessity inconsistent with the occurrence of Pareto optimality (compare Chapter 3).

Implicit in the above set of assumptions are some very peculiar assumptions about the decision process itself. It is treated as though it is an effortless one involving no alternative cost. There are no costs involved in deciding one's preferences and there is no need to search for knowledge; it is freely and fully available without cost.

ONE-WAY GROUP DEPENDENCE

Let us now suppose that group possibility (2) is the only possible one for society. In this case, every (possible) action of at least one member affects the satisfaction of another member or other members but no other member can affect this satisfaction. We also suppose that conditions (b) to (f) above will hold. Assuming that the dependent members can predict the actions of the independent members and that each of the independent members has a uniquely preferred course of action, then, given the preceding conditions, Pareto optimality will occur. However, if at least one member, who is personally independent but upon whom some members of the group depend, has a number of most preferred courses of action (among which there is indifference), Pareto optimality of group behaviour is not assured. In this case, the independent member will be indifferent about the 'best' courses of action and need not select the one which is preferred by other members.[6] The above comments upon the violation of conditions (b) to (f) in the group independence case apply also to this one. If condition (f) is the only one violated then Pareto non-optimality is certain to occur but any other combination of violations can lead to Pareto non-optimality but need not.

COMPLETE INTERDEPENDENCE OF GROUP MEMBERS

The complete interdependence case (3) is of more interest than the preceding ones since it more closely approximates the conditions of our own society. In this case, we assume that a different choice by any member will affect the satisfaction of every other member. In this circumstance, there are new obstacles to the attainment of Pareto optimality and in some cases these seem to be intractable. Nevertheless, complete knowledge need not entail indeterminacy problems in this case.

To illustrate this, the following assumptions may be made:

a. Group possibility (3) is the only possible one for the society.
b. All members of the group have perfect knowledge of all the possible courses of action which can be taken by the group.
c. All members have perfect foresight of the different outcomes (payoffs) which would stem from all the alternative courses of action of the group and which would affect their satisfaction.
d. No members change their preference ordering of the group's courses of action as time elapses.
e. All members have a preference ordering over the group's alternative courses of action which meets the usual consistency requirements, is complete, and is consistent with their ordering of the possible outcomes which attach to these courses.
f. Where it is within their power, individuals will select the most preferred (group) course of action.

Let us suppose that our group consists of n members, that a_i represents the possible courses (strategies) of member i and U_i represents the satisfaction of member i in an ordinal fashion. Further, let us suppose that

$$U_1(a_1^0, a_2, ..., a_n) > U_1(a_1, a_2, ..., a_n) \qquad (a_1 \neq a_1^0)$$

$$U_2(a_1, a_2^0, ..., a_n) > U_2(a_1, a_2, ..., a_n) \qquad (a_2 \neq a_2^0)$$

$$U_n(a_1, a_2, ..., a_n^0) > U_n(a_1, a_2, ..., a_n) \qquad (a_n \neq a_n^0).$$

Since all members of the group have the power to select their own course of action or strategy, the i-th player will select course a_i^0 if this is chosen consistently with the individual's preferences. The joint action of the group will be $[a_1^0, a_2^0, ..., a_n^0]$. Individuals will have no incentive to diverge from their chosen course of action and the joint action will be Pareto optimal. Any divergence of joint action from $[a_1^0, a_2^0, ..., a_n^0]$ will make some individual worse off. Of course, there is no implication in this situation that $U_i(a_1^0, a_2^0, ..., a_n^0) \geq U_i(a_1, a_2, ..., a_n)$ for any member.

STABLE PARETIAN SOLUTIONS

No doubt the above set of conditions can be applied so that a stable and Pareto optimal solution can be obtained for groups having more complex preference patterns. By a process of systematically eliminating dominated courses of action, a group of super-rational beings can in some cases reach a stable and Pareto optimal group strategy by independently choosing their own courses of action.[7] To illustrate this, we suppose a group of two members and assume that each member has two possible courses of action. Player one's alternative courses of action (strategies) are a_1' and a_1^* and player two's alternative courses of action (strategies) are a_2' and a_2^*. We also assume that

$$U_1(a_1', a_2) < U_1(a_1^*, a_2)$$
$$U_2(a_1, a_2') < U_2(a_1, a_2^*).$$

This implies that strategy a_1^* is dominant from player one's viewpoint and a_2^* is dominant from player two's standpoint.

Acting independently the players should choose the joint strategy (a_1^*, a_2^*). Player two will reason that player one will never adopt a_1' and will act accordingly. The position (a_1^*, a_2^*) is obviously stable since no player can have any incentive to diverge from it knowing the other player has selected either the strategy a_1^* or a_2^*, as the case may be. Stability follows (in the sense of Nash) since

$$U_1(a_1', a_2^*) < U_1(a_1^*, a_2^*) \text{ and } U_2(a_1^*, a_2') < U_2(a_1^*, a_2^*).$$

The position is also Pareto optimal. Any joint action involving a_1' would make member one worse off and member two will be made worse off by a joint action which involves a_1^* and a_2' in place of a_2^*. Hence, each alternative joint course of action to (a_1^*, a_2^*) would make at least one member worse off.

It is evident that in some cases involving a larger group and a larger number of strategies stable Pareto optimal solutions can be obtained by the systematic elimination of dominated strategies. Sometimes an iterative procedure can be involved in deciding upon the dominated strategies. Member one may be expected to eliminate a number of strategies and this may lead member two to eliminate some strategies which in turn would cause member one to eliminate further strategies.

In the last set of situations, it is assumed that each individual will know the other members' preference well enough to be able to eliminate their dominated strategies as possibilities. Thus we have implicitly added in an extra assumption to the ones contained in the (a) to (f) group above. It is clear that there are some empirical cases in which this condition is not approximated, and that individuals can sometimes gain an advantage by giving others a false impression of their preferences.[8]

If the set of conditions (a) to (f) hold, if

$$U_i(a_1^0, a_2^0, ..., a_n^0) > U_i(a_1, a_2, ..., a_n)$$

where $i = 1, ..., n$ and $(a_1, a_2, ..., a_n) \neq (a_1^0, a_2^0, ..., a_n^0)$, if each member of the group is aware of this last fact and if communication is costless and sufficiently rapid, then one might expect all members of the group to agree to the joint strategy $(a_1^0, a_2^0, ..., a_n^0)$. This joint strategy will be stable in the sense that if every other individual member of the group adopts the a^0-th course of action, then the remaining individual will find it advantageous to also adopt this course of action. The joint strategy $(a_1^0, a_2^0, ..., a_n^0)$ is Pareto optimal. One fears, however, that there would be cases in which

$$U_i(a_1^0, a_2^0, ..., a_n^0) > U_i(a_1, a_2, ..., a_n)$$

where $i = 1, ..., n$ and $(a_1, a_2, ..., a_n) \neq (a_1^0, a_2^0, ..., a_n^0)$ and yet all members may not be aware of this fact and no member may be willing to reveal his or her most preferred joint strategy for fear that others will not reveal theirs, that their most preferred joint strategies are different and that they may be able to use this small piece of information to their advantage. In this case, ignorance of preferences may persist and members of a group may fail to adopt a joint action which they all consider to be the very best course.

NON-STABILITY OF GROUP RATIONALITY

In all group situations considered so far, the Pareto optimal solutions for them are 'self-enforcing'. They are Nash solutions. No member can obtain an advantage by diverging unilaterally from the group solution. But there are interdependence group situations in which this is not so for any possible Pareto optimal solution. In these cases, at least one individual has a unilateral interest to diverge from any Pareto optimal solution. This is so in the following example: the set of (a) to (f) conditions are assumed to hold and the group is supposed to consist of two members and each is supposed to have two alternative courses of action. The preference orderings which the two individuals have over the possible joint courses of action are indicated by the numbers in the following matrix:

	a_2^1	a_2^2
a_1^1	7,4	3,6
a_1^2	2,5	8,2

All possible joint courses of action except (a_1^2, a_2^1) are Pareto optimal. But individual one has an incentive to diverge unilaterally from the Pareto optimal solution (a_1^1, a_2^2) and individual two has an incentive to diverge unilaterally from the Pareto optimal solutions (a_1^1, a_2^1) and (a_1^2, a_2^2). Hence, it is implied in this case that every agreement which is designed to ensure a particular Pareto optimal solution must rely upon the good faith of the parties for its fulfilment since there is always an 'incentive' for parties to dishonour it by their unilateral action. If there is any doubt about the good faith of the parties, then uncertainty is inescapable in this type of situation. In the above prisoners' dilemma type of game, the Nash equilibrium is the Paretian suboptimal set of strategies (a_1^2, a_2^1).

ADDITIONAL BARRIERS TO GROUP OPTIMALITY

In the class of group situations now to be discussed, alternative Pareto optimal solutions involve a conflict of interest and this conflict may result in group action which is less than Pareto optimal even if conditions are comparatively ideal. If the following conditions are satisfied, Pareto optimality of group behaviour is not assured:

i. The set of conditions (a) to (f) hold.
ii. Members of the group can bargain about the joint course of action which they will pursue as from time, T_0.
iii. There are a number of Pareto optimal courses of joint action and these involve a conflict of interest among members of the group.
iv. In the absence of any agreement regulating their joint action, the group may adopt a joint action which is less than Pareto optimal.
v. There are 'no' technical limitations upon the ability of group members to contact one another. There is no cost of communicating.
vi. Yet there is a time limit upon the bargaining process. If no agreement upon a joint course of action is reached by T_0, then disagreement is a *fait accompli* and a less than Pareto optimal set of joint actions can occur in the interval which commences at T_0.
vii. All members of the group are aware of the group's alternative Pareto optimal courses of action.

Members of the group may fail to reach agreement for the following reasons:

i. In bargaining, individuals make assessments of the willingness of other individuals to make concessions. Sometimes they misjudge this. Bargainers sometimes believe that by holding out they will gain a particular concession but they are sometimes mistaken and as the result of their failure to reach agreement, Pareto non-optimality remains a possibility. A great deal of uncertainty surrounds the outcome of a bargaining process and the process sometimes leads to results which are less than Pareto optimal.[9]
ii. Again, we have not considered the possibility that some members of a group may be able to predict the behaviour of other members of the

group with varying degrees of accuracy. No doubt, the predictive ability which each member feels that he or she has will have an impact upon the member's willingness to make concessions and so upon the possibility of a Pareto optimal agreement. If, in the last matrix example which we discussed above, each member believes that he or she can perfectly predict the other's course of action, then at least one member must be wrong and members will be unable to agree upon a Pareto optimal course of action because no joint action can ensure each member as 'much' as the member believes that he or she can obtain alone. Although this is an extreme example, it illustrates the point that the prevailing opinion of group members about their ability to predict the behaviour of others may be such as to rule out the possibility of a Pareto optimal agreement. Indeed, the prevailing beliefs may sometimes be such that even the minimum demands of all members cannot be satisfied simultaneously. This is so in the extreme example just considered.

iii. Furthermore, it is not always justifiable to assume that a bargaining process is an emotionally neutral one for members of a group.[10] If individuals actually bargain this may bring into play emotions which are absent otherwise and these new factors may render a Pareto optimal agreement impossible. We might crudely make allowance for this new element by varying our utility figures for joint strategies so that they depend upon whether these are a bargained outcome or not. To illustrate this, let us suppose that the circumstances pertaining to the last matrix above are relevant. We assume that the utility figures in that matrix refer either to joint actions which are not the result of agreement or to an emotionally neutral bargaining case. To save the reader the effort of referring back, that matrix is

	a_2^1	a_2^2
a_1^1	7,4	3,6
a_1^2	2,5	8,2

But if bargaining is not a neutral process, a different utility matrix may be relevant to bargained courses of action. For instance, individual one may have the following ordering of 'bargained' joint actions:

		a_2^2
a_1^1	7	2
a_1^2	1	9

This matrix indicates that individual one would most of all like to obtain an agreement to joint strategy (a_1^2, a_2^2), and that this individual would prefer the bargained outcome (a_1^2, a_2^2) to the unbargained outcome (a_1^2, a_2^2). The bargained outcome (a_1^1, a_2^2) is less preferred than the unbargained one. The same is true of the bargained outcome (a_1^2, a_2^1). We expect that individual one will never agree to joint actions (a_1^2, a_2^1) or (a_1^1, a_2^2).

Individual two might have the following ordering of bargained joint strategies:

	a_2^1	a_2^2
a_1^1	2	7
a_1^2	5	1

If this is so, individual two will be unprepared to agree to joint actions (a_1^1, a_2^1) or (a_1^2, a_2^2). Hence there is no joint strategy to which both members are prepared to agree. Our allowance for bargaining emotions makes agreement impossible in the above case if all members insist upon being a little better off in a bargained situation than in the least nasty situation which they can ensure without any agreement.

iv. Furthermore, if we wish to consider all possibilities, we should not assume that members of a group proceed upon the principle that all members (or even some members) are absolutely trustworthy. In most circumstances, one might expect members of a group to be attentive to the probability of being double-crossed, and to consider this probability along with its consequences before entering into an agreement. Indeed, members of a group may sometimes believe that in reaching an agreement they are substituting one uncertain situation for another. In the limiting case where nobody is prepared to fulfil the agreement at all,[11] the position is not materially different to that in the absence of the agreement. Otherwise, the agreement may alter the probability of different joint actions necessarily creating certainty.

As a result of distrust members may reach no agreement at all or curiously enough they may agree to a Pareto suboptimal joint course of action. To illustrate the last possibility, we suppose that the group conditions which were relevant for the first matrix above hold. However, we now suppose that each member of the group of two has three alternative courses of action and we use a different set of numbers to indicate preferences. Preferences are indicated in the following matrix:

	a_2^1	a_2^2	a_2^3
a_1^1	5,3	6,5	0,8
a_1^2	3,5	8,0	1,0
a_1^3	4,4	5,3	3,5

The Pareto optimal courses of action in this case are (a_1^1, a_2^2), (a_1^1, a_2^3) and (a_1^2, a_2^2). We can safely exclude the possibility that parties will agree to either of the last two joint actions (strategies). However, we are not in a position to conclude that they will agree to (a_1^1, a_2^2). If member one breaks the agreement, member two may be faced with the joint course of action (a_1^2, a_2^2) rather than (a_1^1, a_2^2). If member two feels that there is a sufficiently high probability of one's breaking the agreement, this member will not agree to a_2^2. Similarly, individual one may not be prepared to agree to a_1^1. On the other hand, it is conceivable that members of the group may agree to (a_1^3, a_2^1). Consequently, respective parties by maintaining their part of the agreement avoid the possibility of (a_1^1, a_2^3), (a_1^2, a_2^2) and (a_1^2, a_2^3). Of course, the parties could do this without agreement. Individual one can do this by adopting a_1^3 and individual two can do it by adopting course a_2^1. How then can they benefit by an agreement? One possibility is that the agreement changes the subjective probabilities of the joint acts favourably for the members. The agreement may change individual two's subjective probability distribution over (a_1^i, a_2^1), $i = 1$, 2 and 3, and individual one's subjective probability distribution over (a_1^3, a_2^j), where $j = 1, 2, 3$.

If we were to move outside the world which we have just constructed and were to allow the possibility that members of a group may not be cognisant of all their possible courses of action or of all the outcomes stemming from them, we should raise a whole new set of problems. In this new world the flexibility of agreements will be important. One possibility is that agreements will be for much shorter durations so as to permit new agreements to be drawn up as time goes on and possible courses of action and outcomes become clearer. In this world which closely approximates our own, no one can be sure of the Pareto optimal courses of action and everyone stumbles forward in a myopic condition. This is the type of world which our theories must ultimately come to grips with.[12] Indeed, it would be no surprise if Pareto optimality was the exception rather than the rule in such a world for its fulfilment would have to be accomplished by partially blind actors.

MIXED INTERDEPENDENCE OF GROUPS

Instead of exploring the world which has just been mentioned, let us proceed to a discussion of the 'mixed' group cases (4) in order not to lose symmetry. Under this heading have been included all of those cases which do not fall under the other three but which contain a mixture of their elements. There are, of course, a large number of subcases included under heading (iv) but since they raise few new difficulties which stand in the way of Pareto optimality, a systematic consideration of them will not be attempted. One possibility is that each member of the society can choose either to be independent of or to be dependent upon the actions of all other members. There are some courses of action open to all members of the society which will make them independent and some which will make them dependent. However, it could well be that all the Pareto optimal strategies for the society require the members to engage in strategies which make them interdependent. Yet, members may not agree to adopt these strategies since they may feel that the risk of their being double-crossed is such that they would prefer independent strategies. The situation here is similar to one which was discussed under point (iii). Indeed, all of the problems of attaining Pareto optimality which were discussed under the first three headings arise for some type (iv) cases.

BOUNDARIES OF GROUPS, OVERLAPPING GROUPS: INTERGENERATIONAL ISSUES

The term society has been used to designate any group whose satisfaction is independent of the actions of any set of individuals outside of it. Given this usage, then an existing human population does not form a society if at a future date members of it will be affected by the actions of individuals born in the interim. Indeed, there may be human groups such that the term society can only be strictly applied to an existing collection of individuals plus a set which will be born over an infinite or at least very large span of time.[13] This situation can arise if one generation of individuals tends to live for some time along with the next and even later generations so that a chain of interdependence arises.[14] Where a society is like this, explicit allowance ought to be made for the fact that all 'players' are not alive at the 'beginning' of the game. Presumably, since unborn players cannot take part in the earliest agreements and cannot express their preferences for some time, these factors might be expected to impose additional restrictions upon the applicability of the Pareto optimal theory of group behaviour. We must take account of the fact that all groups do not exist in 'splendid isolation' and this requires a more general formulation.

Using the formulation which will soon be presented, we shall consider whether any group can ensure Pareto optimality for itself after allowing for all behavioural possibilities, including the behavioural possibilities of individuals not in the group or not yet born. Let I represent a set of individuals or a group. The set I may consist of just one individual, any combination of individuals or all individuals who exist over some period. We suppose that there are $r = 1, ..., k$ individuals in group I and do not exclude the possibility that $k = 1$. To be general, we assume that group I need not be faced by a single set of alternative courses of action which will be open to it to choose from but may be faced by a number of possible (probable) sets.[15] Its actual course must always be confined to the set of alternative courses which do arise for it. Formalizing, let B represent the set of alternative courses of action which may be open to group I. $B = \{B_1, B_2, ..., B_h\}$, where any element, such as B_1, represents one set of alternative courses of joint action (for the entire future) which may be open to group I. Each element of the sets $B_1, B_2, ..., B_h$ represents a course of action which may arise for group I's choice. Where each b-value represents a course of action (for the entire future) which may arise for group I's choice,

$$B_1 = \{b_{11}, b_{12}, ..., b_{1v(1)}\}$$
$$B_2 = \{b_{21}, b_{22}, ..., b_{2v(2)}\}$$
$$B_h = \{b_{h1}, b_{h2}, ..., b_{hv(h)}\}.$$

Each element of the sets $B_1, B_2, ..., B_h$ can be expressed as a vector which indicates one combination of actions which the members of group I may be able to undertake over their entire future. An element such as b_{11} may be expressed as $[b_{11,t}, b_{11,t+1}, ..., b_{11,t+\pi}]$ where $t + \pi$ extends up to the time when the last member of group I is unable to act. The element b_{11} indicated a combination of acts each of which is performed in consecutive periods.

Let

$$H = B_1 \cap B_2 \cap ... \cap B_{h-1} \cap B_h.$$

Then, set H represents the set of courses of action which are certain to be available for group I's choice. Only for elements contained in the set H

is group I certain to have a choice. If the set H is empty, then there is no course of action which group I is certain to have the opportunity of choosing.

Let

$$K = B_1 \cup B_2 \cup ... \cup B_{h-1} \cup B_h.$$

Then K represents all of the b-values which group I may have an opportunity of choosing. We suppose that there is associated with each b-value which may arise for group I's choice, a set of possible courses of action which may be pursued by all individuals not included in I. For any given value of b, we represent this set by $\xi(b)$ and recognize that the elements of the set may vary with b

$$\xi(b) = \{\xi_1(b), \xi_2(2), ..., \xi_{m(b)}(b)\}$$

where $b \in K$ and where any element such as $\xi_1(b)$ represents one possible course of action which may be pursued by group I given that group I adopts course b.

Although this raises a number of metaphysical problems, it will be assumed that there is for all individuals in group I an ordering which ranks ordinally the actual 'satisfaction' which they would derive from each of the possible $[b,\xi_z(b)]$ combinations. ξ_z represents any element of $\xi(b)$ and b can assume any value in the set K. This 'true satisfaction' ordering for the r-th individual is represented ordinally by $U^r(b,\xi_z(b))$, where $b \in K$ and $\xi_z(b) \in \xi(b)$ and this ordering is assumed to be transitive and complete.

Given these conditions, then, it is impossible for group I to select a course of action which will ensure Pareto optimality for it, unless there is at least one value of b, say b^*, such that

$$[U^1(b^*,\xi_z(b^*)), U^2(b^*,\xi_z(b^*)), ..., U^k(b^*,\xi_z(b^*))]$$
$$\nprec [U^1(b,\xi_z(b)), U^2(b,\xi_z(b)), ..., U^k(b,\xi_z(b))]$$

or more compactly,

$$[U^r(b^*,\xi_z(b^*))] \nprec [U^r(b,\xi_z(b))] \tag{8.1}$$

where $r = 1, ..., k$ and where $\xi_z(b^*)$ can assume the value of every element in the set $\xi(b^*)$ and $(b,\xi_z(b))$ can assume every value for every possible b-value except b^*; and

$$b^* \in H. \tag{8.2}$$

Group I cannot ensure Pareto optimality for itself if there is no $b \in K$ which satisfies conditions (8.1) and (8.2).

Let B^* represent the set of all b-values which satisfy expression (8.1). Then, group I cannot select a course of action, that is, a b-value which will ensure Pareto optimality for it (after allowing for its behavioural environment) unless the set $B^* \cap H$ is non-empty. The non-emptiness of both B^* and H is necessary for the non-emptiness of $B^* \cap H$. Of course, both B^* and H may be non-empty and yet $B^* \cap H$ may be empty. Given our assumptions about U^r, it can be shown that B^* is certain to be non-empty if each individual in group I is indifferent about the $\xi_z(b)$ elements in each set $\xi(b)$ where $b \in K$. Of course, this last condition is automatically satisfied if there is only one element in each of the $\xi(b)$ sets. If any of the individuals in group I are not indifferent about the elements in each of the $\xi(b)$ sets then B^* can be empty. But even if B^* is not empty, for example because there is just one element in each of the $\xi(b)$ sets, H may be empty. However, it will not be empty if there is just one set of possible alternatives. Indeed, if this is so and B^* is not empty, then $B^* \cap H$ is non-empty.

Let P represent the set of b-values which can never be Pareto optimal for group I. Then P will be empty or non-empty depending upon the particular circumstances of the case. Group I is faced by the following position: it will be certain not to achieve Pareto optimality if it selects a b–value in the set P; it will be certain to obtain Pareto optimality if it selects a b-value in the set $B^* \cap H$; and if it selects any other value in the set K, that is, any element in the set $K - (B^* \cap H \cup P)$, it will only have a chance between zero and unity of realizing Pareto optimality. While either the set $B^* \cap H$ or the set

$$D = K - (B^* \cap H \cup P)$$

may be empty, both cannot be simultaneously empty. If both these sets are empty, it is implied that all elements of K belong to set P since $K = P \cup D \cup (B \cap H)$. This would imply that every possible course of action, that is, every $(b, \xi_z(b))$ combination, is less preferred than another possible one in the set K and so would involve a logical contradiction.

Now, there are a number of possible ways in which the above construction can be interpreted. What can the above sets represent? One interpretation is that they refer to some theoretical objective estimate which could supposedly be derived, given what is known at the beginning of period t. By assumption, whatever actually occurs is always consistent with the objective estimate. A grave difficulty for this interpretation is that there may be unique events in very general social systems and these may render it impossible to discover some sets of theoretical possibilities. Unfortunately, the theoretical objective set cannot necessarily be established by a consensus of opinion. But even if we could approximate the objective set in particular instances, I would not be surprised to find that K frequently comprises of more than one set of alternatives and that there is often more than one $\xi_z(b)$ value associated with each b-value. Also, given our assumptions about each of the U^r orderings, I should not be surprised to find that $B^* \cap H$ is often objectively empty. If this does happen to be the case, it clearly limits the applicability of all economic theories (in particular some welfare theories) which are based upon the implicit assumption that $B^* \cap H$ is not empty. Again, we can reinterpret our construction so as to relate it to a subjective domain. Even if individuals in group I were to reach a consensus as to what they think is possible, then they may perceive a number of possible sets in K and $B^* \cap H$ to be empty within this subjective domain. Our conceptions may be of interest in both the subjective and objective spheres.

CHANGING INFORMATION AND GROUP FLEXIBILITY

Now, group I is most unlikely to decide upon an inflexible course of action for its whole future for to do so would be to ignore information which may come to hand in the future. It may only decide upon an inflexible joint action for period t and may leave its later courses of action (more or less) open. It is, then, interesting to pose the question of what are the conditions under which group I can choose (an inflexible or single path) course of action for t and be certain that this chosen course of action is necessary for its Pareto optimality.

$$\text{Let B}_t = \{B_{t1}, B_{t2}, ..., B_{tq}\}$$

represent the set of the sets of alternative courses of action which may be open to group I during period t. We represent each of these sets $B_{t1}, B_{t2},$ ..., B_{tq}, as

$$B_{ts} = \{\beta_{s1}, \beta_{s2}, ..., \beta_{s, p(q)}\}$$

where $s = 1, ..., q$ and each element, such as β_{11}, represents one course of action which may be available to group I for period t.
Let

$$S = \sum_{s=1}^{q} B_{ts}.$$

Then, S represents the set of all courses of action which may be open to group I for period t. β_t represents any element of S and is one course of action which may be available to group I for period t.
Let

$$Z = \prod_{s=1}^{q} B_{ts}.$$

Z represents the set of all courses of action for period t which are certain to be available for group I's choice. There is associated with each element, β_t, which is contained in set S, a set

$$\theta(\beta_t) = \{\theta_1(\beta_t),\ \theta_2(\beta_t),\ ...,\ \theta_{m(\beta_t)}\ (\beta_t)\}$$

where any element, such as $\theta_1(\beta_t)$, represents a course of action other than β_t which may possibly be pursued by group I and $\bar{I}$ given β_t. The set $\theta(\beta_t)$ represents all courses of action which may possibly be pursued by group I and $\bar{I}$ given β_t. Let $\theta_g(\beta_t)$ represent any element of $\theta(\beta_t)$. Then only if there is at least one value of β_t say β^*_t, such that

$$[U'(\beta^*_t, \theta_g(\beta^*_t))] \not\lessgtr [U'(\beta_t, \theta(\beta_t)) \tag{8.3}$$

where $r = 1, ..., k$ and where $\theta_g(\beta^*_t)$ can assume the value of every element in $\theta(\beta^*_t)$ and $(\beta_t, \theta_g(\beta_t))$ can assume every value for every possible β_t value except β^*_t and such that

$$\beta^*_t \in Z \tag{8.4}$$

does there exist at least one β_t which must be consistent with Pareto optimality for group I.

Let β^* represent the set of all β_t values which satisfy condition (8.3). If $\beta^* \cap Z$ is empty, then there is no β_t which is certain to be consistent with Pareto optimality for group I. If it is non-empty, then there is at least one β_t value which is certainly consistent with Pareto optimality for group I. It is clear that the conclusions which were reached for the previous construction apply to this one, *mutatis mutandis*. For example, $\beta^* \cap Z$ is empty if either β^* or Z is empty. Furthermore, if each individual in group I is indifferent about the elements in each of the sets $\theta(\beta_t)$ and if there is only one set in the set S, then $\beta^* \cap Z$ is non-empty. However, $\beta^* \cap Z$ may often be empty.

In the model just considered, period t is assumed to be of some fixed but undefined length. For the period, group I is assumed to pursue an inflexible course of action. Its inflexibility may be the result of its own decision or it may arise because its knowledge does not change during period t, or if it does change, group I may be technically 'unable' to vary its course of action of that period so as to make allowance for it. We are challenged by the fact that in some circumstances the degree of flexibility is a consciously imposed restriction. It is itself often the result of a decision and that decision will in part depend upon expectations about the availability of knowledge in the future. Until we obtain a clearer understanding of these flexibility decisions and relationships, many of our constructions of group behaviour and group behavioural possibilities will be insubstantial. Once we recognize that knowledge is not a fixed thing and realize that members are not completely fixed in a single path which they must follow, we can hardly fail to see that the flexibility of (group) decisions is of great significance. Although I am not going to deal with them in this chapter, flexibility questions deserve more than a perfunctory treatment.

COMMUNICATION AND PARETIAN OPTIMALITY

Even if the members of group I form a closed group, that is, a group in which the members may reach joint agreements among themselves but will not attempt to reach agreements with individuals outside the group, and if $\beta^* \cap Z$ is objectively non-empty, members of the group may not act to attain Pareto optimality for themselves because the factors mentioned for the society case at the beginning of this chapter may operate to rule out a Pareto optimal 'agreement'. Of course, even if $\beta^* \cap Z$ is objectively non-empty, members may not perceive this or their perceptions may diverge to such an extent that they are unable to agree upon its non-emptiness and upon other facts. They may be unable to reach a consensus or to do so might be costly. This raises the question of what effect communication problems have upon the likelihood of Pareto optimality.

While I do not intend to get involved in a detailed discussion of communication questions here, it might be noted that when individuals desire a change in social structure (that is, in the probable actions of a group of individuals), and this could be a change in which all relevant individuals are willing to agree, they may fail to communicate about it. This may happen (i) because the cost to them of the communications may offset their probable gains to such an extent as to deter them or (ii) because, even if costs do not offset to this extent, the individual may feel that it is very probable that some other individual or individuals will initiate communication and bear the major burden or major part of the costs involved in communicating about the change. In the latter case, individuals fail to communicate because they are prepared to take a risk upon the likelihood that some other individual or individuals will initiate and foster communication about the desired changes. If every individual in the group is either in circumstance (i) or (ii), a desired change may fail to materialize. In case (i), a straightforward externality barrier arises; in the second case externality plus a chance element is involved. We can obviously extend these thoughts so that they apply to subgroups rather than to individuals.

There are, as we have noted, other risks tied up with the communication of preferences. Professor Arrow (1963, p. 7) and Professor Morgenstern (1964) have pointed out that it is sometimes to individuals' advantage to give a distorted impression of their preferences rather than to reveal their 'actual' ones. If individuals reveal their actual preferences, either their gains may be less as a result of an imposed system of allocation which varies action with expressed preferences or they may give their 'opponents' strategic information. It should also be observed that individuals will not always be aware of their 'best' or 'approximately best' distortion. Since individuals must often distort or reveal their preferences with some uncertainty, they may fail to reveal their actual preferences when that revelation would be to their advantage. As noted, a whole group may fail to improve its situation because of this problem.

Professor Morgenstern (1964) has indicated that this distortion factor raises some serious problems for the testability of theories based upon the Pareto optimum hypothesis since individuals may not consider an interviewer or observer neutrally. The reaction of individuals will be conditioned by their perception of what the interviewer or observer is likely to do with the material. Is the observer going to try and induce individuals in the economy to act differently on the basis of the material or is it likely to come into the hands of someone who may act differently given the preference material? (One sees an analogy between some problems here and some quantum physics problems.) Also, if information upon the preferences of an individual is sought, one must be aware of the fact that time and effort is involved in expressing them. If the individuals, who are the subject of the research, have preferences about how they wish to spend their time, then if they do cooperate in expressing them, to say a 'neutral' observer, their expression of them may only be perfunctory or may be designed to satisfy the observer in as short a time as possible. No doubt, there are limits to the time which any of us will spend on this matter. Indeed, to express our complete ordering over all of society's possibilities would involve a great deal of time and I, for one, would not care to cooperate. On the other hand, individuals may be prepared to express their preferences upon a few possibilities and theories need to be designed so as to take some account of this. In line with this, I would also suggest that individuals often have a limited vision of their own preferences. To visualize them completely and consistently involves effort (for example, a search for possibilities and the effort of consistently ordering them) and individuals are obliged to reach some 'decision' upon this matter.[16]   Since we know so little about this phenomenon, it is hazardous to venture an opinion as to whether it places practical limitations upon the Pareto optimality approach. This matter cannot be decided either way by abstract thought alone.

INCOMPLETENESS OF PREFERENCE ORDERING

Again, individuals' expressed preference ordering may be incomplete since they may be expected to order preferentially some alternatives which they are not genuinely in a position to compare. Our knowledge of our own preferences depends upon our previous experience. As between two possibilities, one of which has never been experienced, individuals may not know which one they prefer. I believe that this situation is more common than is realized and becomes very important when we are considering preferences for large systems, for example, those for a society, country or large collection of individuals. Of course, even within our framework of limited knowledge, there may be some consistency; one may not know whether one prefers A to B but may be sure that A or B is preferred to C. Hence, upon the rationalist approach, one should never choose C in preference to A or B. Nevertheless on the basis of limited experience, individuals may venture to give a complete preference ordering, which may, for instance, suggest 'their most probable' ordering.

PATH DEPENDENCE OF PREFERENCES

This brings us face to face with the metaphysical problem of whether individuals always perceive their true preferences or the actual satisfaction which they would derive from their alternatives. I believe that it can be safely conjectured that individuals, because of their limited experience, will not always know their 'true' preferences and in some circumstances neither will nor can discover them. In their lifetime, individuals and societies only have one path which they will follow and they cannot experience all the paths which might have been open to them. (As pointed out in Chapters 2 and 3, preferences can be path dependent.) It seems impossible to escape doubt about the closeness which individuals' perceived preference ordering bears to their 'true' one.[17] Consequently, if individuals have or may have a distorted view of their 'true' preferences, this raises an obstacle to the testing of an objective Pareto optimality theory.[18] Hence, it seems that if we press the Pareto optimality theory towards its logical limit, we reach the disconcerting point of view that there are a number of circumstances in which it is not testable, not realistic and does not yield substantial economies in thought or in its application.

CONCLUSION

Although problems of cooperation can create barriers to Pareto optimality for a group, the elimination of such barriers does not ensure Pareto optimality. No matter how avidly a group may seek to cooperate so as to ensure Pareto optimality for itself, the realization of this goal may be impossible for no one may know which course of action will be Pareto optimal. In circumstances where this is so, anyone who advises a group to act Pareto optimally is requiring them to perform miraculous deeds. There are some welfare and normative economic, game and social theories which do require some miraculous transformations of the social universe before they can be applied and which ought to be treated with great scepticism. But besides being sceptical, we need to, and can, develop theories which make allowance for the limitations of man's knowledge. Although one may employ a limited Pareto optimum concept in developing such theories, and in this case one should specifically clarify its limited nature, I cannot, in view of the problems which have been raised, escape the conclusion that we ought to examine and search in addition for other bases of social behaviour.

NOTES

1. A restricted estimate of its range of application can be obtained by considering von Neumann and Morgenstern (1944), Luce and Raiffa (1957), Shubik (1959) and Buchanan and Tullock (1962).
2. Professor Morgenstern has published a thought-provoking article upon this subject – see Morgenstern (1964). Other contributions are, however, numerous. Since I do not wish to compile a long bibliography on this subject, let me mention just two other interesting articles. They are Simon (1955) and Shubik (1952).
3. By the Pareto optimality hypothesis of group behaviour, I mean the postulate that a group will organize itself and act so that it will be impossible to make any member of the group better off without making another member worse off.
4. In the society considered here, this change in preferences may be a result of learning by experience. In a society in which there are dependencies among individuals, social interaction may cause changes in preferences. On this point, see Knight (1935). T. Veblen (1924) and J.M. Clark (1936) also stress that social interaction and learning influence preferences.
5. Where these gaps arise, there may be a random element in behaviour. Since the decision process involves effort and is subject to technical limitations, the random element may be significant and may be especially so in those cases where social interaction is possible. On the presence of random elements in behaviour, see Karlsson (1958).
6. Such indifference may annoy the dependent members greatly. It might also be noted that the decision processes are not always value or emotionally neutral. If an independent decision maker consults with a dependent member and appears to have some regard to his or her interests, this may create a favourable impression upon the dependant. Over long periods, interdependencies may change and annoyed dependent members may search for and find ways which will enable them to exert an influence.

7. Compare Harsanyi (1962).
8. Not only may individuals give false impressions of their preferences but they may bluff if they are in a bargaining situation.
9. Sometimes, bargainers miscalculate the extent to which they can press their advantage and are disappointed that their opponent does not yield earlier. For a theory which takes into account the learning of bargainers, see Cross (1965).
10. Deutsch (1962) suggests that factors involved in the possible 'loss of face' of negotiators may be important in affecting their behaviour.
11. Upon the influence of trust on behaviour, see Schelling (1960, especially p. 45), also de Finetti (1963) and Heiss (1963).
12. Constructive attempts in this direction are now fairly common. Although he was concerned with 'optimal' actions of a firm operating under conditions of uncertainty, Hart (1942) illustrates some general points about the importance of flexibility. It is apparent that the nature of the learning processes and optimal flexibility arrangements are closely connected. For an 'early' explicit introduction of learning processes into decision making see Flood (1954).
13. This interdependency creates a large number of theoretical problems. Graaff has indicated that the need to define a time interval for welfare maximization sets limitations upon the 'New Welfare Economics'. He states that 'the plain fact of the matter is that a value judgment is required to determine the location of the horizon' for welfare maximization. See Graaff (1957).
14. Not only does this interdependence place limitations upon the 'New Welfare Economics' since future generations are not available to express their preferences, but also because the preferences of future generations bear some relationship to the actions of existing generations. For instance, such a relationship enters through the education process which influences the attitudes and values of individuals.
15. This allows for the possibility that there may be some chance outcomes for the group which will limit its future alternatives. These chance elements may enter in the growth of technology, in seasonal conditions affecting production, and so on. Haavelmo (1954) considers a number of ways in which random elements can affect future possibilities.
16. Compare Buchanan and Tullock (1962, pp. 97–8).
17. In this respect Knight (1935, p. 35) pessimistically suggests that 'human beings . . . neither know what they want – to say nothing of what is "good" for them – nor act very intelligently to secure the things which they have decided to try to get'. This, however, may be an exaggeration.
18. This does not imply, as we have already seen, that there are no problems for testing a subjective Pareto optimality theory.

REFERENCES

Arrow, K.J. (1963), *Social Choice and Individual Values*, 2nd edn, New York: John Wiley & Sons.

Baumol, W.J. and Quandt, R.E. (1964), 'Rules of Thumb and Optimally Imperfect Decisions', *American Economic Review*, 54, 23–46.

Buchanan, J.M. and Tullock, G. (1962), *The Calculus of Consent*, Ann Arbor: University of Michigan Press.

Clark, J.M. (1936), *Preface to Social Economics*, New York: Farrar & Rinehart.

Cross, J.G. (1965), 'A Theory of the Bargaining Process', *American Economic Review*, 55, 67–94.

de Finetti, B. (1963), 'La teoria dei giochi', *Civiltá delle macchine*, 11(4 and 5).

Deutsch, M. (1962), 'Some Psychological Assumptions of Game Theory', *Recent Advances of Game Theory*, Princeton University Conference (October 1961), Princeton, New Jersey: Princeton University Press, 57–9.

Flood, M.M. (1954), 'On Game-Learning and Some Decision-Making Experiments', in Thrall, R.M., Coombs, C.H. and Davis, R.L. (eds), *Decision Processes*, New York: John Wiley, 139–58.

Graaff, J. de V. (1957), *Theoretical Welfare Economics*, Cambridge: Cambridge University Press.

Haavelmo, T. (1954), *A Study in the Theory of Economic Evaluation*, Amsterdam: North-Holland.

Harsanyi, J.C. (1962), 'Rationality Postulates for Bargaining Solutions in Cooperative and in Non-Cooperative Games', *Recent Advances in Game Theory*, Princeton University Conference (October 1961), Princeton, New Jersey: Princeton University Press, 223–47.

Hart, A.G. (1942), 'Risk, Uncertainty, and the Unprofitability of Compounding Probabilities', in Lange, O., McIntyre, F. and Yntema, T.O. (eds), *Studies in Mathematical Economics and Econometrics*, Chicago: University of Chicago Press, 110–18.

Heiss, K. (1963), 'Bruno de Finetti on Game Theory and Human Behavior', *Research Memorandum 78*, Econometric Research Program, Princeton University.

Karlsson, G. (1958), *Social Mechanisms*, Stockholm: Almqvist & Wiksell.

Knight, F.H. (1935), *The Ethics of Competition and Other Essays*, New York: Harper & Brothers.

Luce, R.D. and Raiffa, H. (1957), *Games and Decisions*, New York: John Wiley & Sons.

Morgenstern, O. (1964), 'Pareto Optimum and Economic Organization', in Kloten, N., Krelle, W., Müller, H. and Neumark, F. (eds), *Systeme und Methoden in den Wirtschafts-und Sozialwissenschaften*, Tübingen: J.C.B. Mohr.

Schelling, T.C. (1960), *The Strategy of Conflict*, Cambridge, Mass.: Harvard University Press.

Shubik, M. (1952), 'Information, Theories of Competition and Theory of Games', *Journal of Political Economy*, 60, 145–50.

Shubik, M. (1959), *Strategy and Market Structure*, New York: John Wiley & Sons.

Simon, H.A. (1955), 'A Behavioral Model of Rational Choice', *Quarterly Journal of Economics*, 79, 99–118.

Veblen. T (1924), *The Theory of the Leisure Class*, London: Allen and Unwin.

von Neumann, J. and Morgenstern, O. (1944), *Theory of Games and Economic Behaviour*, Princeton, New Jersey: Princeton University Press.

9. Optimal Slack and Efficient Budgeting within Organizations

As indicated in the previous chapter, the contributions in this book rely on a variety of assumptions about group behaviour. In this chapter, it is assumed that a group or organization wishes to maximize its expected net benefit as a whole but is limited in this possibility by uncertainty and short-term inflexibility in its allocation of funds or resources to units or divisions within the organization; taking such factors into account it considers the optimal allocation of funds or resources to the units of the organization. It will be shown that in such circumstances it is sometimes optimal to allocate excess funds to units or divisions as compared to that which would be optimal under conditions of certainty equivalence. The budget allocation should build in slack. However, under other circumstances the opposite policy is optimal.

Sub-units or divisions of organizations such as companies, government departments, universities and so on are often allocated resources or entitlement to purchase resources, for a forthcoming period, usually a year, by a central body of the organization. The sub-unit or division of the organization may be given a budget to purchase specified types of items as it sees fit, or it may be allocated a particular quantity of labour, materials, inventories or other items that affect its operation during the relevant execution period. These allocation decisions are made in advance of the execution period and allocations can either not be changed during the execution period, or only at great difficulty or cost on the part of the sub-unit or division which, in the case of an emergency, may be able to prevail on the centre to give it a supplementary grant. It will be supposed, as a first approximation, that once an allocation has been made for a period, then it cannot be altered.

Given this inflexibility, various questions arise about the optimal allocation to sub-units in terms of the goals or aims of the organization, which we assume for simplicity operates as a team,[1] that is, each sub-unit has the same objective as the overall organization. Allocations to sub-units are made during the planning period (prior to the execution

147

period) at a time when the world external to the sub-unit or its environment for the execution period is imperfectly known or subject to uncertainty. Bearing this in mind, to what extent is the interest of the whole organization best served by allocating more funds or resources to a sub-unit than would be optimal (on average) under certainty, or best served by budgeting fewer funds or allocating fewer resources to the sub-unit than this? Given the team assumption, the first-mentioned type of allocation would provide the sub-unit with slack on average and in the latter case the sub-unit would experience strain on average. This contribution considers the conditions under which it is optimal for an organization to introduce slack or strain, on average, in its allocation of resources to a sub-unit.

Hart (1942) observed several decades ago that when uncertainty and the possibility of learning are allowed for, the expected gains by individuals or organizations can be raised by their holding more resources such as cash, inventories or labour than required to maximize their (expected) gain based solely on the expected value of the non-controlled random variables influencing their gain. In Theil's (1961) terms, Hart pointed to the possible absence of certainty equivalence in the objective function of an organization. The holding of reserves which, on the face of it, look excessive may not be evidence of organizational slack but may be a rational response to the existence of uncertainty and the possibilities for learning. Leibenstein (1978)[2] does not discuss this possibility in his outline of organizational slack.

Theil's approach (1961) to maximizing the expected value of the objective function is based on the assumption that the independent variables in the objective function can be divided into controlled and non-controlled ones (see also Chapter 6 or Tisdell, 1973). The non-controlled variables are assumed, as a rule, to be random. In the decision problem formulated below, controlled variables are retained but random functions, rather than random non-controlled variables, are employed to allow for uncertainty.

GENERAL ASPECTS OF OPTIMAL BIAS IN THE INTERNAL ALLOCATION OF AN ORGANIZATION'S RESOURCES

It may be useful to formulate the problem generally, seek solutions to it and then illustrate it by particular cases. Assume that the central body allocating resources to sub-units is concerned only with one controlled variable, x, and that only one sub-unit is under consideration. The controlled variable, x, might be the size of budgeted expenditures for the sub-unit, or the level of its inventories, or its allowed level of employment of labour, or allowed input of raw materials, or the level of cash balance permitted.

Suppose that the net benefit (in dollars, utility or other appropriate measure) received by the organization from a sub-unit varies with the amount of x allocated to it. However the actual net benefit received depends upon events that are probable only at the time the allocation is made. Let there be i possible sets of events or states of nature and let p_i be the probability of the i-th state of nature at the time the allocation is being planned. Assume that the net benefit received by the organization when the i-th state of nature prevails is

$$z_i = f_i(x) \tag{9.1}$$

where $f_i'' < x$, that is, the marginal net benefit received declines with the size of x; for example, the size of the sub-unit's allocated budget. When the i-th state of nature prevails, the optimal value of x is that for which

$$z_i' = f_i'(x) = 0. \tag{9.2}$$

Let this be satisfied for

$$x = \hat{x}_i \tag{9.3}$$

and let

$$\bar{x} = \sum p_i \hat{x}_i. \tag{9.4}$$

Given a stationary probability distribution for the states of nature, $\bar{x}$ represents the average value of x that would prevail, x being optimally adjusted to the states of nature as they occur.

However, when the allocation is being made by the central body only the probability distribution of the states of nature are known, and the allocation cannot be changed during the execution period. Supposing that the organization wishes to maximize its expected net benefit (gain in dollars, utility or some other measure), then it needs to maximize

$$y = \sum_{i=1}^{n} p_i f_i(x). \tag{9.5}$$

The necessary condition for this to be at a maximum is that

$$\frac{dy}{dx} = \sum p_i f_i(x) = 0. \tag{9.6}$$

The second-order conditions hold when this condition is satisfied because of the assumption that $f_i'' < 0$. Let equation (9.6) be satisfied, or equation (9.5) reach a maximum for

$$x = x^*. \tag{9.7}$$

The problem being posed, therefore, is under what circumstances is x^* equal to, greater than or less than $\bar{x}$, that is, under what circumstance (on average) is no bias, slack or strain optimal.

The size of x^* (say, the budget) for the sub-unit should be increased until the marginal expected net benefit from increasing it is equal to the marginal expected net benefit forgone. If there are $i = 1,..., h$ functions for which $x_i < x$, this amounts to the requirement, rearranging equation (9.6), that

$$\sum_{i=h+1}^{n} p_i f_i'(x) = - \sum_{i=1}^{h} p_i f_i'(x). \tag{9.8}$$

The faster the function declines on the left-hand side of equation (9.8) compared with the rate of increase of the function on the right-hand side, the lower is the optimal value of x^* if the possible states of nature remain unchanged. If the probabilities of the states of nature remain unaltered, so does $\bar{x}$ in this case, and the likelihood that $x^* < \bar{x}$, that strain on average is optimal, increases. This can be illustrated by the cases considered below.

ILLUSTRATION OF OPTIMALITY OF SLACK AND STRAIN IN ALLOCATION

If the z_i functions in equation (9.1) are quadratic, the corresponding p_i $f_i'(x)$ functions are linear and decreasing, given that $f_i'' < 0$. The optimal allocation of x can be found by solving the linear equation

$$y = \sum_{i=1}^{n} p_i a_i - \sum_{i=1}^{n} p_i b_i x = 0 \tag{9.9}$$

for x, where a_i and b_i are the coefficients of the relevant linear expressions. If only two states of nature are possible,

$$y = p_1 (a_1 - b_1 x) + p_2 (a_2 - b_2 x) = 0. \tag{9.10}$$

Solving this for x,

$$x^* = \frac{p_1 a_1 + p_2 a_2}{p_1 b_1 + p_2 b_2}. \tag{9.11}$$

Since

$$p_1 a_1 - p_1 b_1 x = 0. \tag{9.12}$$

for

$$\hat{x}_1 = a_1/b_1$$

and

$$p_2 a_2 - p_2 b_2 x = 0 \qquad (9.13)$$

for

$$\hat{x}_2 = a_2/b_2, \qquad (9.14)$$

$$\bar{x} = p_1 \hat{x}_1 + p_2 \hat{x}_2 \qquad (9.15)$$

$$= p_1(a_1/b_1) + p_2(a_2/b_2). \qquad (9.16)$$

If state of nature one is equally as likely as state of nature two, $p_1 = p_2 = 0.5$ and $x^* = x_1$, if $b_1 = b_2$. This case is illustrated in Figure 9.1.

Figure 9.1   *Illustration of circumstances in which slack or strain in allocation of a resource or a budget to a sub-unit is optimal for the organization*

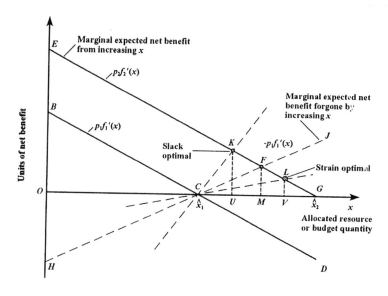

In Figure 9.1, the expected net benefit to the organization of x for state of nature one is indicated by line *BCD*, and for state of nature two by line *EFG*. Both these lines have equal slope and, given that $p_1 = p_2 = 0.5$, $\bar{x} = x^*$ at point *M*. The value of $\bar{x}$ corresponds to the mid-point between $\hat{x}_1$ and $\hat{x}_2$ and x^* corresponds to the point where line *HFJ* intersects *EFG*. Line *HFJ* is obtained by rotating line *BCD* on the fixed point *C*. *HFJ* represents the marginal expected net benefit forgone from increasing x and line *EFG* represents the marginal expected net benefit from increasing x, and these are equal at points of intersection of the lines.

If *BCD* should happen to decline at a faster rate than *EFG*, the rotated line corresponding to *BCD* increases at a faster rate than *HJ*. For example, the rotated line corresponding to *BCD* might be like *CK*. Consequently, x^* corresponds to *U* and $x^* < \bar{x}$. Hence it would be optimal to introduce strain on average in the allocation. It would be optimal to allocate a total budget, for example, that is less than the absolutely optimal one on average.

On the other hand, if *BCD* should happen to decline at a slower rate than *EFG*, the rotation of *BCD* corresponds to a line such as *CL* in Figure 9.1 and x^* corresponds to a point such as *V* and $x^* > \bar{x}$. Then it is optimal to allocate a budget, for example, that provides the sub-unit with slack on average. A larger budget is allocated in this case than in the previous one.

Thus it can be seen that the second derivative of the expected net benefit functions plays an important role in determining the optimal degree of bias in allocating resources to sub-units. In the above case, when these are equal no bias is called for, but when they are unequal it is optimal to introduce either slack or strain on a systematic bias. When the marginal expected net benefit forgone from increasing x increases at a faster rate than the marginal expected gain from increasing x, it is optimal for the organization to build strain into its allocation to the sub-unit. On the other hand, when the opposite relationship holds, it is optimal for the organization to build slack into its resource allocation to a sub-unit.

DISCUSSION

This chapter indicates that in order to allow rationally for uncertainty and the inability of organizations to adjust promptly to changing states of information, it can be optimal to allocate resources to sub-units in a way which allows them to enjoy slack on average, or subjects them to strain on average. Circumstances such as differences in the rate of change of marginal benefits to the organization, favouring one policy or the other were considered. Although the argument needs to be generalized further, it has enabled us to identify elements that can be important in managerial decision making.

It might also be desirable in further work to relax the assumption that an organization operates as a team. Conflict and deception are not uncommon within organizations. Also the possibility of varying an allocation during the execution period should be allowed for. To allow for these factors would complicate the analysis. Nevertheless, the present analysis illustrates that even in relatively uncomplicated situations it may be optimal from the point of view of an organization for central management in its allocation of resources to sub-units or divisions within the organization to provide sub-units either with slack or impose strain on them on average. This is so, taking into account the uncertainties that the sub-units have to cope with and the relative penalties imposed upon the whole organization by being generous or niggardly on average in allocating resources to the sub-units.

NOTES

1. See, for example, Marschak (1955) and Marschak and Radner (1972).
2. See, for example, Leibenstein (1978), especially Chapter 2. Leibenstein (1975) recognizes the existence of 'inert' areas of behaviour in a multidivisional firm but does not follow the rational approach adopted here.

REFERENCES

Hart, A.G. (1942), 'Risk, Uncertainty and the Unprofitability of Compounding Probabilities', in *Studies in Mathematical Economics and Econometrics*, Lange, O., McIntyre, F. and Yntema, F. (eds), Chicago: University of Chicago Press, 110–18.

Leibenstein, H. (1975), 'Aspects of the X-Efficiency Theory of the Firm', *Bell Journal of Economics and Management Science*, 6, 580–606.

Leibenstein, H. (1978), *General X-Efficiency Theory and Economic Development*, New York: Oxford University Press.

Marschak, J. (1955), 'Elements for Theory of Firms', *Management Science*, 1, 127–37.

Marschak, J. and Radner, R. (1972), *Economic Theory of Teams*, New Haven: Yale University Press.

Theil, H. (1961), *Economic Forecasts and Policy*, 2nd rev. edn, Amsterdam: North–Holland.

Tisdell, C.A. (1973), 'Certainty Equivalence and Bias in the Management of Production', *Review of Marketing and Agricultural Economics*, 41(4), 166–78.

10. Information Transmission and Optimal Advice for Groups

The knowledge possessed by different individuals within an organization is generally not available to all individuals in the organization, for knowledge does not automatically flow from one individual to another. Indeed, within a large organization it may be impossible for any single individual to comprehend all of the knowledge within the organization. Within large organizations it is likely that no individual possesses or could comprehend all the information possessed by the whole organization. This is because of the limited capacity of individuals or their bounded rationality.

Since the transmission of knowledge, as well as the collection and processing of it, within an organization involves a cost, there is a need to give consideration to the economics of information within organizations. For example, it is clear that it is not always economic to collect and transmit all information of value. The costs of such activities must be weighed against their benefits.

In addition, within organizations and for groups it is usually not optimal, because of the extra cost involved, to tailor advice, recommendations or information finely to the situation of individual members. Coarse transmission of recommendations may be economic. Given that communication is not tailored to individual situations, it may pay, from an economic point of view, to slant the advice given compared to the average situation faced by members of the group. Such a circumstance may, for example, arise for advice from central management to units within a decentralized firm or for government providing recommendations to economic producers, for example, to farmers about optimal rates of fertilizer application.

Let us consider communication of information generally in organizations before taking up the issue of slanting or biasing recommendations.

OPTIMAL COLLECTION AND TRANSMISSION OF INFORMATION IN ORGANIZATIONS

Consider the economics of collecting and communicating information in organizations. For example, let us suppose that an organization acts as a team (Radner, 1962; Marschak, 1955) and is out to maximize its collective net benefits or net gains. Clearly, the greater are the marginal costs of transmitting information in an organization, the less information it is worthwhile collecting and communicating. This can be illustrated, for example, by Figure 10.1.

There, *MB* represents the marginal benefit to the organization of transmitted information within a group. MC_1 represents the marginal cost of collecting information by the group and the curve *MC* indicates the marginal cost of collecting plus transmitting the information to elsewhere in the organization. In the absence of transmission costs, it is optimal for the relevant collecting group to obtain an amount of knowledge equivalent to x_2. However, if marginal costs of transmission occur (these might involve costs in preparing material for transmission, explaining it and so on) and curve *MC* applies, it is optimal for the collecting group to collect only x_1 of information and transmit it. The greater are the marginal costs of communicating, the less information, other things equal, is it optimal for an organization to obtain.

Figure 10.1   Costs of transmitting information tend to reduce the value of collecting it in an organization

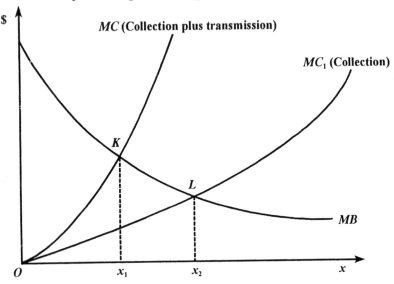

Amount of information or knowledge

Given the costs of transmitting information in organizations and the types of rules that have evolved to cope with it (such as annual budgets for subgroups within an organization) it can be efficient to build slack in subsections of the organization. For example, a subsection may be given a budget slightly greater than needed, on average, to carry out its duties, thus providing it with some slack on average. It may, however, be more efficient to do this than to interact with it continually concerning its requirements and its experience of unforeseen circumstances. Such interaction involves costs and delays and the total costs on average can well exceed those from providing some slack for a subsection to give it some capacity to react from its own resources to changing circumstances. Looked at in this way some degree of slack on average in organizations can be a means for achieving greater efficiency in their operations (Tisdell, 1984, or see Chapter 9 of this book).

SOME FURTHER ASPECTS OF THE ECONOMICS OF SUPPLYING INFORMATION TO OTHERS

There is, of course, a good deal of further work required on the economics of supplying information to others. Issues which can be discussed under this heading include the role of the government in supplying information and the incentive of private individuals and groups to provide information, for example through advertising.

It is sometimes claimed that governments have an important role to play in the supply of information because of various types of market failure involved in the supply of knowledge (Arrow, 1962). Any person originating knowledge or information finds it extremely difficult to retain private property rights in it and enforce those rights. Hence, in a market system some types of information and knowledge will be undersupplied from a social point of view. Both the generation and communication of knowledge may be less than is socially optimal. As illustrated in Figure 10.2, the marginal cost of knowledge generation and transmission might be as indicated by curve *MC* and the marginal private gain by private suppliers might be as indicated by the curve identified by *MBP*. Private supply would, therefore, amount to x_1. If the social marginal gains from supply are as indicated by the curve identified by *MBS*, the socially optimal supply of knowledge is x_2. Government intervention may, therefore, be called for.

Figure 10.2 Market failure in knowledge generation and transmission

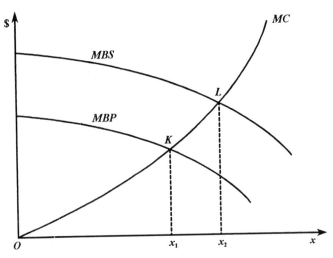

Amount of knowledge generation and transmission

Although an organzation, such as a business firm, may have a commonly agreed objective, units or individual members of it may still tend to act in accordance with their own perceived benefit.   For example, in the generation of knowledge, they may act in accordance with a curve like MBP in Figure 10.2, whereas the marginal benefit of generation and communication of knowledge in the whole organization could be higher and similar to curve MBS in Figure 10.2.   In the absence of intervention, failure in information and generation and transmission may occur within the organization.

In many organizations, fiat or command is used to make sure that information is collected and transmitted by members or the sub-units. This may be an improvement on a *laissez-faire* approach but it can sometimes lead to economically excessive transmission of information. An alternative might be to consider economic incentives for information generation and communication.

Given that a government and units or members within an organization play a role in the supply of information, then specific economic problems arise in determining what information to provide and how to transmit it.   For example, in agriculture the response of a crop to fertilizer may vary between different farms.   How finely tailored should government advice to farmers be about the 'optimal' rate of fertilizer application?   If a recommended rate is to be determined for a group of farmers experiencing different response rates in practice, should it be the best fertilizer application on average for them? (See Tisdell and De Silva, 1983.) Similar situations can arise in business organizations, for example, when central management wishes to give advice to its decentralized units. Let us therefore consider this advisory problem.

NATURE OF THE ADVISORY PROBLEM

Governments frequently provide information and advice to economic agents such as small firms and farmers, to enable them to improve their decisions. However, individual economic agents may not be faced with uniform conditions and the advice given to one may not be optimal for others. But to tailor information or advice to individual circumstances or even to differentiate it by sets of conditions can be costly and uneconomic. The advice tendered by government may be optimal only for an average situation or for one set of circumstances. A similar situation exists for central management within an organization or business firm.

Given that only a point recommendation (that is, advice optimal for only one set of economic circumstances) is to be made and that this recommendation is followed by all relevant economic agents irrespective of the conditions faced by them, how should this advice be tailored to maximize aggregate economic gain? Should economic agents be advised to set their relevant controlled variable (for example, quantity applied or used of an input, such as fertilizer by a farmer) at the level corresponding to its average optimal level for them as a group or should it be slanted or biased away from this value? This part of this chapter identifies circumstances that make different types of slanting optimal from an aggregate point of view (Kaldor–Hicks viewpoint)[1] and also identifies conditions under which greater disaggregation of advice may be called for.

Single-point recommendations may be made not only because it is costly to differentiate advice for individuals, but also because issuing multiple recommendations may be confusing to some recipients. Simplicity in presentation may make for more effective communication.

One question which is not taken up here is the slanting of advice either to allow for the discounting of its credibility by recipients or to attract their attention. It may be optimal from an economic point of view and adopting the philosophy that the ends justify the means, to slant information to allow for such considerations.

The problem envisaged here is relevant when there are economic constraints on the provision and dissemination of information by government. These constraints exist in all economies but may be more restrictive in developing countries. In developing countries, agricultural extension advice is of particular importance given that the majority of individuals in most developing countries are economically dependent upon agriculture. Uniform-point recommendations are not uncommon in LDCs. In Sri Lanka, where agricultural extension services are comparatively well developed, uniform-point recommendations are made, for instance, by the Coconut Research Institute of Sri Lanka to coconut growers about the amount of fertilizer to apply (CRISL, 1980) and the spacing of mature palms, even though actual economic and biological optima vary depending upon soil types and other conditions.

In the remainder of this chapter, the optimal biasing of point recommendations from a collective point of view is considered first and then factors that may make it worthwhile to differentiate information or recommendations are discussed. The scope for making the approach operational is also considered. It is developed on the assumption that the government is providing advice to farmers or decision units but can be adapted for application to advice by central management in a multidivisional firm to its divisions.

OPTIMALLY BIASED RECOMMENDATIONS

The problem of optimally biasing recommendations is complex but a simple formulation of the problem is considered here. In this section, the optimal recommended value from a collective point of view of a variable controlled by farmers or other decision units is compared with the average of its optimal value for individual farmers or decision units to determine whether bias is optimal and the desirable direction, if any, of the bias in recommendations.

Suppose that each relevant economic agent has a net benefit function that depends quadratically on the magnitude of a controlled variable x. The dependent variable might be the firm's profit or in a subsistence economy the level of the subsistence unit's production for the use of a given amount of resources or, more generally, utility for the relevant decision-making unit. Suppose further that the welfare of the economic agent is maximized when its net benefit function is maximized with respect to its controlled variable. The net benefit function of this i-th economic agent might be represented by

$$y_i = a_i x_i^2 + b_i x_i + c_i \qquad (10.1)$$

which implies a diminishing marginal benefit from increasing the size of x. For example, depending upon the problem, this function could represent utility, production or net benefit from application of fertilizer by a farmer. Each economic agent would maximize their economic net benefit by setting x at a level for which

$$dy_i /dx_i = 2a_i x_i + b_i = 0 \qquad (10.2)$$

that is at

$$\hat{x}_i = - b_i / 2a_i. \qquad (10.3)$$

Differentiating equation (10.3) twice, it can be seen that the second-order conditions for a maximum are satisfied. If there are n relevant agents, this implies that on average the optimal values of x of the n agents are

$$\bar{x} = 1/n \sum \hat{x}_i. \qquad (10.4)$$

Now suppose that the government wishes to maximize aggregate welfare in the sense that it wishes to maximize

$$W = \sum y_i \qquad (10.5)$$

(see 10.1) but is only able to recommend one level of x to all the economic agents. This 'welfare function' implies that the net benefits of each of the individual decision-making units are weighted equally. If net benefits are perfectly transferable, this criterion is equivalent to the Kaldor–Hicks criterion.[2] Note that decision-making units need not have the same y-functions.

Should the recommended level of x be $\bar{x}$, larger, or smaller than this? If the marginal benefit functions of the agents differ only by a constant, then point recommendation $\bar{x}$ is optimal. Aggregate welfare averaged over the agents is

$$1/n \ W = - E[a_i]x^2 + E[b_i]x + E[c_i], \qquad (10.6)$$

where E represents averages and all agents are assumed to adopt the same level of x. Aggregate welfare reaches a maximum when (10.6) does. Differentiating and solving in the usual way, this expression reaches its maximum for

$$x^* = E[b_i] / E[2a_i], \tag{10.7}$$

where the sufficient condition is, in fact, satisfied. From (10.4),

$$\bar{x} = E[b_i / 2a_i]. \tag{10.8}$$

If all the marginal net benefit functions have the same slope, all values of $2a$ are the same and consequently $x^* = \bar{x}$.
It would be optimal to give point advice equal to $\bar{x}$. Thus when

$$E[b_i / 2a_i] = E[b_i] / E[2a_i] \tag{10.9}$$

no slanting of information or advice is called for assuming that only a point recommendation is made and that it is followed.

This case is illustrated in Figure 10.3. Suppose that there are only two economic agents (or two groups of agents each facing identical conditions and equal in number). Suppose that the marginal benefit curve for one agent is as indicated by line *ABC* and for the other, by *DEFG*. These lines are parallel. The optimal value of x for agent 1 is $\hat{x}_1$ and for agent 2, $\hat{x}_2$ and the average of these values corresponds to point *H*.

Figure 10.3 Case in which aggregate welfare is maximized by not biasing recommended value of controlled variable

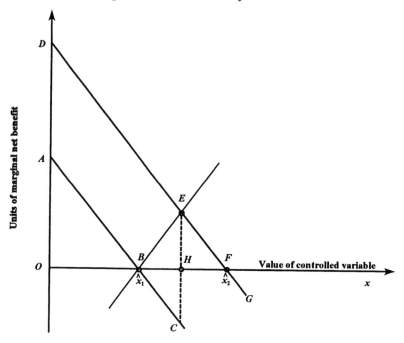

Suppose that only one value of x can be recommended by the government. The recommended value of x should be increased until the aggregate net marginal benefit from doing this equals zero. This occurs at point H. At this point $EH = HC$, or the marginal benefit forgone by agent 1 is equal to the increase in marginal benefit obtained by agent 2. The optimum can also be identified by rotating line ABC through 180 degrees on fixed point B to form the line BE. Line BE represents the marginal benefit forgone by agent 1, and at E equals that obtained by agent 2. To advise the x-value corresponding to H is optimal. If

$$E[b_i]/E[2a_i] < E[b/2a_i], \tag{10.10}$$

it is optimal to recommend an x-value less than $\bar{x}$, and if this equality is reversed to recommend an x-value greater than $\bar{x}$. This can be illustrated by the case shown in Figure 10.4. Let there be two economic agents (or groups suitably defined) and let the marginal benefit curve of agent 1 be as shown by line ABC and that of agent 2 be as shown by line $DEFG$. The marginal benefit received by agent 1 from x declines at a faster rate than that for agent 2, and consequently relationship (10.10) holds. The value of $\bar{x}$ corresponds to M and is the mid-point between points B and F. The optimal advisory value of x, x^* corresponds to point K. It is the value of x for which the marginal benefit forgone by agent 1 from an increase in x equals the marginal benefit obtained by agent 2. At K, $CK = KE$ or rotating ABC on fixed point B through 180 degrees, it is the value for which line EB equals line DG. Since $OK < OM$, it is optimal in this case to slant the recommendation about x so that it is less than the average optimal value, $\bar{x}$.

This illustration is readily modified to show that if the marginal benefit of the agent receiving higher marginal benefit should decline at a faster rate than that of the other agent, it is optimal to bias the recommended value of the controlled variable upwards, that is above $\bar{x}$. In this case, the line DG declines at a faster rate than the line AC and an analogous argument to that just outlined applies.

It might be noted that the slanting of advice has income distributional consequences. Those receiving lower marginal benefits have their potential income reduced by the advice tendered. While it is also true that point recommendations do not maximize the benefits of those receiving higher marginal benefits, a government may wish to tailor its advice to favour the former group if members of it happen to have lower incomes (which, of course, they need not have). This will tend to bias the recommended value of x downwards.

Figure 10.4 Case in which it is optimal to bias recommendation for controlled variable

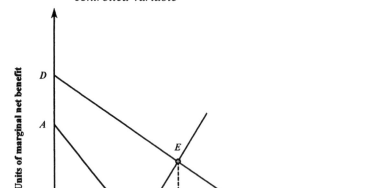

OBSERVATIONS ON THE VALUE OF DIFFERENTIATING INFORMATION

One may wish to consider the circumstances that increase the likely gain to be obtained by differentiating recommendations according to the conditions faced by the recipients of this information. The more divergent are the marginal benefits of recipients from variations in the controlled variable and/or the greater the rate of decrease of their marginal benefits, the greater the aggregate benefit forgone as a result of a point recommendation and the greater the benefit – other things equal – from differentiating information. This is illustrated in Figure 10.5, for a case in which there are two economic agents and for which marginal benefits from changes of their controlled variable are equal.

Given that the marginal benefit curve for agent 1 is AC and for agent 2 is DG, the aggregate net welfare 'forgone' by giving the point recommendation corresponding to H rather than B for agent 1 and F for agent 2 is equal to the area $\triangle BHC$ + area $\triangle HEF$. Should the marginal benefit curves become more divergent, other things equal, for example, shift for agent 1 from AC to $A'\,C'$ and for agent 2 from DG to $D'\,G'$, aggregate net welfare 'forgone' as a result of the point recommendation increases. It increases to the area of $\triangle B'\,HC'$ + area $\triangle E'\,HF'$.

The effect of an increase in the slope of the marginal benefit curves can also be illustrated in Figure 10.5. Let *MP* be the marginal benefit curve for agent 1 and *QS* be that for agent 2. The optimal point recommendation then corresponds to *U* given that the marginal benefit curves are parallel. The welfare benefit forgone by not giving perfect advice is equal to the area of Δ*NUP* + area Δ*RUS*. Now suppose that both marginal benefit curves increase in slope but remain parallel to become *M'P'* and *Q'S* respectively. The welfare benefit forgone now increases to area Δ*NUP'* + area Δ*R'US*.

Figure 10.5   *The more divergent the marginal benefits for agents and the steeper the marginal benefit curves, the greater the aggregate benefit forgone by not differentiating recommendations*

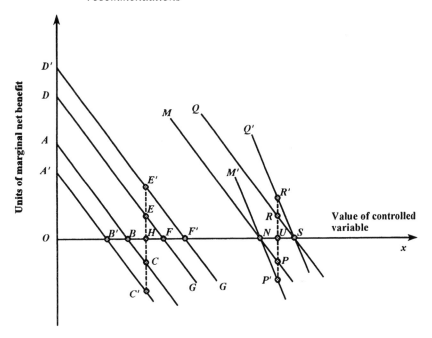

OPERATIONAL ASPECTS, CONCLUSIONS AND QUALIFICATIONS

One may wonder how operational use could be made of this theory, particularly in LDCs. Some information is needed about the nature of the different net benefit functions faced by different producers. While undoubtedly knowledge can be so imperfect as to rule out any application of this theory, even in LDCs such as Sri Lanka, India and the Philippines, experimental data is available for crops, enabling estimates to be made of production (and/or profit) responses on different farms in relation to controlled variables such as fertilizer. Agricultural experimental results are often available, for example, for production responses to fertilizer on different soils, for varying rainfall patterns and other variables. These may come from experimental plots in different regions or they may be deduced from experimental results in a particular locality.

The greatest difficulty is liable to occur in practice when one deviates from using either production or profit as an indicator of net benefit. If one employs some type of utility indicator, sampling in the field may be needed to construct the relevant utility functions. It might be observed that there are some subsistence or peasant economies in which production by a farm or decision unit may roughly be taken as an indicator of welfare (utility is, approximately, a linear function of output over a range) and in these circumstances application of the theory appears least complicated.

Differences in net benefit functions (for example, production, utility, or profit functions) between decision units can occur for a wide variety of reasons. They can occur because of differences in factor endowments including cross-country differences in climate, weather variables and soils. Furthermore, differences in human capital reflecting itself in the quality of management, especially the likelihood or otherwise of complementary resources being used in the case of high-yielding varieties of crops, can give rise to significant differences in net benefit and productivity relationships. Responses conditioned by differences in cultural factors may also give rise to heterogeneity of effective net benefit and production relationships. Both natural and cultural factors can therefore give rise to considerable diversity in the net benefit or production relationships faced by different individual decision-making units, and make it worthwhile to take account of the issues considered above.

Thus one can see that it may be optimal from a welfare point of view to bias point recommendations. This contribution has outlined circumstances under which biasing is optimal. It also points to conditions under which the economic 'losses' or benefits forgone by adopting point recommendations rather than differentiated advice can be considerable. Thus it is a small start in investigating a subject that appears to have been neglected but which has policy significance, especially as far as agricultural extension advice by government and its advice to small firms is concerned.[3]

However, it needs to be remembered that mechanisms for transmitting advice and information patterns of the diffusion of information and means of eliciting action by economic agents on the basis of communications can be complex (Ozga, 1960; Kotler, 1971). This chapter abstracts from such complexities by assuming that extension advisers communicate their advice precisely (and directly) to economic agents who blindly follow it. A number of communication mechanisms are possible (distribution of leaflets and bulletins to economic agents, on-farm visits by advisers, demonstrations, the use of different types of media and the possibility of learning from others in the group) and differences in the receptivity of different group members to advice needs to be taken into account. It may, for example, be most important to target information or advice first to those who are likely to be most receptive to it, especially if there are likely to be flow-on benefits by others in the group following these leaders (Reekie, 1975). Another factor to be considered is the distortion of messages in transmission and in their diffusion (Williamson, 1967). These considerations should be taken into account in more detailed studies.

Another important factor is the possibility of individuals learning from their own trials and seeking out their own optimum once they have been convinced to try a new technique. In some cases, it may, for instance, be not so important to advise farmers precisely about the optimal amount of fertilizer to apply but to convince them to apply it at all and in sufficient quantities for them to see that it is beneficial so that they start their own trial and error process of finding the optimal application for their own circumstances. Nevertheless, the assumption that once individuals try a technique they will quickly or eventually discover its optimal level of use is a special one. A spectrum of patterns exist for learning by experimentation or trial, a process to be distinguished from learning by doing (Arrow, 1962). Ideally the spectrum should be allowed for in building models of the social value of extension advice.

Despite the possibility of learning by experimentation or by trial and error, individuals often fail, given uncertainty, to discover the optimal level of utilization of a technique from their point of view. Furthermore, there are circumstances (but not all) in which greater social gains from communication of advice are made by encouraging the improved utilization of existing employed techniques rather than by urging the adoption of superior techniques. Conditions making for the social superiority of one type of extension strategy rather than the other can be specified but even superficial consideration of the problem indicates that the appropriate strategy varies with the circumstances.

NOTES

1. A Kaldor–Hicks optimum is achieved for a group when its economic organization is such that it is impossible to make any change that results in aggregative gains to any set of group members exceeding losses to the remainder of the group, it being assumed that gains are transferable.

2. Maximizing function (10.5) will maximize welfare in the Kaldor–Hicks sense described in note 1, and if actual transfers are made costlessly, a Paretian welfare gain would be made, that is, some individuals in the group would be made better off and none would be worse off as a result of maximizing (10.5) (compare Little, 1957; Mishan, 1981). Furthermore, if y_i represents the profit of the i-th division of a multidivisional firm, maximizing (10.5) will maximize the total profit of the firm.

3. While it is true that Theil (1961), (compare Tisdell, 1973), investigates the matter of certainty equivalence or bias in relation to the expected value of a non-controlled variable, his problem differs from that outlined above. Mathematically, the above problem involving bias is similar to that in Tisdell (1984). For complementary but different problems dealing with the value of extension advice, see De Silva and Tisdell (1981), and Tisdell and De Silva (1983).

REFERENCES

Arrow, K.J. (1962), 'The Economic Implications of Learning by Doing', *Review of Economic Studies*, 29, 275–82.

Coconut Research Institute of Sri Lanka (CRISL) (1980), 'The Manuring of Adult Coconuts', *Coconut Research Leaflet*, 36, rev. edn, Colombo: Coconut Research Institute.

De Silva, N.T.M.H. and Tisdell, C.A. (1981), 'Response of Coconuts to Fertilizer and Advice to Sri Lankan Growers; An Aggregative Approach', *Ceylon Coconut Quarterly*, 32, 72–9.

Kotler, P. (1971), *Marketing Decision Making: A Model Building Approach*, London: Holt, Rinehart & Winston.

Little, I.M.D. (1957), *A Critique of Welfare Economics*, London: Oxford University Press.

Marschak, J.M. (1955), 'Elements of a Theory of Teams', *Management Science*, 1, 127–37.

Mishan, E.J. (1981), *Introduction to Normative Economics*, New York: Oxford University Press.

Ozga, S.A. (1960), 'Imperfect Markets Through Lack of Knowledge', *Quarterly Journal of Economics*, 74, 29–52.

Radner, R. (1962), 'Team Decision Problems', *Annals of Mathematical Statistics*, 22, 857–88.

Reekie, W.D. (1975), *Managerial Economics*, Oxford: Philip Allen.

Theil, H. (1961), *Economic Forecasts and Policy*, 2nd edn, Amsterdam: North-Holland.

Tisdell, C.A. (1973), 'Certainty Equivalence and Bias to the Management of Production', *Review of Marketing and Agricultural Economics*, 41, 160–87.

Tisdell, C.A. (1984), 'Slack and Strain in Efficient Budgeting and Resource Allocation by Organizations', *Managerial and Decision Economics*, 5(1), 54–7.

Tisdell, C.A. and De Silva, N.T.M.H. (1983), 'The Value to Producers of Extension Advice about Optimal Resource Use', *Sri Lankan Journal of Agricultural Sciences*, 20, 67–78.
Williamson, O.E. (1967), 'Hierarchical Control and Optimum Firm Size', *The Journal of Political Economy*, 75, 123–38.

11. Transfer Pricing and the Management of Multidivisional Firms

Because managers are subject to conditions which make for bounded rationality, decentralization of management in large businesses is essential for their economic success and survival. Even if top managers were able and did receive all the information generated (or which could be generated in an organization), they would soon become overloaded with information and their managerial decision making could suffer. Furthermore, as an organization becomes larger, it becomes more difficult for top management to monitor and control the behaviour of subordinates. In these circumstances, 'slippages' occur in the organization with adverse economic consequences. Because of increasing asymmetry of information in the organization, opportunities for private goal seeking are increased. Some of these problems can be overcome by decentralizing the organization and providing suitable economic incentives to individuals or managers of the divisions of a business with a view to increasing the correspondence between their own personal goals and those of the business. The mechanism of transfer pricing and the payment of bonuses to managers rising with the profit imputed to their divisions (using transfer prices) provides one possible means of doing this.

Use of transfer prices, which in effect creates an internal market for the firm, is regarded by many writers as an efficient means of management of multidivisional firms. While its value as a management technique is known to be subject to a number of limitations of the type discussed in the general economic theory of market failure, two important limitations of transfer pricing have been neglected in the literature: (1) imputed profit/loss based on optimal transfer prices can be a poor guide to the economic value of a division to a firm when market transaction costs are important (for instance, even if a division shows an imputed loss, it may not be optimal to dispose of it), and (2) transfer pricing can retard technical change, innovation and productivity enhancement within a division to the detriment of the firm as a whole. Both aspects are examined here.

171

As mentioned above, several writers regard transfer pricing as a useful mechanism for assisting in profit maximization by multidivisional firms (Hirshleifer, 1956; Gould, 1964; Naert and Janssen, 1971; compare Williamson, 1975). Using optimal transfer prices, each division of the firm independently maximizes its profit and in this decentralized setting maximizes the profit of the firm as a whole as a byproduct. At least, this is the standard theory.

Under certain conditions, it is true that the profit of the firm can be maximized by this method in a static setting. However, in a vertically integrated firm if divisions supplying inputs to processing or distributing divisions have decreasing per-unit costs, the optimal transfer price implies a loss for the supplying divisions and the usual complications associated with decreasing costs apply. Again, if (profit) externalities occur between divisions of the firm, account must be taken of these in determining transfer prices. For instance, there is evidence that vertically integrated textile firms sometimes find that their fabric (and, in some cases, garment) divisions provide a vanguard for the market introduction of their new yarns, and so have a favourable impact on demand for yarn from their yarn divisions. In addition, one must consider whether there is sufficient knowledge to determine optimal transfer prices in practice. If bonuses are paid to divisions on the basis of an imputed profit, each division may have an incentive to conceal actual costs in order to secure a higher transfer price than otherwise. Furthermore, while an iterative trial and error pricing procedure can be used to search for optimal transfer prices, supplies are still subject to manipulation by divisions with a strategic interest in obtaining a favourable transfer price (compare the theory of incentives in state-owned or socialist firms), and, of course, in the real world conditions change with time and so do optimal transfer prices. In addition, note that if economies of scope are important (Baumol et al., 1982) the imputed profit from a division or activity based on optimal transfer price is likely to understate its real economic value to the firm as a whole.

Most of the above limitations are known or are quickly perceived from a knowledge of standard microeconomic theory. However, there are two further limitations of transfer pricing that are less obvious but are important:

1. imputed profit or loss can be an inadequate guide to the value of a division to the firm if market transaction costs are important; and
2. the transfer price system, when combined with bonuses based on imputed profit, can slow down technical change and innovation and provide a disincentive to productivity increase.

We will consider each of these matters in turn. The existence of market transaction costs is important to the argument (see Coase, 1937; Demsetz, 1968; Cheung, 1969; Alchian and Demsetz, 1972; Williamson, 1975, 1979; De Alessi, 1983). Further issues related to market transaction costs are discussed in Chapter 15.

VALUE OF A DIVISION

Let us consider a vertically 'integrated' firm consisting of two divisions: an input supplying division (I) and an input using one (II). In Figure 11.1 let the line identified by *MC* represent the cost to division I of supplying an essential input *X* for the production of division II and let the line identified by *NMR* represent the net marginal revenue obtained by division II by using *X*.

Figure 11.1   The value of a division in terms of its contribution to the global profit of a business

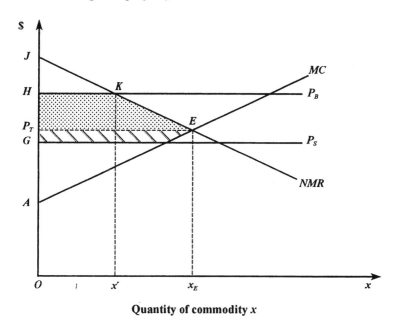

Quantity of commodity *x*

Market transaction costs of *HG* per unit of *X* traded are assumed. The firm is assumed to be able to sell the input on the market at P_S or buy it in at P_B. In the case shown, the gap between the selling and buying prices straddles the intersection of lines MC and NMR, and it is optimal for the firm not to trade in X. The optimal transfer price is P_T, and this imputes a profit equal to the area of $\triangle AEP_T$ to division I and of $\triangle P_TEJ$ to division II. However, the value of each division to the firm is greater than is indicated by these areas. The value of division I is greater by the dotted area, and the value of division II is larger by the hatched one. For instance, suppose that the fixed costs of division I equal the area of $\triangle$ AEP_T. Division I might then appear to make no contribution to profit of the company, and it may be thought that its closure would be a matter of indifference. However, this is not the case. Closure of the division will reduce the firm's or company's profit by the dotted area. This is the case, since, with the closure of division I, division II has to purchase commodity X in the market and in so doing incurs market transaction costs which result in its purchase price of X being effectively P_B. In order to maximize its profit, division I reduces its use of commodity X from x_E to x'. Consequently, the firm's profit falls from an amount equal to the area of $\triangle P_TEJ$ to an amount equal to the area of triangle HJK if the fixed costs of division II are ignored. The other case in which the value of division II is considered involves similar factors which can easily be overlooked.

The buying and selling price will not always straddle the intersection point of MC and NMR. When the selling price is above this point it becomes the transfer price, and the input is sold, to some extent, on the outside market. The profit imputed to division I underestimates its value. When the buying price is below this intersection point the imputed profit on the basis of the transfer price underestimates the value to the firm of division II. Thus, one can see that there is a need for caution when market transaction costs are important.

INNOVATION AND TRANSFER PRICING

If there are no market transaction costs and the firm is unable to influence the market price of the commodity being transferred within the firm, the commodity's optimal transfer price from the viewpoint of maximizing the global profit of the firm is the market price of the commodity. Under these conditions, each division can increase its profit by reducing its cost of production. Hence, there is an incentive to adopt new profit-raising techniques and to increase productivity if divisional managers obtain bonuses, either pecuniary or non-pecuniary, which are positively related to the profit of their divisions. This can be illustrated by Figure 11.2, assuming that the earlier situation applies, *mutatis mutandis*. P_M is the market price of X and therefore $P_T = P_M$. Suppose that division I can reduce its marginal cost from that indicated by lines $ABMC_1$ to $ABMC_2$, either by adopting a new technique or otherwise raising its productivity. To do so will raise both the profit of the division and the global profit of the firm. Division I will find it profitable to increase its production from x_3 to x_4, and its profit (and the global profit of the firm) will rise by the equivalent of the hatched area in Figure 11.2. Similarly, if division II increases its productivity so that its net marginal revenue rises from the line indicated by $CDNMR_1$ to $CDNMR_2$, its profit rises by the dotted area. However, such rises in imputed profit need not occur when market transaction costs are important.

Figure 11.2   Cost-reducing innovation or productivity increase by a division raises its imputed profit if the optimal transfer price remains constant

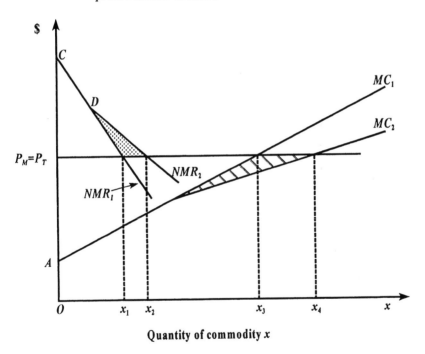

Quantity of commodity x

Consider the situation, illustrated in Figure 11.3, where market transaction costs are important. Conditions similar to those in Figure 11.1 are assumed. In this case the marginal costs of production of division I are initially as indicated by line $ABMC_1$ and market transaction costs are such that the firm makes no use of outside markets for X. Initially, the optimal transfer price is P_T. Now suppose that division I can reduce its marginal cost to that represented by line $ABMC_2$, either by adopting a new technique or by improving productivity. If this is done, the optimal (static) transfer price becomes P'_T and the profit imputed to division I falls. Division I's profit falls by the difference between the dotted and the hatched areas in Figure 11.3, despite the fact that the profits of the firm as a whole rise. The global profits of the firm increase by the equivalent of the area of ΔBLN. Division II now appropriates an amount equal to the dotted area in Figure 11.3 and makes a 'stemming' profit equal to the area of ΔMLN so that its total profit rises by the equivalent of the area of quadrilateral $P'_T P_T LN$. Division II gains without 'sowing', whereas division I in innovating loses imputed profit. Therefore, if bonuses are positively related to imputed profit, division I has no incentive to adopt the new technique because its profit is down. A similar situation can be illustrated for productivity rises obtained by division II. This is not to say that all reduction in market costs or rises in net marginal revenue will lower the profit of the division initiating them, but that some such changes, especially when tilted towards the margin, will do so (Duncan and Tisdell, 1971).

Figure 11.3   *Cost-reducing innovation or productivity change which alters the transfer price may reduce the imputed profit of the innovating or productivity-enhancing division*

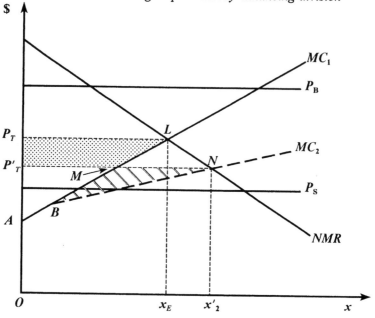

Quantity of commodity x

While market transaction costs may be large enough to prevent a firm using an outside market for an input, this is not always so, for example, the case shown in Figure 11.2 could apply. When non-straddle cases occur, there may be no impediment to technical change through variations in profit imputed to the innovating division. Indeed, the general rule is that provided the optimal transfer price remains unchanged after the cost-reducing or productivity-raising technological change by a division takes place, there is no impediment to technical change because the imputed profit of the innovating division rises. The incentive problem can only occur when the initiation of the technical change turns the terms of trade against the innovating division through the variation in the optimal transfer price, that is, the transfer price falls from division I's point of view if it is the innovator or rises from the point of view of division II if it is the innovator. In such a case, the imputed profit of the innovating division may fall.

CONCLUSIONS ABOUT THE ABOVE ISSUES

As has been seen, transfer prices have limitations when they are used to impute profits to divisions and if used as the main basis to decide whether or not to close down divisions. Transfer pricing may, in certain circumstances, retard technical progress and innovation within the firm, impede productivity increases and result in the global profit of a multidivisional firm not being maximized. Of course, there would be scope for bargaining between divisions. A division which would experience a fall in its imputed profit by adopting a technique which would increase global company profit but lower the division's imputed profit may demand a bribe from other divisions to compensate it for its loss. Whether this would be a practical way to manage a firm is unclear. It would raise severe management problems given the small numbers involved in the bargaining process. It might be noted that the problems raised here are not peculiar to capitalist firms but would apply with equal force to those in socialist countries when a transfer price system is used.

The analysis outlined here concerning the impact of technical change on profits or producers' surplus has similarities to analyses in quite different contexts, for example, the impact of technological progress on the surpluses obtained by primary producers (Duncan and Tisdell, 1971; Akino and Hayami, 1975; Lindner and Jarrett, 1978; Taylor, 1980).

SOME FURTHER OBSERVATIONS

The theory of transfer pricing, although it allows for some impediments such as the transaction costs involved in using markets and implicitly recognizes the limited possible span of control of top management, is still relatively static. Furthermore, its proponents do not give substantial attention to the presence of spillovers or externalities between divisions of companies and how best to allow for these. For example, should those divisions with a favourable effect on the returns of other divisions be imputed a subsidy with a deduction being made from the imputed profit of the divisions benefiting? How should such 'transfers' be determined? Or are there more desirable ways of taking spillovers between divisions into account in imputing the profit or 'worth' of divisions? Much of the economic theory of externalities is in fact relevant to 'markets' within multidivisional firms, that is, for taking into account symbiosis between divisions where it in fact exists.

Also, more attention needs to be given to what functions are best centralized or decentralized within organizations, including business firms. To what extent, for example, should finance and investment be centralized? To what extent should research and development be centralized? For example, in the case of research and development, centralization could yield economies of scale and scope. However, this might be at the expense of important information generated at the plant level or through direct contacts with suppliers or customers. Partial centralization (but with some decentralization) of such activities and the development of suitable information networks may turn out to be the most appropriate solution in many cases.

Central management may be an important source of information for the divisions of a company and questions of what to communicate and how to present it so that it is of the greatest net benefit for the company continue to be important. As yet the theory of transfer pricing does not seem to have been linked with the economics of information and transmission of information in organizations.

Schumpeter (1942) was concerned that with the growth of larger corporations under capitalism they would tend to become ossified and rule ridden and that this would stifle innovation and hamper the efficient operation of capitalistic economic systems. There is, of course, always a danger of this occurring. In any organization, the problem is how to allow constructive freedom to its individual parts yet sustain its collective purpose and cohesion via inputs and controls from the central management of the organization. The appropriate balance is important for the survival and well-being not only of organizations but of society as a whole. An assessment of organizations needs to take into account their ability to cope with and adapt to changing circumstances. This can often be more important for their survival and efficient functioning than their optimal adaptation to a static situation such as that portrayed by much of the theory of management based on transfer pricing.

REFERENCES

Akino, M., and Hayami, Y. (1975), 'Efficiency and Equity in Public Research: Rice Breeding in Japan's Economic Development', *American Journal of Agricultural Economics*, 57, 1–10.

Alchian, A.A., and Demsetz, H. (1972), 'Production, Information Costs and Economic Organization', *The American Economic Review*, 62, 777–95.

Baumol, W.J., Panzer J.C. and Willig, R.D. (1982), *Contestable Markets and the Theory of Industry Structure*, New York: Harcourt, Brace & Jovanovich.

Cheung, S.N.S. (1969), 'Transaction Costs, Risk Aversion and the Choice of Contractual Arrangements', *Journal of Law and Economics*, 12(1), 23–42.

Coase, R.H. (1937). 'The Nature of the Firm', *Economica*, New Series 4, 386 *et seq.*

De Alessi, L. (1983), 'Property Rights, Transaction Costs and X-efficiency: An Essay in Economic Theory', *American Economic Review*, 73, 64–81.

Demsetz, F. (1968), 'The Cost of Transacting', *Quarterly Journal of Economics*, 82, 33–53.

Duncan, R.C. and Tisdell, C.A. (1971), 'Research and Technical Progress – the Returns to Producers', *Economic Record*, 47(117), 124–9.

Gould, J.R. (1964), 'Internal Pricing in Firms where there are Costs of Using an Outside Market', *Journal of Business*, 37, 61–7.

Hirshleifer, J. (1956), 'On the Economics of Transfer Pricing', *Journal of Business*, 20, 172–84.

Lindner, R.K. and Jarrett, F.G. (1978), 'Supply Shifts and the Size of Research Benefits', *American Journal of Agricultural Economics*, 60, 48–58.

Naert, P.A. and Janssen, C.T.L. (1971), 'On Suboptimization in Decomposition Approaches to Transfer Pricing', *Journal of Industrial Economics* 19(3), 220–30.

Schumpeter, J. (1942), *Capitalism, Socialism and Democracy*, 2nd edn, New York: Harper Brothers.

Taylor, C.R. (1980), 'The Nature of Benefits and Costs of the Use of Pest Control Methods', *American Journal of Agricultural Economics*, 62(5), 1007–11 .

Williamson, O.E. (1975), *Markets and Hierarchies: Analysis and Antitrust Implications*, New York: The Free Press.

Williamson, D.E. (1979), 'Transaction-cost Economics: The Governance of Contractual Relations', *The Journal of Law and Economics*, 12(2), 233–62.

12. Game Theory and Group Behaviour

INTRODUCTION

Since the publication of von Neumann and Morgenstern's *Theory of Games and Economic Behaviour* (1944), game theory has become a well-established part of economic theory and receives coverage in all major microeconomic texts (for example, Varian, 1993; Mansfield, 1994). While it does undoubtedly provide valuable insights into group behaviour and is useful for decision-making purposes, it is far from able to provide a general theory of group behaviour. This is because it relies on the assumption of comparatively unbounded rationality by the social participants in the games and on fluidity in and costless mechanisms to achieve group cooperation where members of the group desire Paretian optimality for the group. As mentioned later, in many respects it places more demands on the limited decision-making capabilities of individuals than does standard neoclassical economic theory.

At the outset there are some interesting observations that can be made:

1. There are several group situations in which optimizing behaviour by individuals or coalitions of individuals result in outcomes that are not perfectly predictable. This is the case, for example, when mixed strategies are used. In cases where such strategies are necessary for resolution of conflict in a group, but are not used, the outcome is even less predictable. This illustrates the limits to using individual rationality to predict social behaviour.

2. When coalitions in games are possible, and are easily formed and altered, there may be no solution to a game that can assure each potential coalition of members of a group as much as this coalition could obtain by its creation. This implies that the core of the game is empty. This again highlights limits to using unbounded rationality assumptions as a means to predict social behaviour.

181

3.   It may also be said that the theory of games indicates limits to using the deductive approach as a way to predict social behaviour. While a considerable amount of research has been done on experimental games, particularly by psychologists, the situations considered are highly simplified. The bulk of publications on the theory of games uses the mathematical deductive approach rather than the empirical. Little attention has been given to incorporating institutional constraints into the theory of games. Whether or not developments in the evolutionary theory of games (see Weibull, 1995) will break out of these shackles is unclear. Whether or not a shift in paradigm occurs in evolutionary games will depend on how their dynamics are structured and on how they make allowance for institutional constraints, learning and historical experience. In any case, the use of equilibria as solutions to games remains a central part of game theory and therefore is a limitation in the minds of those evolutionary economists opposed to the use of equilibrium concepts in economics.

Except for the discussion in Chapter 8, it has been assumed that organizations or groups are either teams or foundations. A team has a common objective and all members are motivated to promote this objective by their actions. No special incentives are required to ensure this. However, even a team cannot act with unbounded rationality because its members have limited decision-making ability, information is costly to transmit and so on. In a foundation there is a common agreed objective but members may not promote it unless provided with appropriate incentives. From this point of view, a multidivisional firm might be regarded as a foundation if all members (or relevant decision makers), for example, are agreed on profit maximization of the whole company as a goal. However, appropriate rewards or incentives may have to be given to managers of divisions to ensure that they promote the collective goal. In strategic games, however, no common objective of group members may exist. This at least will be the case unless games are cooperative games.

Von Neumann and Morgenstern divided games into cooperative and non-cooperative games. However, their theory does not provide a detailed guide as to when games are likely to be cooperative or non-cooperative, except to point out that cooperation will not occur unless all parties can gain from it. It follows that cooperation is impossible for some types of games, for example, for two-person zero-sum games. However, even in cases where cooperation is possible, it may not occur or it may not be complete. Thus a whole range of social possibilities arise, not all of which are captured by current theories of games.

Since there is now such a large body of literature on the theory of games, it is impossible to review it fully here. I shall therefore concentrate on von Neumann and Morgenstern's basic theory and some simple extensions of it. Despite the limitations of the theory, it has done much to enhance our understanding of social and economic interdependence.

GAME THEORY AND ITS EARLY SETTING

The outcome for any one individual as a rule depends not only upon his or her own strategy but also upon the strategies of other individuals. Rational individuals will take account of this interdependence and this creates new possibilities, many of which can be analysed by constructs from the theory of games.

As Morgenstern and von Neumann put it:[1]

> [In a social economy,] every participant can determine the variables which describe his own actions but not those of the others. Nevertheless those 'alien' variables cannot, from his point of view, be described by statistical assumptions. This is because the others are guided, just as he himself, by rational principles whatever that may mean – and no *modus procedendi* can be correct which does not attempt to understand those principles and the interactions of the conflicting interests of all the participants. Sometimes some of these interests run more or less parallel – then we are nearer to a simple maximum problem. But they can just as well be opposed. The general theory must cover all of these possibilities, all intermediary stages, and all their combinations.

The problems dealt with in the theory of games of strategy have been largely ignored by neoclassical economists or treated only under highly restrictive assumptions such as those of the theory of perfect or pure competition. Theories of perfect competition frequently assume that the equilibrium exists and that each individual, since his or her trading is small in relation to the market, is faced by fixed conditions. Even traditional theories which depart from the assumption of perfect competition ignore game-like interdependence, for example, the theories of Joan Robinson (1969) and Edward Chamberlin (1950) and the standard textbook analyses of cartels, treat these as monopolist. An early and important exception was Frances Edgeworth (1881) who analysed coalitions in some detail and predicted that, as a result of the tendency for economic agents to combine, solutions to economic problems would become increasingly indeterminate. However, the traditional economic theory of market competition is deficient in so far as it does not explain the conditions under which economic agents combine. Their degree of coalition is taken as datum, not as something to be explained.

Let us consider how far the theory of games, operating with various rationality postulates, can remedy some or all of these deficiencies. In the discussion which follows, I shall be considering two questions:

1. How far can the treatment of the theory of games of interacting agents generate determinate predictions of their behaviour?
2. How far is the theory of games dependent on or committed to unrealistic assumptions or simplifying omissions concerning the circumstances and condition of the interacting agents?

INDIVIDUAL RATIONALITY IN TWO-PERSON GAMES

In a two-person zero-sum game, a loss for one player is a gain for the other. Interests of the players are diametrically opposed and there is no scope for cooperation. In this type of game, it is rational for players to try to minimize the gain of their opponent. If any player, A, believes that the opponent, B, is able to minimize A's gain for whatever strategy is adopted by A, it is rational for A to adopt the strategy which maximizes the minimum of this gain. The same is true, *mutatis mutandis*, for B. If both act in this way, the saddlepoint value for the game is reached and von Neumann and Morgenstern regard this as the solution for the game.[2] As von Neumann (1928) has shown, every two-person zero-sum game has a saddlepoint for either pure or mixed strategies. A mixed strategy requires players to select their strategy by chance. If all their opponents can know is the probability with which players make their selection, this randomization raises the players' minimum expected payoff. The rational solution requires players to build into their behaviour an element of unpredictability, if players wish to maximize their (constrained) expected utility.

But as Simon (1955) has observed, the knowledge attributed to the players by this theory is greater, and the attribution even more unreasonable, than in neoclassical economic theory. Each player is assumed to know all the available strategies, outcomes and preferences of the other players. In practice, each of these assumptions is likely to be violated. Once again, however, it can be argued that the assumptions are stronger than is necessary for von Neumann and Morgenstern's proposed solution. Under certain conditions, strategies need only be evaluated in the neighbourhood of the saddlepoint; or if the game is repeated and replicated the solution of von Neumann and Morgenstern might be approached in the limit. The arguments are analogous to those which were outlined in Chapter 3.

Nevertheless, the formulation of the game situation by von Neumann and Morgenstern leaves out of account a number of strategic factors which may be important. In practice, an astute player can take advantage of other players' misperceptions and weaknesses. If an opponent does not know all of your strategy set, this can be advantageous and it may be in your interest to keep your opponent suitably ignorant. One can gain an advantage by making information selectively available to an opponent. There may also be advantages in misleading an opponent about your preferences and your probable actions. Players can sometimes obtain an advantage by tricking their opponent into believing, for instance, that they will adopt a particular strategy, while actually planning another which will be very advantageous if the opponent falls for the ruse. While economic situations rarely satisfy the conditions for zero-sum games, the strategy of misinforming competitors is common in business competition. Multinational corporations, for example, may indicate to competitors that they intend building plants in particular countries when they have no such aim. Their aim is to deter competitors from establishing competitive plants in these countries. To carry out their ruse they may purchase land, begin negotiations with governments, and so on. The point is so elementary and obvious that it is puzzling why strategic aspects of information have been given so little attention in the theory of games of strategy. Even in zero-sum games, differences in the beliefs and knowledge of the players can be decisive for the outcome of the game.

THREE OR MORE PERSON GAMES

Games involving three or more players hold out the possibility that a subset of players can form an alliance or coalition to their mutual advantage. This introduces new barriers to rational behaviour and may make it impossible to find any completely rational settlement for a game.

a.   The weakest von Neumann and Morgenstern rationality postulates for an n-*person game* Von Neumann and Morgenstern make only modest claims for their theories of *n*-person games and they clearly believed their ideas to be just a starting point. They try to predict the behaviour of rational well-informed players and to narrow down the likely behaviour and outcomes by invoking successively more restrictive rationality postulates. Throughout their theory they assume that coalitions and cooperative agreements are reached outside the game and that these are respected by the contracting parties. This is a weak spot in their theory and they indicate that they would like to develop an approach which does not rely on this assumption (von Neumann and Morgenstern, 1964, p. 224). Let us, however, accept it at this stage.

In the opinion of von Neumann and Morgenstern, a group of rational individuals will cooperate if cooperation is Paretian better than non-cooperation for that group, that is, if at least some members of the group gain from cooperation and no individual in the group loses by it. Thus, the entire group forms a grand coalition when it is in their Paretian interest to do so.

Clearly this is a theory with limited explanatory and predictive power since nothing is postulated about the behaviour of every other possible coalition, as is done under stronger postulates. But in any case it seems to be untrue as a statement of the way rational individuals would act in even the limited range of cases covered by the theory. A group may fail to form a grand coalition when it is in their Paretian interest to do so (Tisdell, 1966 or Chapter 8). Conflict about sharing the grand coalition payoff, or mere ignorance, may stand in the way of Paretian optimal agreement. Again, the costs of forming a coalition must be taken into account. Communication and discussion are not costless and if the cost tends to fall on initiators, their expected gains may be less than their cost, even though, taking account of overall gains and cost of arranging a coalition, there might be a net benefit to the group. Because of this externality, it is in the interest of no set of individuals to begin the process required for a grand coalition. This difficulty is likely to be more important the larger the group, since communication costs rise and individual gains from a grand coalition tend to be smaller. Enforcement of agreements may be difficult or impossible. The larger the group the more costly and difficult it is likely to be to police violations of agreements, and enforce sanctions.

There is another limitation of the theory of coalition formation. The theory of games of strategy assumes that parties can enter into coalitions and dissolve these without influencing their range of choices of strategy. Coalitions are reversible at will and do not alter the strategic possibilities of a game. In practice, however, entry into a coalition may reduce available strategies of the cooperating individual players, that is, reduce the flexibility of the participants. In an uncertain world in which conditions are changing, individuals can often endanger their expected gains by adopting a policy which reduces flexibility.

In a business cartel, for example, the members are rarely able to adopt strategies which maximize their combined profit because these mostly result in a loss of (future) options for some members. For example, joint profit may be maximized by closing down all the plants of some companies in the cartel and by not advertising and selling the variety of products originally produced by some member companies. Members without productive capacity and market goodwill will not be in an easy situation to re-establish themselves within the market should other cartel members take advantage of them. They are, therefore, not likely to agree to such extreme optimizing procedures for the cartel as a whole.

Yet another limitation of the analysis of coalition formation in the theory of games is its failure to take account of the effect on the behaviour of members of the experience which they obtain from membership of a coalition. Their information about other members of the coalition improves, they are subject to new social pressures as the result of their membership of a group and their attitudes may change as a result of common propaganda and information. For instance, if workers join a trade union their attitude towards their employer and towards non-trade union workers may change. The implications of such factors for coalition formation and the type of coalition organization which might be agreed to, require study.

It might be argued that there is one kind of coalition which does not raise some of the theoretical difficulties discussed above. Marschak (1954) and Radner (1961 and 1962) distinguish coalitions in which incentives are required to ensure that individual actions are brought into line, from coalitions (teams) in which group and individual interests coincide and no such incentive is required. Team situations are rare. However, there may, for example, be situations in which company managers, individually and collectively, desire a common goal such as maximizing the profit of their company, or maximizing the sales of their company subject to the profit of their company reaching a commonly agreed level. Each is so committed to the common goal that no incentives are required to direct the behaviour of the members of the team towards this goal.

But even in the case of a team, problems for group rationality are not absent. In a team, different members control different action variables and generally have different sets of information. A team has the problem of coordinating its actions and disseminating its collective knowledge. Since the dissemination of information is not costless, it generally does not pay an organization to keep its members fully informed even in respect of knowledge which could improve their appropriate response. In Radner's model, designed for studying the optimal transmission of information and action in teams, the transmission of information is to some extent random, and the actions of the team are to that extent random (Radner, 1961). He examines various procedures for sharing information. These are: no transmittal of information by members, partitioned communication, management by exception and reporting of exceptions only. In the system which he studies, the methods are of ascending value for a group of a given size and the last method becomes relatively more valuable as the size of the group increases. It is possible, then, that group rationality results in an increase of randomness in a team's behaviour in relation to the outside world as the size of the organization (team) increases, and may necessitate predictable changes in its administration.

b.   Von Neumann and Morgenstern's stronger postulates – the equilibrium concept   In order to further narrow the range of possible solutions (outcomes) to a game played by rational individuals, von Neumann and Morgenstern suggest that a solution should not only satisfy the condition mentioned in the previous section, but should also be a set of possible payoffs to the players which is not dominated by any other set of payoffs. One set of payoffs dominates another if there is at least one group of players which by forming an alliance can ensure that its members earn more than in the dominated set. Any rational individual would prefer to form such an alliance.

Nevertheless, the type of coalition which emerges in a game can rarely be completely explained by the rational behaviour of the participants. It is useful to illustrate this idea of a solution by taking a particular example. Assume three players, A, B and C in a constant-sum game and let the constant value of the game be 6 units of payoff ($6, if you like). If the players do not form any coalition, each receives 2 units. However, if any two players form a coalition, the coalition receives 5 units *in toto*, so that the excluded player receives only one unit. Thus, by forming a coalition and cooperating any two players can gain one unit between them at the expense of the excluded player.   On the basis of von Neumann and Morgenstern's theory, it follows that if communication is possible, a coalition of two players will form. But it is impossible to determine which two players will form the coalition.

How will the members of the coalition share their gain? Von Neumann and Morgenstern suggest that it will be shared equally so that each member of the coalition obtains 2.5 units. The three sets of payoffs (payments to players A, B and C respectively) which form possible solutions according to von Neumann and Morgenstern's theory are:

$$[2.5, 2.5, 1], [2.5, 1, 2.5] \text{ and } [1, 2.5, 2.5].$$

Other agreements on sharing are possible but are, it is argued,[3] unlikely. Their argument is based upon a 'stability' property. No players will take less than they could get by going it alone (that is less than 1), and none will take less than they can obtain by forming a counter-coalition with another player. Imputations of the set above dominate imputations not in the set. No player is likely to break away from a coalition giving him or her 2.5 units because the other two players (in a three-person game) are likely to form a coalition on mutually advantageous terms, for example, they might agree to an equal division of gains and their coalition might last. This gives some support for the von Neumann and Morgenstern solution. Again, a coalition of two players should be stable, for if coalitions regularly form and breakdown, and if breakdown is achieved at minimum cost, in the long run players achieve on average the same amount as if they had not cooperated. Thus the fruits of cooperation are frittered away. Rational players should foresee this. If a player's heresy begins an unstable movement, the player ought not to turn heretic if offered more than 2 units by a coalition.

Thus, although a coalition of two players is likely to occur there may be more indeterminacy in the payoff to individual coalition members than von Neumann and Morgenstern suggest.

We might note that in an attempt to reduce indeterminacy, some game theorists adopt the strong rationality concept (or core concept) that no potential alliance should receive less than it can obtain by forming the alliance. However, for many games (including the above zero-sum example) players are unable to obtain a set of payoffs which satisfy this condition.

NASH EQUILIBRIUM

The Nash equilibrium is stressed in some microeconomic texts (for example, Varian, 1993) as a likely solution for a number of games of strategy if the game is a one-shot game or in the normal form. A Nash equilibrium is a choice of a set of strategies in a game such that given the set of strategies chosen by other players, no players would wish to change their chosen strategy. It has been shown that all two-person zero-sum-games have a solution in this sense for either pure or mixed strategies. Several non-zero sum games (which provide potential for cooperation between players) also have such a solution either in terms of pure or mixed strategies. Nevertheless, the applicability of the theory for the mixed strategy case requires the acceptance of expected utility maximization or expected gain maximization as an objective of the individual players.

The type of problems mentioned in Chapter 8 apply. In addition, note that the Nash equilibrium is not necessarily a Paretian optimum. For example, in the prisoners' dilemma problem the anti-social set of strategies dominates the Paretian preferred strategy for both of the players. However, in a replicated game, that is a game in the extensive form where learning is possible and retaliation can be engaged in, the behaviour of the players may not accord with the Nash equilibrium of the one-shot (normal form) case. Nevertheless the Paretian solution may be very unstable. Its stability depends on the likelihood of retaliation, the possibility for re-establishing trust, and so on.

COOPERATIVE GAMES – SOME SIMPLE ANALYTICS

Von Neumann and Morgenstern consider two possibilities for cooperative games, namely games with side payments and those without such payments. Side payments involve the transfer of income, benefits or payoffs from one set of players to other players, for example to compensate players who would otherwise lose by adopting cooperative behaviour. It is supposed that players will cooperate to maximize their joint gain. In the case of a duopoly, for instance, this would involve cooperation to maximize their joint profit. When side payments are possible, von Neumann and Morgenstern suggest that the actual division of profits is indeterminate, except that no player will accept less than the player could definitely obtain in the absence of cooperation (compare Shubik, 1959, pp. 42–4).

In Figure 12.1, let $OB = OH$ equal the total joint benefit to be obtained from cooperation of two players. Let M_1 represent the gain to player one (for example, duopolist one) and let M_2 represent that to player two. If there are no limits on side payments, any distribution of payoffs along the line BH is possible. Suppose that player one is assured of M_1^* in the absence of cooperation and that player two is assured of M_2^* in the absence of cooperation. According to von Neumann and Morgenstern's theory, each player must be offered at least these respective sums to cooperate. Therefore, the von Neumann and Morgenstern solution must lie on the segment CG. The exact position is indeterminate according to von Neumann and Morgenstern. However, it might be argued that the division of payoffs should in some way reflect what the players could ensure themselves without cooperating. If it were to reflect their *relative* gains in the absence of cooperation, the division would be along the line OAJ. Thus it would correspond to the division indicated by point F. Such a division preserves the relative benefit of the players. On the other hand, it might be argued that the players should share the gains from cooperation equally. In that case, the line AK through A at 45 degrees to the horizontal would be relevant and the division corresponding to point D would be optimal. Player two is advantaged by this solution compared to the previous one. It preserves the *absolute* difference between the payoffs to players in the non-cooperative situation.

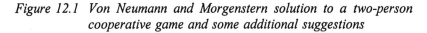

*Figure 12.1   Von Neumann and Morgenstern solution to a two-person
cooperative game and some additional suggestions*

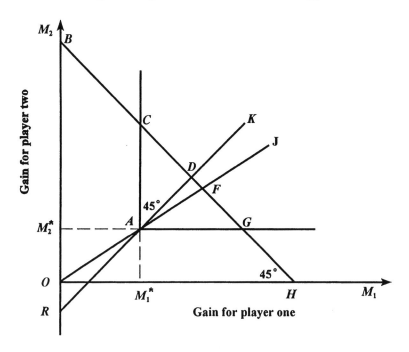

THREATS AND THE SOLUTION TO COOPERATIVE GAMES

The possibility that the payoffs or gains of players in the absence of cooperation could be used as a basis for dividing gains after cooperation is only one suggestion. Another possibility is to divide the benefits of cooperation, taking into account those threats which individual players can pose to other players in a non-cooperative situation. Observation suggests that players with the greatest threat power are likely to obtain the largest share of the cooperative cake. But how can threat power be measured? Several decades ago, Nash (1950) suggested that it might be evaluated by considering differences in the payoffs of players and using these to establish a zero-sum threat game, the solution to which becomes the basis for dividing the gains of the players from cooperation (compare Shubik, 1959, pp. 48–51; 1964).

This approach can be explained as follows. Supposing a two-person game, for example, a duopoly, let the respective payoffs of player one and of player two be represented by

$$P_1 = P_1(\alpha, \beta) \tag{12.1}$$

and

$$P_2 = P_2(\alpha, \beta) \tag{12.2}$$

where α represents the strategies available to player one and β those available to player two.

To evaluate the threat which a player can bring to bear upon an opponent, it seems clear that this threat action should be evaluated not only in terms of the damage that can be done to the opponent, but also taking account of the cost or damage to the threatener. For example, suppose that a business person has a set of alternative strategies which yield the same final profit but have different effects on the profits of an opposing firm. The strategy which gives the opponent the least profit would then be the best threat strategy for the business person to adopt.

Nash in fact proposes that threat be measured by the difference in payoffs to players. Consequently, the possible threat posed by player one is evaluated as

$$T_1(\alpha, \beta) = P_1(\alpha, \beta) - P_2(\alpha, \beta). \tag{12.3}$$

Hence, the greater is the payoff to player one in comparison to player two's payoff, the greater is player one's threat for the strategies adopted, using Nash's measure. The 'matrix' of player two's threat is

$$T_2(\alpha, \beta) = P_2(\alpha, \beta) - P_1(\alpha, \beta). \tag{12.4}$$

These threat values can be used to specify a threat game. If players were to adopt strategies to threaten one another to the maximum extent possible, what would happen? Might not the solution to this hypothetical (possible) game be used as the basis for dividing up gains from cooperation? Nash suggests that this is quite possible.

Although players would like to threaten with their maximum threat policies in order to obtain the greatest possible share of joint profit from cooperation, each only controls one of the variables upon which their threat depends. In relation to $T_1(\alpha, \beta)$ player one only controls α and in relation to $T_2(\alpha, \beta)$ player two only controls β. Yet each player can take it for granted that in the hypothetical threat game, players aim to maximize their threat. Hence, player one should maximize $T_1(\alpha, \beta)$ subject to

max T_2 (α, β) and player two should maximize T_2 (α, β) subject to
β

max T_1 (α, β).
α

Given this, we can now specify the threat games which in fact turn out to be a zero-sum game because

$$T_1 (\alpha, \beta) = - T_2 (\alpha, \beta) \qquad (12.5)$$

as can be seen from equations (12.3) and (12.4). The threat posed by player two is the negative of that coming from player one.

The threat power of player two can therefore be restated as

$$\max_{\beta} T_2 (\alpha, \beta) = \max_{\beta} [-T_1(\alpha, \beta)] = - \min_{\beta} [T_1(\alpha, \beta)]. \qquad (12.6)$$

Hence, when T_1 (α, β) is at a minimum with respect to β, player two's threat is at a maximum.

Given the above, the optimal strategies for the players in the hypothetical (possible) threat games are for player one to maximize T_1 (α, β) subject to the condition that player two is trying to minimize it, and for player two to try to minimize T_1 (α, β) subject to the condition that player one is trying to maximize it. This is a classical zero-sum game and therefore has an equilibrium solution either in terms of pure or mixed strategies. The solution occurs at the saddlepoint for function T_1 (α, β) and satisfies the condition

$$\max_{\alpha} \min_{\beta} T_1 (\alpha, \beta) = \min_{\beta} \max_{\alpha} T_1(\alpha, \beta). \qquad (12.7)$$

Suppose that equation (12.7) is satisfied for the strategies α^* and β^*. This implies that α^* is player one's best threat strategy and β^* is player two's best threat strategy.

For their optimal threat strategies, player one has a payoff of $P_1(\alpha^*, \beta^*)$ and player two has a payoff of $P_2(\alpha^*, \beta^*)$. These two values play a central role in the 'fair' division of joint benefits in a cooperative game. Nash suggests that maximum joint profit in the cooperative game will be divided so as to preserve the same absolute payoff advantages of each player in the 'optimal' (equilibrium) threat situation.

If M_1 represents the payoff to player one and M_2 equals the payoff to player two in the cooperative situation, the Nash threat solution requires that

$$M_2 - M_1 = P_2(\alpha^*, \beta^*) - P_1(\alpha^*, \beta^*) = k \qquad (12.8)$$

or that rearranging,

$$M_2 = k + M_1 = P_2(\alpha^*, \beta^*) - P_1(\alpha^*, \beta^*) + M_1. \qquad (12.9)$$

This will be satisfied by all coordinates on a straight line which passes $[P_1(\alpha^*, \beta^*), P_2(\alpha^*, \beta^*)]$ at 45 degrees to the horizontal.

Reinterpreting Figure 12.1, let point A correspond to the threat equilibrium of the game. Thus $P_1(\alpha^*, \beta^*)$ corresponds to M_1^* and $P_2(\alpha^*, \beta^*)$ corresponds to M_2^*. All combinations along line AK satisfy equation (12.9).

In addition, this particular Nash model requires that the cooperating players maximize their joint benefit. Where max π represents the maximum joint benefit of the players, in theory all distributions of benefits satisfying

$$M_2 = \max \pi - M_1 \qquad (12.10)$$

are possible. This equation corresponds to line BH in Figure 12.1. However equations (12.9) and (12.10) must be satisfied simultaneously. These equations are satisfied simultaneously for

$$M_1 = \tfrac{1}{2}(\max \pi - k) \qquad (12.11)$$
$$M_2 = \tfrac{1}{2}(\max \pi + k). \qquad (12.12)$$

Given the way in which the Figure 12.1 is reinterpreted, this solution corresponds to point D in Figure 12.1. In other words, after each player receives the amount the player would have received in the equilibrium threat situation, the gains from cooperation are shared equally. If the two players happened to be duopolists, the benefits shared might be their joint profits.

SOME LIMITATIONS OF THE NASH THREAT SOLUTION

While we might expect threat power to influence bargained solutions to cooperative games, the special status of absolute difference in payoffs in the equilibrium situation is not apparent intuitively. Is it not possible that relative payoffs rather than absolute differences in payoffs in this situation could be more pertinent? If this is so, it would require the equation

$$M_2 = P_2(\alpha^*, \beta^*)/P_1(\alpha^*, \beta^*)M_1 \qquad (12.13)$$

to be satisfied rather than equation (12.9). For reinterpreted Figure 12.1, this would correspond to line *OJ* and thus the optimal cooperative solution would correspond to point *F*. This approach gives greater benefits from cooperation to the relatively more threatening player as compared to the Nash threat solution.

In practice, the division of benefits will depend very much on perceptions as to whether players are likely to adopt a threat strategy if their demands are not met. In such circumstances, it can be advantageous to have a reputation for being 'tough'. In effect this means that historical experience will play a role.

The question of appropriate reference points for division of gains from cooperation is far from resolved. Note that the suggestions raised in the previous section give quite different reference points for determining division of payoffs from those based on threat possibilities. This subject could benefit from empirical research.

The Nash threat approach requires interpersonal comparisons of utility or benefits because differences in these are used to evaluate threats. Note that my suggestion for distribution of benefits to be based upon *relative* payoffs to players in an appropriate reference position (for example, threat or non-cooperative position) would be less demanding of information.

LIMITATIONS APPLICABLE TO BOTH THE THEORIES OF VON NEUMANN AND MORGENSTERN FOR COOPERATIVE GAMES AND THOSE OF NASH

The theory of cooperative games as outlined by von Neumann and Morgenstern and by Nash gives little attention to the conditions under which players will engage in cooperative games. As is clear from Chapter 8, the ability of players to make a Paretian gain from cooperation is not sufficient to ensure cooperation but it seems to be necessary. In fact, Chapter 8 suggests that rationality alone does not determine whether a group is likely to cooperate. Trust and past experience, for example, play a role. Cooperation is likely to lock players into the status quo as it is perceived at the time of cooperation. It introduces a degree of specificity. In such circumstances, players who believe that they can increase their threat power relative to other players or enhance their relative non-cooperative position are unlikely to enter into cooperation on bases determined by the status quo, because as a rule cooperation involves institutional constraints and limits the future possibilities for individual players. Thus from an individual player's point of view, the timing of agreements for cooperation is important. Most cooperative agreements limit the future flexibility available to participants.

An extreme case of the above might be that involving a duopoly in which the economic activity of production and marketing units involves decreasing costs per unit as a function of volume. A cooperative von Neumann and Morgenstern solution would require the operation of only one economic unit. A new company in which the duopolists hold shares might be set up for the purpose of operating the unit, the proportion of shares allocated to each player being negotiated at the time of agreement. A 'weak' company at that time would tend to receive a smaller proportion than a stronger partner. Once the cooperative agreement comes into existence, little or no scope exists for altering the sharing arrangements. So a currently weak company expecting to improve its relative economic position would want to defer any cooperative agreement. Nevertheless cooperative arrangements of the above type have sometimes been entered into by companies, for example, by manufacturers of electric light bulbs. Another example is two regional producers of beer in Brisbane, Queensland. They have agreed to joint production but will continue to advertise and market their products independently. Although marketing involves decreasing costs, presumably the 'weaker' partner at least thought that this would help to maintain its flexibility after the agreement. Thus we need to consider the flexibility of strategies and development possibilities before and after cooperative agreements. In addition, threat power prior to agreement and subsequent to cooperative agreement is likely to be a major consideration in whether to cooperate or not.

Von Neumann and Morgenstern, and Nash in following them, treat the sharing of gains from cooperation and the maximum gain from cooperation by players in a dichotomous manner. It is assumed that cooperating players will adopt a Paretian optimal or efficient solution and that their joint gains will then be shared in some prescribed manner. The possibility is overlooked that sharing arrangements may prevent a Paretian optimal outcome being achieved. In many cases, sharing and the size of collective benefits are interdependent. This has some interesting implications for the solutions to cooperative games, and it is possible that suitable sharing arrangements may not exist for some games able to generate the theoretically attainable Paretian optimum.

SHARING OF BENEFITS MAY AFFECT THE SOLUTIONS OF COOPERATIVE GAMES

In their solution to cooperative games, von Neumann and Morgenstern overlook the possibility that arrangements for sharing benefits may affect the incentives of players and therefore the level of collective benefit available for sharing. For example, this could arise in relation to a joint business venture where the contribution of the parties, for example, in terms of knowhow and other contributions cannot be exactly specified in advance (see Tisdell, 1993, Chapter 4). Agreements of this nature tend to be incompletely specified.

In Figure 12.2 where *OA* represents the maximum joint benefit of players from cooperation, side payments may not make all points on the 45 degree line *AF* attainable. Rather, for instance, a sharing curve such as *HJCKL* could apply. Each point on this curve corresponds to a possible sharing ray from the origin. If this is so, no players will rationally agree

Figure 12.2   Von Neumann and Morgenstern suggested solution to cooperative games may not be Paretian efficient if sharing has a disincentive effect

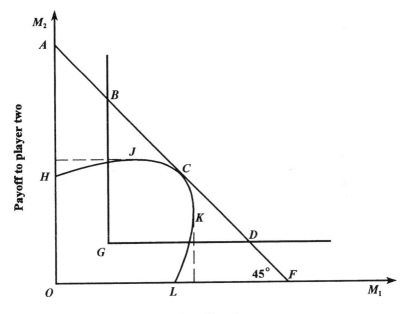

Payoff to player one

to a sharing arrangement which would locate them outside the segment *JCK* of this curve. If *G* represents the payoffs which players could assure themselves of in the absence of cooperation, the solution will not necessarily be anywhere along interval *BD*, the von Neumann and Morgenstern solution. Rather the solution will be along the segment *JCK*. Note that very unequal sharing arrangements are not Paretian efficient in this case. Note that it is even possible for sharing to cause the sharing curve to be everywhere below the Paretian frontier attainable in theory. Consequently the sharing curve in Figure 12.2 could be everywhere below the line *AF*.

For similar reasons, the Nash threat solution may not be optimal, nor similar solutions designed to preserve differences between players in non-cooperative situations. For example, if point *G* in Figure 12.3 is the non-cooperative base point for division of benefits (for example, a Nash threat equilibrium), the solution which preserves the same absolute difference in payoffs as at point *G* cannot be optimal, nor can that which preserves the same relative payoffs if the situation depicted in Figure 12.3 holds. There the curve *HJCKL* represents the sharing curve of benefits from cooperation.

Figure 12.3   Nash threat and similar solutions may not be Paretian efficient in some situations involving sharing

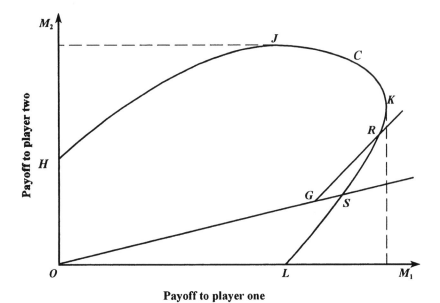

Payoff to player one

The 45 degree line *GR* preserves the same absolute difference in payoffs as at *G*. But clearly *R* is not optimal. It does not pay player one to press his or her advantages because both parties can be better off with the sharing that corresponds to *K*, which is specified by the slope of the ray *OK*. Line *GS* represents conditions which preserve the relative payoffs of players in position *G*. Once again, it is not optimal for player one to press his or her relative advantage because point *S* is inferior to point *K*. It would be preferable for both parties to agree to sharing corresponding to point *K*.

Conceivably in some circumstances the sharing set of possibilities could have a re-entrant section like that indicated by the curve *HJKLR* in Figure 12.4. In that case no solution inside segment *JKL* is optimal because all players can receive more by going to point *J* or *L*. This merely underlines the point that, depending upon the structure of the problem, some sharing arrangements give Paretian inferior results because of their impact on incentives.

*Figure 12.4 A re-entrant sharing possibility set limits possible solutions
to a cooperative game*

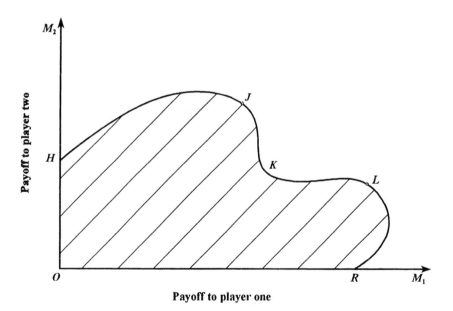

COOPERATIVE GAMES WITHOUT SIDE PAYMENTS

The above analytics have mostly been based upon the assumption that side payments between players are possible. However, sometimes side payments are not possible or there may be restrictions on them, for example of an institutional type. When side payments are not possible, this restricts the range of possible cooperative agreements. In Figure 12.5, for example, the hatched set *OABC* represents all possible payoffs from a game in the absence of side payments. Paretian efficient solutions would therefore be confined to the frontier *ABC*. But if side payments are possible, the set of possibilities is extended to the *ΔOFG* and any distribution of payoffs along the line *FG* can be attained in theory. *FG* is the highest attainable collective iso-benefit curve of the players. In the absence of cooperation, players may be at a point in the interior of set *OABC* and even without side payments, mutual gains are possible by cooperation. Similar methods for obtaining solutions to those already discussed can be applied to the set of possible payoffs ruling out side payments. However, it is conceivable that not every point in set *OABC* is attainable in practice.

Figure 12.5 The possibility of side payments extends the range of bargained payoff possibilities

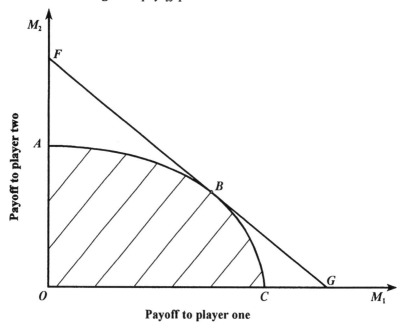

Payoff to player one

Consider the case shown in Figure 12.6. There the payoff possibility set in the absence of side payments is the set *OABC* and point *A* maximizes joint benefit. Side payment distributions along *AG* are possible. However, without side payments player one would obtain no benefit, so this 'solution' is unlikely to occur.

Figure 12.6   A corner point maximizes collective gains in this case making such a cooperative solution unlikely in the absence of side payments

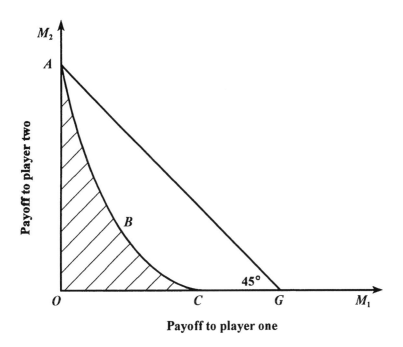

CONCLUDING COMMENTS

While the simple analytics above and similar analysis hold a degree of fascination, they are essentially static and therefore the amount of insight that they can give is limited. In particular, they are unable to come to grips with the flexibility and reversibility problems involved in cooperation. Cooperation can reduce the future options of individual players, and in some cases can make them more vulnerable to future threats. Furthermore, just as arrangements for entering into cooperation are usually not costless, disengagement in cooperation may also have a cost. Thus institutional arrangements are not perfectly reversible. This is particularly so for groups consisting of larger numbers of people. It seems a particular weakness of game theory that it does not give some attention to such factors. Nevertheless, it has contributed significantly to our understanding of group behaviour since von Neumann and Morgenstern (1944), and in fact has helped to make us aware of limits to rationality as a predictor of or basis for group behaviour.

NOTES

1. Von Neumann and Morgenstern (1964, p. 11). See also Morgenstern (1935).
2. The saddlepoint (equivalent to the centre point of some types of saddles) defines a mathematical property of the payoff function such that when one individual is minimizing his or her maximum loss, the other individual is maximizing his or her minimum gain. If the interests of the players are diametrically opposed, players cannot do better than select strategies corresponding to the saddlepoint and von Neumann and Morgenstern consider that these give the solution to a two-person zero-sum game involving rational players.
3. Von Neumann and Morgenstern (1964), Chapters 5 and 6.

REFERENCES

Chamberlin, E. (1950), *The Theory of Monopolistic Competition*, Cambridge, Mass.: Harvard University Press.

Edgeworth, F. (1881), *Mathematical Psychics: An Essay on the Application of Mathematics to the Moral Sciences*, London: Kegan Paul & Co.

Mansfield, E. (1994), *Microeconomics*, New York: Norton.

Marschak, J. (1954), 'Towards an Economic Theory of Organization and Information', in Thrall, R.M., Coombs, C.H. and Davis, P.L. (eds), *Decision Processes*, New York: Wiley, 187–99.

Morgenstern, O. (1935), 'Perfect Foresight and Economic Equilibrium', *Zeitschrift für Nationalökonomie*.

Nash, J.F. (1950), 'The Bargaining Problem', *Econometrica*, 18, 128–40.

Radner, R. (1961), 'The Evaluation of Information in Organization', in *Proceedings of the Fourth Berkeley Symposium on Probability and Statistics*, Berkeley: University of California.

Radner, R. (1962), 'Team Decision Problems', *Annals of Mathematical Statistics*, 33, 857–81.

Robinson, J. (1969), *The Economics of Imperfect Competition*, London: Macmillan.

Shubik, M. (1959), *Strategy and Market Structures*, New York: Wiley.

Shubik, M. (1964), *Game Theory and Related Approaches to Social Behaviour*, New York: Wiley.

Simon, H.A. (1955), 'A Behavioral Model of Rational Choice', *Quarterly Journal of Economics*, 69, 99–118.

Tisdell, C.A. (1966), 'Some Bounds upon the Pareto Optimality of Group Behaviour', *Kyklos*, 19, 81–105.

Tisdell, C.A. (1993), *Economic Development in the Context of China*, London:

Macmillan.

Varian, H.R. (1993), *Intermediate Microeconomics*, 3rd edn, New York: Norton.

von Neumann, J. (1928), 'Zur Theorie Gesellschaftsspiele', *Math. Annalen*, C, 295–320.

von Neumann, J. and Morgenstern, O. (1944), *Theory of Games and Economic Behaviour*, 1st edn, Princeton, New Jersey: Princeton University Press. 3rd edn by the same publisher 1953.

von Neumann, J. and Morgenstern, O. (1964), *Theory of Games and Economic Behaviour*, New York: Wiley.

Weibull, J.W. (1995), *Evolutionary Game Theory*, Cambridge, Mass.: MIT Press.

13. Symbiosis, Assistance and Cooperation in Business

INTRODUCTION

In the previous chapter, game theory was used to consider possibilities for formalized cooperation between players. This chapter will concentrate on business cooperation and assistance of one business by another which may be less formalized in character than envisaged in game theory. It will be shown that a business, particularly a large business, may benefit in various circumstances by providing economic assistance to its suppliers or, in certain circumstances, to purchasers or users of its product downstream in the production chain. Such assistance is a possible alternative to vertical integration in an industry.

Factors which may lead a company to cultivate symbiotic relationships with selected firms having business dealings with it, include gains from beneficial externalities or spillovers including economies in the provision of services connected with these, provision of market security to suppliers thus enabling them to have an opportunity to take advantage of learning and reduce the costs of retaining flexibility or keeping options open, and reduced market transaction costs. These possibilities will be explained shortly and Marks & Spencer will be taken as an example of a company which has established symbiotic business relationships.

As discussed, fostering of symbiotic relationships between independent firms can be an alternative to vertical integration of a business, and franchising is a possible alternative to horizontal business integration. Sometimes cooperative arrangements or means of assistance of one business to another evolve informally over time, with networking and bonding playing a role in their evolution and maintenance.

EXTERNALITIES OR SPILLOVERS AS A BASIS FOR ONE BUSINESS ASSISTING OTHERS

Just as in a multidivisional firm, a division up the processing chain can benefit from innovation, technological change and productivity increase in a division supplying it with inputs (see Chapter 11), so can a purchaser of inputs from independent suppliers. Furthermore, it may be profitable for such a purchasing firm to promote innovation by its suppliers. This it may do by carrying out research and development (R & D) of value to suppliers, by providing them with information services, for example, about methods to improve their productivity, providing training courses in better management and so on.

The possible benefits to the purchasing firm can be seen from Figure 13.1.

Figure 13.1 It may pay a processor or purchaser of an input to assist a supplier to innovate

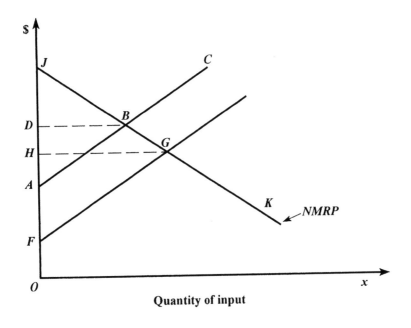

Quantity of input

Suppose for simplicity that there is a single supplier of an input, *x*, to a single purchaser of it that uses it to produce a final product. Let line *JK* represent the net marginal revenue product curve of the processor and let *ABC* represent the marginal cost of production of *x* by the supplier. Suppose that this supplier is a price taker and the price of the input is set at *OD*. The processor makes a profit equal to the area of △*DBJ* and the supplier of the input obtains a profit equivalent to the area of △*ABD*. However, suppose an innovation is possible that reduces the supplier's marginal cost of production to the line *FG*. The processor's or purchaser's profit now increases to the equivalent of △*JHG* and the profit of the supplier becomes equivalent to the area of △*FGH*. Hence, the processor's profit is up by the equivalent of the area of quadrilateral *HGBD*. If the supplier will not innovate without assistance from the processor, the processor will find it profitable to spend a portion of area *HGBD* to induce the supplier to innovate.

There may also be circumstances in which it pays a supplier to assist a purchaser to innovate because the innovation raises the demand for the supplier's product. This can be illustrated by Figure 13.2. Here *ABC*

Figure 13.2 In some cases, suppliers of inputs can gain by assisting processors or purchasers of these to innovate

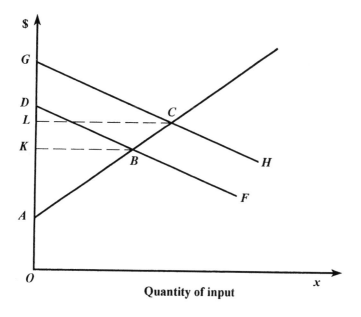

represents the marginal cost of supply of input *x* and *DBF* is the net marginal revenue product curve of the processor or purchaser prior to innovation whereas *GCH* is the curve after innovation by the processor. Supposing similar conditions to the previous ones, the profit of the supplier of *x* is equal to the area of $\triangle ABK$ prior to this innovation and that of the processor is equal to the area of $\triangle KBD$. After the innovation the relevant triangular areas for profit become *ACL* and *LCG*, respectively. The profit of the supplier of the input increases by the equivalent of the area of quadrilateral *KBCL*. Thus the supplier has a margin to induce or assist the processor(s) or purchaser(s) to innovate.

Note that the above examples have been constructed so that the businesses involved gain from the innovation. Although mutual gain is possible in many circumstances, it does not always occur, for example, if the innovation shifts a supplier's marginal cost curve downwards but it becomes much more elastic in the process. Such a case is shown in Figure 13.3. In this case, *FD* is the processor's net marginal revenue product curve and *ABC* is the supplier's marginal cost curve prior to innovation and *ADE* is the curve afterwards. If optimal transfer prices are used, the supplier's profit falls from the area of $\triangle ABK$ to that of *ADH*. If the supplier is not forced by market conditions to innovate (as is supposed here), the processor will need to make a side payment of some kind to the

Figure 13.3 Some innovations may reduce the profit of the innovator but raise those of an industry or a buyer; side payments may then be needed for cooperation

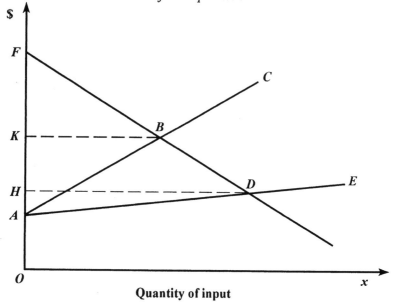

supplier to induce the innovation. It would, of course, be profitable to make a side payment given that the innovation would increase the profit of the processor or purchaser by the equivalent of the area of the quadrilateral *HDBK*. Similar situations can be illustrated for innovation on the processing side: if the net marginal revenue product curve becomes more elastic, the chances rise that the profit of the processor from innovation will decline.

Other circumstances are also possible where buyers may find it advantageous to assist sellers and vice versa. Consider, for example, a processor who relies on supplies of inputs from his or her neighbourhood because import of supplies from elsewhere is not profitable due to market transaction costs. Suppose that production by the processor causes local pollution. This pollution may reduce the productivity of the processor's independent local suppliers. It may, therefore, pay the polluting processor to moderate this pollution in order to increase the productivity of local suppliers and reduce the price being paid by him or her for local supplies. Figure 13.1 can be readily adapted to explain this situation.

ECONOMIES OF BUYERS PROVIDING SERVICES TO SELLERS AND VICE VERSA

In some cases, a purchaser of supplies, especially if large, finds it profitable to supply its suppliers with services. These may be R & D services, advice or information about likely market requirements, quality testing, managerial training and so on. The same can be true of a larger supplier of products to many small firms. In providing such services, a large buyer or seller may experience economies of scale and scope (compare Baumol *et al.*, 1982). Small buying or selling firms in an industry, because of start-up costs and economies of scale, may find it unprofitable to supply such services themselves.

An alternative possibility might be for an independent firm to supply such services. However, this might involve greater transaction costs and such a firm may not have continuing in-house experience in the industry. For this reason, it may not be the most economical option. The provision of such services provides some opportunity for large firms to subsidize dependent small firms where this is to the advantage of the large firm.

ADVANTAGES OF PERMANENT OR PREFERRED BUSINESS RELATIONSHIPS

From a long-term profitability point of view, there can be advantages in businesses establishing permanent preferred business relationships with one another. This can provide suppliers and buyers with a degree of security, reduce the need to build in costly flexibility in production to cope with uncertainty and assist the learning process of each party. Where competition causes rapid entry and exit of firms in an industry, economic advantages from learning are forgone.

In addition, preferred business relationships can significantly reduce market transaction costs and this can be an advantage to both parties to such an arrangement. It may also benefit the consumer, as discussed in Chapter 15.

Permanent or preferred business relationships do not imply that competition has no influence on behaviour. Where a partner fails to perform in a reasonable manner, then an alternative partner may be found in the longer term. Nevertheless, in most cases, informal business partnerships are not broken casually. For one thing, there are always risks with new partners and an industry partner may be able to reform if put under pressure. This all implies that in many business situations, cooperation through partnerships of a stable nature is likely to be to the long-term economic advantage of firms. From this viewpoint, these arrangements can be preferable to ruthless short- term competition for supplies or sales. Such factors are, as a rule, overlooked in neoclassical economic theory and in its application.

AN EXAMPLE: MARKS & SPENCER

The large British retailer, Marks & Spencer, follows the type of behaviour outlined above in providing assistance to its suppliers of merchandise. A detailed study of this company has been undertaken by Tse (1985) who emphasizes that Marks & Spencer, founded in 1884, is much more than a retailer and may also be considered to be a manufacturer without factories given the close links between it and its suppliers (compare Tse, 1984, a and b).

Marks & Spencer sell only one brand, their St. Michael brand. But this is probably not so much the distinctive feature of this company as the fact that it has been convinced since the 1920s that as a retailer it must assume the role of an interpreter to industry (manufacturers) of the demands and tastes of the market. It has become convinced that it must be a supplier of market knowledge and appropriate technological knowledge to its suppliers.

Deciding what the market wants is not a passive reaction on the part of Marks & Spencer but involves creativity, and at the same time it aims in its decisions to sell only quality products priced at a level which its target customers can afford. The latter view of the company, the view that it gives value for money, is well established among consumers and this means that it spends little on advertising.

Marks & Spencer decides on the products that it wants to have manufactured and ensures that they are manufactured to its quality standards. In this regard, Dr Tse says

> Unlike other retailers, Marks & Spencer takes upon itself the decision of what to manufacture, not simply what to buy from the manufacturer. It has its own team of designers working closely with the supplier to design or redesign the product. It is important to note that the design of the product is not simply a question of taste and fashion or technical feasibility and details, it is also a commercial decision involving judgements pertaining to market trends, hidden and potential needs, cost and price elasticities of demand, impact on existing lines, etc. Moreover, it is also very much a question of having the ability and vision to capitalise on the most recent scientific advances and technological breakthroughs which may have a bearing on the final production of the product. (Tse, 1985, p. 31)

Marks & Spencer therefore plays a major role in transfer of market information, in product innovation and in ensuring the technological progress of its suppliers.

When earlier this century Marks & Spencer began to concentrate on what the customer really wanted it found it difficult to obtain the requisite products because in many cases they did not exist. Tse points out that the required products were not being produced by manufacturers in sufficient quantity and at realistic prices for the mass market. This led Marks & Spencer to develop its primary objective:

> to discover, and where necessary create, such products. It became convinced that the greatest stumbling block lay in the fact that manufacturing and retailing had been operating as two distinctly separate business entities. This the company saw as a fundamental flaw. It believed that in order to serve the customer effectively and efficiently, mass manufacturing and mass retailing must somehow be organically linked together. The history of Marks & Spencer since the 1920s is best summed up as the relentless effort to achieve precisely this. (Tse, 1985, pp. 71, 72)

Marks & Spencer is said to be in a partnership with its suppliers for a common purpose. This symbiotic relationship means gains to both Marks & Spencer as well as to its suppliers. It acts as production consultant to its suppliers and maintains a team of more than 350 technologists for this purpose. It indicates customer demands for them, provides technical services designed to achieve innovation, improvement in quality and lowering of costs, provides means to ensure strict quality control in production and is on the lookout for new materials, packaging technology and so on that may assist its suppliers to produce a better quality article at lower cost. There is a technological approach to its suppliers and it also tries to ensure that they achieve economies of scale through standardization of product, continuity of demand and adequate utilization of production capacity. The company engages in specification buying. Buying agreements specify to manufacturers the material to be used in manufacture and the process to be employed.

While the relationship of Marks & Spencer to its suppliers has benefited it by its being able to obtain better quality products at lower prices and products wanted by consumers, the question remains open of whether its suppliers have benefited by this relationship. The dominant position of Marks & Spencer could lead it to squeeze the profit margin of its suppliers and the possibility of single-buyer exploitation could arise. Tse (1985) points out that Marks & Spencer is extremely demanding on suppliers as far as quality is concerned, and does expect some of the advantages of the suppliers' relationship with Marks & Spencer to be passed on in the way of lower prices which in turn mean lower prices to consumers. However, Marks & Spencer still wants its suppliers to make a profit to maintain its long-term relationship with them and to provide finance for their business expansion and technological progress. The main aim is to have a long-term cooperative arrangement by which all parties gain. Short-term economic exploitation by either set of parties to the cooperative arrangement would jeopardize their long-term benefits. The fact that more than a hundred manufacturing suppliers have been on Marks & Spencer's supply list for more than 30 years, indeed 60 have been on it for more than 50 years, indicates the long-term benefits flowing from the cooperative strategy. Dr Tse provides specific examples of how mutual benefits have been obtained by Marks & Spencer. Examples range from garments to tomatoes.

Marks & Spencer is said to be more dependent on its suppliers than most retailers. While Marks & Spencer does not have any financial stake in the manufacturers, it does invest very substantially in them in terms of technical support, management advice, and, above all, a thorough educational process to bring the manufacturers' outlook and operating philosophy close to that of Marks & Spencer' (Tse, 1985, p. 81). While some suppliers supply Marks & Spencer exclusively, or almost so, many do not. It is, however, in Marks & Spencer's interest not to lose reliable suppliers as a source. Considerable cost is involved in finding and 'training' new suppliers and its investment in the 'human capital' of previous suppliers is lost when they no longer supply Marks & Spencer. On the other hand, it is unlikely to be to the advantage of a supplier to take Marks & Spencer off its list because it will lose the long- term advantages of sales to Marks & Spencer and technical and market advice from this source.

It might be thought that Marks & Spencer might find it advantageous to become vertically integrated with some of its suppliers, so that all become a part of the same company. However, the management of Marks & Spencer has resisted this, on the grounds that it could lead to reduced managerial efficiency because it could reduce managerial specialization and lead to decision-making overload.

If a symbiotic relationship between Marks & Spencer and its suppliers is to survive, Marks & Spencer must continue to provide them with information and opportunities of value. As a part of this, Marks & Spencer has tried to ensure that what it does, it does well, after adequate learning and experience on its part. It begins, for instance 'the merchandising of a limited range of products in the early stages of development to ensure that both the merchandising departments and the food technologists concentrate their efforts on raising and establishing the standards of a number of basic products before advancing further' (Tse, 1985, p. 93).

Lord Israel Sieff, former Chairman of Marks & Spencer, has emphasized that it is not a mere shopkeeper. He says:

> We came to regard ourselves as a kind of technical laboratory. We felt it was one of our functions to provide our suppliers with expert technical information about the new materials and processes which the advance in technology was making available. We saw ourselves, in our limited way, as production engineers, industrial chemists, laboratory technicians. We learned to exercise an active influence on production generally and on the textile industry in particular. (Sieff, 1970, pp. 146–7)

However, Marks & Spencer does not engage in basic research. Rather, its scientific and technical staff maintains contacts with research institutes and other sources of technical progress so as to help transfer appropriate knowledge and ensure its application.

WIDER ISSUES RAISED BY THIS EXAMPLE

Technological transfer, especially to small manufacturers, has always been a problem in science and technology policy for governments. The approach of Marks & Spencer indicates a new way in which knowledge and technology transfer can take place without necessarily involving governments at all.

The method used by Marks & Spencer need not be confined to larger retailer or manufacturing supplier relationships. The method is also workable in other areas. For example, a large manufacturer may be assembling or using components supplied by many small manufacturers. There is scope for the larger assembler or manufacturer to develop a symbiotic relationship with its suppliers. Again, in the construction industry there may be scope for a large building contractor to develop a symbiotic relationship with subcontractors. By ensuring technological transfer and appropriate knowledge to such subcontractors, a large contractor can improve the quality and reduce the cost of the contribution of subcontractors.

The line of technological and knowledge transfer need not always be from the user of inputs to the supplier. Sometimes it pays a supplier to be the active party. For example, a car manufacturer may find it worthwhile to provide market information and other services gratis or at less than cost to retailers of the manufacturer's cars. Again the supplier of a raw material may play a similar role. For instance, the International Wool Secretariat has had an active policy of providing technical information and advice to textile manufacturers using wool (Tisdell and McDonald, 1979), and synthetic fibre manufacturers adopt a similar policy. This is a reflection of the fact that common gains can be made by one tier of economic activity helping at least one other tier in the chain involved in the production or marketing of a product. However, few firms have developed the symbiotic market, production and technological relationship to the extent of Marks & Spencer.

VERTICAL INTEGRATION VERSUS VOLUNTARY BUSINESS SYMBIOSIS – FRANCHISING AND HORIZONTAL INTEGRATION

As raised in connection with the case of Marks & Spencer, vertical integration is a possible alternative to assistance to businesses involved in symbiotic relationships. However, vertical integration would require greater capital investment by a company adopting this route and could result in some economic inefficiencies. The expertise of a large company having a central role in an industry may not be in managing small businesses. Integration may reduce decentralization and increase inflexibility in the industry. Vertical integration is not always the best economic choice as far as the economic operation of an industry is concerned, nor does it always assist the economic position of the major firm in the industry.

A similar point can also be made in relation to horizontal integration of firms. Firms, for example retailers in the same line of business, may obtain economies of scale in marketing promotion and advertising by merger. However, franchising arrangements may attain that goal more efficiently. The expertise of the franchisors may be in marketing and product presentation and they may be able to achieve economies in this. This, then, is the franchisor's basic source of 'rent' rather than any expertise in managing individual retail outlets. Nevertheless, from a long term-point of view, franchisor and franchisees are in a symbiotic relationship.

CONCLUDING COMMENTS

The importance of cultivating lasting relationships between potentially symbiotic businesses should not be underestimated, particularly in less than perfect markets constrained by market transaction costs. Market self-centred economic competition involving maximization of current gains without regard to the impact of this on symbiotic economic relationships can, in the long term, be expected to be to the economic detriment of a business engaging in it. Because of these elements, it is often important for a business to have a list of preferred suppliers or in some cases buyers. In addition, it is likely to pay to assist smaller associated firms with knowhow and in other ways. Consequently, a group of businesses evolve which support one another. This is a far cry from the 'tooth-and-claw' type of competition extolled in a mechanistic manner by some neoclassical economists.

REFERENCES

Baumol, W.J., Panzer, J.C. and Willig, R.D. (1982), *Contestable Markets and the Theory of Industry Structure*, San Diego, California: Harcourt, Brace & Jovanovich.

Sieff, I. (1970), *Memoirs*, London: Weidenfeld and Nicolson.

Tisdell, C.A. and McDonald. P.W. (1979), *Economics of Fibre Markets: Interdependence Between Man-Made Fibres, Wool and Cotton*, Oxford: Pergamon Press.

Tse, K.K. (1984a), 'The Technological Approach to Retailing: Some Insights for Hong Kong/China Collaboration', *Hong Kong Engineer*, 29–32.

Tse, K.K. (1984b), 'A Manufacturer Without Factories – The Marks and Spencer Story and Its Relevance for Hong Kong – China Economic-Technological Collaboration', *Hong Kong Manager*, 10–21.

Tse, K.K. (1985), *Marks & Spencer*: Anatomy of Britain's Most Efficiently Managed Company, Oxford: Pergamon Press.

PART IV

Wider Economic and Social Issues

14. Values, Preferences, Economic Choice and Welfare

INTRODUCTION

Part IV deals with wider economic and social issues than the earlier portion of the book. This chapter raises some doubts about the treatment of values and preferences in neoclassical theory, including the new welfare economics. The subsequent chapter questions a number of accepted methods of measuring economic efficiency. Attention is then given to market transaction costs, especially their possible effects on economic welfare, and some of their consequences and those of information asymmetries for markets in science, technology and knowhow are considered. Evolutionary approaches to research and development and innovation are discussed and compared with other paradigms before general observations are made about diversity of behaviour and economic evolution.

THE PREVAILING POSITIVIST VIEW IN ECONOMICS

In this chapter, I intend to consider the way in which mainstream economists treat the values and preferences of decision makers, components which play an important role in economic models of choice and welfare, and will discuss the dissent of some economists from the conventional treatment.

The prevailing positivist view in economics, so well expressed by Robbins, discourages economists from studying values and suggests that they should take values as given. The following quotations from Robbins clarify his position:

> Economics, we have seen, is concerned with that aspect of behaviour which arises from the scarcity of means to achieve given ends. It follows that

219

> economics is entirely neutral between ends; that, in so far as the achievement
> of *any* end is dependent on scarce means, it is germane to the preoccupation
> of the economist. Economics is not concerned with ends as such. (Robbins,
> 1952, p. 24)

> Economics is not concerned at all with ends *as such*. It is concerned with
> ends in so far as they affect the disposition of means. It takes the ends as
> given in the scales of relative valuation, and enquires what consequences
> follow in regard to certain aspects of behaviour. (Robbins, 1952, p. 30)

Robbins criticizing Marxian and other institutionalists claims that the
study of changes in relative valuations is outside the scope of economics
and criticizes Hawtrey's claim that economics cannot be disassociated
from ethics. He says:

> Unfortunately it does not seem logically possible to associate the two studies
> in any form but mere juxtaposition. Economics deals with ascertainable
> facts; ethics with valuations and obligations. The two fields of enquiry are
> not on the same plane of discourse. Between the generalisations of positive
> and normative studies there is a logical gulf which no ingenuity can disguise
> and no juxtaposition in space or time bridge over. (Robbins, 1952, p. 148)

However, it is by no means clear that the subject of economics can be
divorced from study of values and the study of the formation and
change of values. Social actions within a society may change some
values, and it may be possible to engineer or transform some values by
social or institutional means. Within a society,

1. the feeling of well-being of its citizens depends in part upon the
   relationship between their values and their economic achievements;
2. economic development or economic change (and thus welfare)
   depends upon the values held by citizens; and
3. the composition of production, the needs catered for by production
   depend upon the values of its citizens.

If we accept the proposition that values are in part formed by social
relationships over which the individual has no or only limited control as
such, formation of and change of values would appear to be a subject of
general concern, and of possible interest to economists. Given the same
resources and the same initial values in a society, differing 'random' (or
non-random) social events may give rise to different value systems with
different implications for the development and welfare of society and its
citizens. Economists may need to face the possibility that a society may
develop a constellation of roles, institutions and values which are
inappropriate to its future development. These factors may block certain

types of economic development considered to be desirable, either by a select few or on occasions by all individuals. The individual values held in a society may be inappropriate to its agreed ends. In this respect, consider the prisoners' dilemma problem in which each individual by following their own self-interest renders all worse off than they need be.

PROBLEMS ASSOCIATED WITH TAKING VALUES AND PREFERENCES AS GIVEN

Robbins's view raises the question that if values or preferences are to be taken as given by economists, whose values or preferences are to count and how are the preferences of individuals to be counted in the process of economic choice? Robbins's apparent view is that this is not important. Economic problems are purely technical ones to be solved by economists using the values suggested by those who employ them to solve such problems. Economics is neutral about the choice of values used by the decision makers employing economists.

However, this is not the Paretian welfare point of view, a view which has had a dominant position in economic thought in recent times. According to this view, in matters of social choice:

1. the welfare of all members of society must be taken into account; and
2. the individual is the best judge of his own welfare.

The preferences of individuals are to be respected and any change in the allocation of resources which increases the welfare of at least one individual without reducing that of another increases social welfare. An individual's preferences accord with his judgement of his welfare, and his behaviour reflects or reveals his preferences. The Paretian view has not gone unchallenged. For instance, Rescher says:

> Values (as we have seen) are given stability and solidity by their essential relationship to benefits; preferences can be things of the fleeting moment, and at that, things which fly in the face of consciously reckoned benefits. Preferences are just that – preferences – and perfectly legitimate preferences need not be reasoned. (Rescher, 1969, p. 109)

> The talk of some economists about preference – combining schemes in terms of 'social *welfare* functions' rings a hollow note. Welfare is indeed an important consideration – but there is nothing sacred about preferences. ... Welfare has to do with our realisation of genuine benefits and our achievement of what is in our real interests. What relates to welfare is objective and interpersonally debatable. ... To assign *central* importance to the project of distilling a conception of social

welfare out of individual *preferences* is to espouse a highly questionable ideology in the economic political sphere. (Rescher, 1969, p. 110)

In Rescher's view, preferences may not conform with welfare, even in the long run.

The view has also been expressed that individual preferences may not be worth respecting because they are manipulated by established power groups and institutions. These groups and institutions may vary individual preferences so that they do not reflect the welfare of individuals, a point of view expressed by Galbraith (1967), by Marcuse (1969) and various radical economists. Traditionally economists have not regarded this possibility as an important one and have assumed that either individual preferences and values are beyond corruptible influence or that individual preferences should be respected no matter how they are formed. On the face of it there would appear to be some evidence that preferences are subject to social influences. Otherwise, measures, for instance to curb the advertising of cigarettes, would appear to be misdirected.

Another example of misguided preferences according to Marcuse (1969), Scitovsky (1976), Galbraith (1967) and various radical economists, is the urge for overconsumption in developed countries. One version of this theory is that 'additional (private) consumption is from the point of view of society as a whole, without utility or even a source of disutility; thus the marginal utility of consumption is in fact said to be zero, or even negative, though people have not yet discovered this for themselves' (Lindbeck, 1971, p. 83). This has at least two possible interpretations:

1. The collective effect of increased consumption by all individuals has an undesirable effect upon the environment or the possibilities for future generations which is either imperfectly recognized by consumers or which consumers feel they individually are powerless to counteract (an externality effect).

2. Even in isolation individuals may be tempted to overconsume, regardless of their own welfare. For instance, appropriate advertising could lead individuals to overeat and to eat foods detrimental to their health, or consumers may be lured into financial difficulties by being encouraged to purchase durable goods beyond their means. Or again they may be lured into buying durables such as motor boats and 'off-road' vehicles which take time to enjoy and to maintain thus placing great pressure on the available time of the consumer and causing possible dissatisfaction.

How important is the sort of manipulation of consumption mentioned above? Economists have done little or no research on this subject. In this respect, Lindbeck (1971, p. 13) says:

> As long as research in this field is in its present 'underdeveloped' state, speculations will presumably always fill the vacuum erected by lack of scientific knowledge; this means that both the 'ultraliberal' notion of the basic autonomy of individual preferences and its opposite of the manipulated consumers, may well co-exist for a long time to come.

The above discussion suggests that achieved consumption may give rise to unwanted effects; to 'diswelfare'. At the same time, expectations or aspirations may run so far ahead of what is actually possible that this may give rise to tension and dissatisfaction. From the psychological point of view, welfare may decline because this gap rises, say because of advertising pressures in society, and welfare (as perceived by the individual) may fall despite a rise in consumption. This view has been expressed by Marcuse (1969, p. 51) in the following way:

> This same trend of production and consumption, which makes for the affluence and attraction of advanced capitalism, makes for the perpetuation of the struggle for existence, for the increasing necessity to produce and consume the non necessary necessity. ... Former luxuries become basic needs, a normal development which, under corporate capitalism, extends the competitive business of living to newly created needs and satisfaction.

This breeds aggressiveness and 'opposition is directed against the totality of a well functioning, prosperous society – a protest against its form – the commodity form of men and things, against the imposition of false values and false morality' (Marcuse, 1969, p. 51). The problem or possibility of economic aspirations getting out of line with economic possibilities is not, however, peculiar to capitalism.

Economists have paid little attention to the possibility that aspirations or values affect welfare. One notable exception is Weckstein (1962) and I shall discuss his theory shortly.

ECONOMIC GROWTH AND DEVELOPMENT – VALUES AND PREFERENCES

While the construction of economic theories of price formation may not require economists to consider the values of market participants in detail, theories of, and strategies for, economic development are likely to be unsatisfactory unless they take specific account of values. Most economists believe that the values held by a population of a country help to determine whether the country will develop from an economic viewpoint, the speed at which it will develop and the direction of development. It has been claimed that the Protestant ethic has had an influence on Western economic development. Whether or not this is so, there is nevertheless some consensus among economists that values are important determinants of economic growth and that the values held by a population constrain its possibilities or the successful strategies which can be used by a planner to induce economic development. For instance, Bauer (1971), has claimed that planning is unlikely to be successful in many underdeveloped countries because of the values of the population.

However, even our market system depends upon the existence of appropriate values in society for its workability. For instance, Boulding (1968, p. 234) has commented:

> The first thing to note is that there are certain individual value systems which undermine the institutions of exchange and are, therefore, extremely threatening to a business system. An exchange system, for instance, cannot flourish in the absence of a minimum of simple honesty because an exchange system is an exchange of promises, and honesty is a fulfilment of promises. If we extend the concept of honesty a little further into the fulfilment of the role expectations, we see this also is essential for the successful operation of a system based on exchange. This is why the institutions of capitalism cannot operate successfully in the total absence of what might be called the Puritan virtues. Thus, if capitalism is to work successfully, there must be defences in the society against dishonesty. These defences may lie in part in the judicial system; that is, in the system of law and police. But I suspect that a good part of the burden must be carried by the integrative system in the internalisation of these moral systems in the individual.

Clearly the existence of various values helps or hinders the achievement of specific economic or other ends and this can be studied from a positive point of view. Economists may need to make judgements about this, and some have. For instance, Myrdal (1956) has claimed that underdeveloped countries have sometimes imported inappropriate values and tastes from more-developed countries, inappropriate given that the LDCs wish to speed up their economic development. In part this suggests that some of the appropriate values for society may alter with the stage of its economic development. Thrift, investment and concern with productivity may be important in a less-developed country and therefore, values supporting these are worth cultivating, but in a developed country these values may be less important; indeed, as Bernard Mandeville suggested, thrift may not be a virtue at all in a developed country, or in certain economic circumstances.

Another aspect to be considered is whether a pluralism of values is conducive to favourable economic development and change. In this respect, one may need to consider the constellation of values held by different groups in society and the amount of conflict and tension, if any, caused by differences in these values. If economic growth or certain types of economic change are desired, there may be an optimal degree of tension.

Conflicts between personal values can also be a source of constructive or destructive change. In this respect, Boulding (1968, pp. 230–31) has suggested:

> Where an overt ethical system, such as the Christian ethic, contains elements which are inappropriate to the social system in which it is embedded, it may remain the overt system because the covert system by which people really act is different. On the other hand, the overt system exercises a constant pressure on the society in which it is recognised. The dynamic character of a society, in fact, often depends on there being a certain tension between its overt and covert ethical systems. A culture in which the overt and covert ethic coincide and in which there is no hypocrisy is likely to be deplorably stable. .... A society with impossible ideals is likely to be highly dynamic, whereas a society with possible ideals is likely to stagnate.

While one may argue about whether economic growth or certain types of economic growth are desirable, the influence of values and conflict of values on this process is a positive question – one in which economists should presumably be interested.

The proposition that more goods and services are preferred to less and that the satiation of consumers is impossible with existing resources is a fundamental tenet of economics. (Note that even if goods and services are not in short supply an economic problem will continue because time is in short supply and has alternative uses.) This is very often taken to imply that more income is preferred to less and that increases in real income increase welfare. But it is by no means self-evident that welfare of individuals is increased by their being able to purchase more goods and services. Such purchases may cause an individual's values or aspirations to change in a way which reduces the individual's psychological welfare, or at least does not increase it, or purchases of greater quantities of goods may reduce a consumer's long-term welfare through their detrimental side-effects, for example, on health, all of which may not be known to the consumer.

Weckstein has considered the possibility that welfare may depend upon the difference between an individual's actual income and the income to which the individual aspires. In conventional economics, aspiration levels play no role in welfare because in a sense the aspirations of individuals are infinite. In Weckstein's model (1962), an individual's welfare (*W*) depends only on the difference between the level of income to which the individual aspires (*A*) and the individual's actual income (*Y*). Weckstein believes that the typical relationship is like that depicted in Figure 14.1 by curve *KLMN*.

Figure 14.1 Weckstein's welfare relationship depends only on the difference between income aspired to and actual income

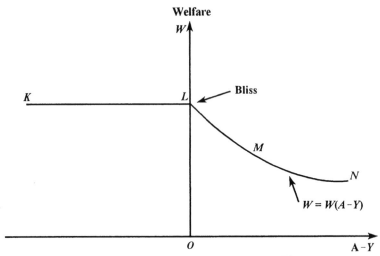

Difference between income aspired to and actual income

One may argue, as I would:

1. about whether the individual's welfare function is typically of this form[1] (for instance, for some individuals values are associated with striving so that their welfare function may reach a maximum at a point where $A > Y$); and
2. about whether an individual's welfare depends solely on the difference between *A* and *Y*, income aspired to and actual income respectively. It may, for example, depend on the level of actual income also.

Nevertheless, provided individuals' aspirations and actual values affect their welfare, this can be adversely affected if aspirations and actual values diverge too much. Welfare can be influenced either by a change in aspirations (reflecting a possible change in values) or by a change in actual results.

Weckstein considers the possibility that a government can, through communication and other means, increase the aspirations of a population for higher incomes.   There is some level of aspiration which can be achieved, but higher aspirations often cannot be fulfilled though they may induce greater effort and thus raise income as individuals attempt to meet them.

In Figure 14.2, the income Y_c can be achieved if individuals aspire to it.   If they achieve it they obtain bliss.   This is obtained for any combination along the 45 degree line in Figure 14.2, that is, at all points where aspiration income equals actual income.   If higher levels of income than Y_c are aspired to, this will call forth greater effort.   How much greater effort is expended may depend on values.   But actual income will fall short of the level of income aspired to.   For instance, the relationship between actual income and the level of income aspired to might be like *OCD*.   As the economy moves from *C* to *D* the gap between actual income and income aspired to increases so that welfare declines if the welfare function is of the type shown in Figure 14.1.   A government may need to choose between welfare and a greater level of national income (see Figure 14.3).

Figure 14.2   Relationship between income level aspired to and actual level of income obtained

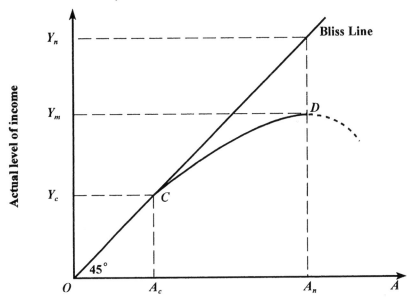

Income level aspired to

There may also be dangers for a government in manipulating aspiration levels and values. The curve *OCD* is likely to fall beyond *D*. Unrealistic levels of aspiration may lead to aggression against the whole productive process, a breakdown in the normal functioning of a social system and in extreme cases, to revolution. It is clear that the Chinese Maoist government influenced aspirations and values as a part of its growth policy, for example, in the 'Great Leap Forward'. It had to face the danger of aggressiveness in its population as a result of pushing aspiration levels too high. Possibly a 'managed' revolution, such as the Cultural Revolution, gave an outlet for such aggressiveness.

If it is true that aspiration levels and values can be altered by governments and social groups and that these have an influence on economic development, is it appropriate for economists to ignore the welfare and other possibilities of this? Is the welfare relationship suggested by Weckstein and outlined in Figure 14.3 a subject for discussion in economics? In my view, yes.

Figure 14.3 Trade-off between welfare and actual income as a result of interaction between aspiration for and actual income

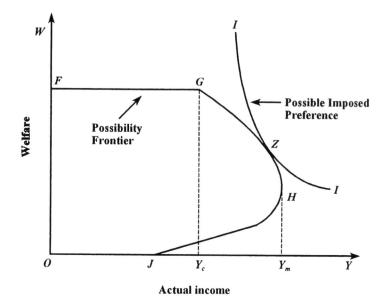

Weckstein's theory implies a possibility frontier between welfare[2] and actual income like the one shown in Figure 14.3. Given this relationship, what level of income should a nation aspire to? The preferences of its leaders may shunt it somewhere along the interval *GH*, for example, to a point such as *Z*, or it may be moved along that interval by uncoordinated advertising in corporate capitalism. For instance, the propositions of Marcuse (1969) or Galbraith (1967) mentioned earlier may hold. Even though individuals become richer their aspirations for consumption outrun their possibilities under the influence of advertising by corporations, and their welfare, at least from their subjective point of view, declines.

Weckstein's models suggest that variables which economists have conventionally regarded as being the determinants of an individual's welfare are not the relevant ones. It also raises the question of whether real welfare and subjective welfare diverge. The problem of what is to be valued from a welfare point of view does not appear to be solved.

DEMAND AND THE ENGINEERING OF PREFERENCES AND VALUES

Economy-wide aspects of the engineering of demand have already been touched upon. But there are also microeconomic aspects of this which may be worth considering. However, economists have paid very little attention to these.

To some extent, Leibenstein's contribution (1950) gives a basis for exploring the possibilities for engineering preferences and the values attached to commodities. Leibenstein was able to show that various social influences such as snob effects, bandwagon effects and the Veblen effect can influence the slope and nature of the demand curve for a product. Can a firm, by using advertising techniques, create a snob or bandwagon effect around its product depending upon which it chooses? Which effect is most profitable for it to create? Should it create from a profit point of view a different effect in different markets? For instance, it may be most profitable for Mercedes to be marketed as a snob product in Australia and as a bandwagon product in Germany, because the manufacturer is at a price disadvantage in Australia after paying the import tariff and the Australian market is small.

Some advertising may lead a buyer to associate certain non-functional, even make-believe, characteristics with a product, and yet in the final analysis the buyer is under no delusion. Nevertheless, the consumer values the association. A phenomenon of this type may occur for cigarettes and cosmetics. The subjective welfare of the buyer would appear to be increased by such advertising. Ironically many conventional economists are critical of such advertising. This criticism would appear to be at odds with the basic nature of Paretian economics that an individual's subjective welfare is the measure of welfare that counts. However, this is not to say that the constellation of advertising in the world today is socially optimal but to suggest that advertising other than informative advertising may also be valued.

It could also be that economists should look more closely at values within firms and economic organizations. Large firms consisting of many individuals and large economic organizations are characteristic of the present world. Do different groups within these organizations hold different values? How are their values formed, changed and maintained? What is the purpose of these values and how do they aid or hinder the economic activity of the organization?

A NOTE ON SCITOVSKY'S JOYLESS ECONOMY

Scitovsky, who has made important contributions to traditional welfare economics, subsequently (Scitovsky, 1976) rejected the conventional approach of economists to human behaviour as unscientific because of the failure of economists to observe and explain behaviour. He says:

> People's tastes, the way they spend their money and arrange their lives, are matters economists have always regarded as something they should observe, but must not poke their noses into. They seem to feel that analysing people's tastes and their motivation would be an invasion of privacy and an abrogation of consumer sovereignty, and that it might expose them to the charge of pretending to know better than the consumer himself what is good for him. Instead, economists assume that the consumer is rational; in other words, they assume that whatever he does must be the best thing for him to do, given his tastes, market opportunities, and circumstances, since otherwise he would not have done it. (Scitovsky, 1976, p. vii)

Scitovsky prefers to draw inspiration from motivational psychology to consider whether or not increasing affluence leads to increased pleasure. His view is that it need not and the economy of the United States is becoming a joyless one. He appears to correlate pleasure with welfare or at least consider pleasure to be desirable.

He is of the opinion that affluence in the United States is reaching levels where it can, and for many does, yield complete and continuous comfort, and therefore little pleasure. His view is summarized as follows:

While comfort hinges on the level of arousal being *at* or *close* to its optimum, pleasure accompanies *changes* in the level of arousal being the optimum. That is why the satisfaction of need gives both pleasure and comfort. But the continuous maintenance of comfort would eliminate pleasure, because, with arousal continuously at its optimum level, there can be no change in arousal toward the optimum. In other words, incomplete and intermittent comfort is accompanied by pleasure, while complete and continuous comfort is incompatible with pleasure. (Scitovsky, 1976, p. 71)[3]

Thus, comfort gained in Scitovsky's view is pleasure lost, and comfort is gained by the satisfaction of wants. But 'the pleasures of stimulation, unlike those of want satisfaction are *not* eliminated by their too persistent and too continuous pursuit' (Scitovsky, 1976, pp. 77–8) and individuals seek stimulation to avoid the boredom and lack of pleasure stemming from their continual fulfilment of wants. In Scitovsky's view, there is insufficient stimulation and novelty in American society. Thus boredom and frustration can build up, in some instances finding an outlet through crime. (Incidentally, this is almost the reverse explanation to Marcuse's for frustration in an advanced corporate economy. Also Weckstein's welfare function is not compatible with Scitovsky's view of pleasure.) In Scitovsky's case, pleasure may be at an all-time low when aspiration levels are met.

Scitovsky believes that the need of consumers for novelty, because of the stimulation it gives, has become inadequately realized. As far as America is concerned, Scitovsky (1976, pp. 282–3) says:

Our consumption of stimulation, variety and novelty is lower than average, and I have discussed some of the cultural, educational and economic influences to account for such a consumption pattern. We could say that there is nothing wrong with seeking comfort rather than stimulus if that is one's ideal of the good life, except for the following reasons. First, we overindulge in comfort; second, in the modern economy, the economies of scale impose the majority's tastes on the whole society, and when the majority chooses to sacrifice the stimulus of novelty for the sake of comfort, the creation of novelty and the minority's seeking new ways of attaining the good life are both impeded.

As will be apparent, this raises the awkward question of the extent to which the preferences of the minority should be sacrificed to those of the majority.

SOME CONCLUDING COMMENTS

Both Weckstein's theory and Scitovsky's theory throw doubt upon the variables which economists have conventionally assumed to be valued from a welfare point of view. Other writers such as Hollis and Nell (1975) and Gintis (1972), drawing inspiration from Marx, argue that the conventional economic approach is deficient because it fails to take account of welfare achieved by individuals in social or institutional roles, that is, from the nature of the role *per se*. In conventional economic theories, welfare depends essentially on commodities. To the extent that Rowley and Peacock (1975) in their book put personal freedom (liberty) before the attainment of Paretian economic efficiency as a desirable welfare goal, they also support the view that traditional welfare economics is too narrow in its conception of the variables which are or are to be valued.

By adopting a particular theory of rational behaviour, economists appear to have opted out of the in-depth study of values and preferences. The positivist view of Robbins appears to have deterred many economists from giving more than a superficial consideration to values and preferences. This has blinded many to important issues. However, there are unresolved problems in values and preferences of relevance to economics which can in principle be studied along positivist lines. An economist could deal with or speculate about these problems without pontificating on ultimate ends. Even the alteration of values and preferences through variations in the economic system to meet higher-order values would seem to fall into a part of economic enquiry. These high-order values may be taken as given in the sense suggested by Robbins. Whether or not the economist *qua* economist has any claim to be able to formulate the appropriate ultimate values better than anyone else is doubtful. In this respect, I agree with Benn and Mortimore (1976, pp. 292–3). They say:

> There is no reason to suppose that the arguments necessary to establish such prescriptive claims would be any easier to formulate or more reliable in practice than those by which economists who accept Humean–Weberian limitations warrant their merely hypothetical prescriptions. An opportunity to ask bold questions is not itself a guarantee of right answers.

However, this is no excuse for an economist ignoring values.[4] In addition, note that the above indicates possible deficiencies in the Paretian approach to economic welfare based upon the aim of attaining efficiency in the fulfilment of preferences conceived in a relatively narrow and static manner.

NOTES

1. I would suggest that it is more likely to be of the form, $W = W(A - Y, Y)$ where $\partial W/\partial(A - Y) < 0$ and $\partial W/\partial Y > 0$.
2. This raises the awkward question of whether there is a difference between perceived or psychological welfare and real welfare and the nature of the difference.
3. This suggests that there may be an optimal rate at which individuals should become comfortable over their lifetime.
4. Issues raised by values are of course much wider than those covered in this chapter contribution. For example, it does not cover values and the relationship between humankind and nature, intergenerational welfare and so on. Some of the issues raised in this regard are covered in Tisdell (1990, 1991, 1993) and in Tisdell and Harrison (1995).

REFERENCES

Bauer, P.T. (1971), *Dissent on Development: Studies and Debates in Development Economics*, London: Weidenfeld & Nicolson.

Benn, S.I. and Mortimore, G.W. (1976), 'Can Ends be Rational? The Methodological Implications', in Benn, S.I. and Mortimore, G.W. (eds), *Rationality and the Social Sciences*, London: Routledge & Kegan Paul.

Boulding, K.E. (1968), *Beyond Economics*, Ann Arbor: University of Michigan.

Galbraith, J.K. (1967), *The New Industrial State*, London: Hamish Hamilton.

Gintis, H. (1972), 'A Radical Analysis of Welfare Economics and Individual Development', *Quarterly Journal of Economics*, 86, 572–99.

Hollis, M. and Nell, E.J. (1975), *Rational Economic Man*, London: Cambridge University Press.

Leibenstein, H. (1950), 'Bandwagon, Snob and Veblen Effects in the Theory of Consumer's Demand', *Quarterly Journal of Economics*, 64, 183–207.

Lindbeck, A. (1971), *The Political Economy of the New Left: An Outsider's View*, New York: Harper & Row.

Marcuse, H. (1969), *An Essay on Liberation*, Boston: Beacon Press.

Myrdal, G. (1956), *An International Economy: Problems and Prospects*, London: Routledge and Kegan Paul.

Rescher, N. (1969), *Introduction to Value Theory*, Englewood Cliffs: Prentice-Hall.

Robbins, L. (1952), *An Essay on the Nature and Significance of Economic Science*, 2nd edn, London: Macmillan.

Rowley, C.K. and Peacock, A.T. (1975), *Welfare Economics: A Liberal Restatement*, London: Martin Robertson.

Scitovsky, T. (1976), *The Joyless Economy*, New York: Oxford University Press.

Tisdell, C.A. (1990), *Natural Resources, Growth and Development*, New York: Praeger.

Tisdell, C.A. (1991), *Economics of Environmental Conservation*, Amsterdam: Elsevier.

Tisdell, C.A. (1993), *Environmental Economics*, Aldershot, UK: Edward Elgar.

Tisdell, C.A. and Harrison, S.R. (1995), 'Livestock, the Environment and Sustainable Development with Illustrations of Issues for Thailand', Research Papers and Reports in Animal Health Economics (5), Brisbane: Department of Economics, University of Queensland.

Weckstein, R.S. (1962), 'Welfare Criteria and Changing Tastes', *American Economic Review*, 52, 133–53.

15. Concepts of Economic Efficiency: Measurement and Limitations

Economic efficiency is highly valued in modern economies and interest in attaining economic efficiency is a major preoccupation of much contemporary economics given the central role of Pareto's concept of economic welfare in neoclassical economics. Satisfaction of the Paretian criterion for measuring welfare requires that there be efficiency in satisfying the wants of individuals in society which in turn requires technical efficiency to be achieved. Thus economic efficiency (allocative and technical) is a dominating concern in contemporary economics and economies, so much so that it often leads to other values being ignored, such as those connected with equity and social justice.

However, the ways of achieving, relieving and measuring economic efficiency are not nearly as straightforward as many writers on this subject would have us believe. This is particularly so when knowledge limitations, transaction impediments and so on are taken into account. Mechanistic (engineering-like) procedures can only carry us a limited way in achieving economic efficiency, which indeed may be unattainable in an uncertain changing world of only partially overlapping generations (see Chapter 8).

One means of coming to grips with the limitations of the concept of economic efficiency is to consider difficulties involved in measuring it. This is the main focus of this chapter.

Because the concept of economic efficiency is central to economic thought, it is not surprising that economists have attempted to measure the extent to which economic efficiency is achieved in actual economies, within industries and by particular firms. Such measurement is a formidable task, not least because the dimensions of economic efficiency are much greater than have been commonly realized.

Before rushing into econometric work, the economist should decide exactly what is to be measured. Measurement without theory and forethought is a dangerous and often futile exercise, even if a tempting one, given computing advances.

The purpose of this chapter is to show that there are many dimensions to economic efficiency and that measurement based upon simplistic mechanical interpretations can be misleading (compare Gurzynski, 1984). Alternative concepts of efficiency are discussed, together with their shortcomings. Examples of the latter are shortcomings of productive efficiency measurement by Farrell (1957) and limitations of survivorship as an indicator of efficiency.

PARETIAN OR STATIC EFFICIENCY

Possibly the most important concept of efficiency in economics is that of Pareto. If an economy is to be Paretian efficient, it must be efficient in satisfying the wants of individuals in relation to scarce resources. In the absence of interpersonal comparisons of utility and within the static setting usually assumed, this requires: (a) efficiency in production; (b) efficiency in the exchange of commodities; and (c) optimal conformity between the composition of production and the wants or tastes of individuals. Otherwise efficiency in satisfying wants can be improved – someone can be made better off without making anyone else worse off.

The requirement for static Paretian efficiency is technical efficiency in production, implying that firms should adopt techniques giving them the greatest amount of production for their employed quantity of inputs. Firms should therefore be producing on their production function. As defined by economists it is a best-practice or efficiency frontier. In reality, such productive 'efficiency' is not always achieved and writers such as Farrell (1957) have tried to measure the extent to which this is so. Farrell's approach is considered later.

Pareto's approach is useful in demonstrating that technical efficiency in production by individual units does not ensure efficiency in collective production. Even if firms are fully efficient in an engineering sense of employing the most efficient techniques, resources may be poorly allocated between firms or firms may not specialize according to their comparative advantage. This is not always appreciated, and frequently productive efficiency of a firm or industry is presented as a sufficient argument in favour of government assistance.

Paretian efficiency also requires an optimal conformity between the composition of production and the wants of consumers. Normally this implies that rates of product transformation and rates of indifferent substitution should be equal, or the level of production of each product be such that its marginal cost of production be equated with its price. Harberger (1954) has tried to measure the extent of the deadweight loss arising from this allocative efficiency in the United States. Harberger concluded (on the basis of industry rates of profit and assumed demand elasticities) that the social deadweight loss through allocative inefficiency due to monopoly in the Unites States amounted to less than one-tenth of one per cent of GNP. His results, however, have been questioned. For example, Kamerschen (1966) suggests that Harberger's approach fails to take full account of the social loss due to monopoly because imperfectly competitive firms engage in a considerable amount of wasteful advertising. Furthermore, no account is taken of organizational slack and X-inefficiency.

Neoclassical theory suggests that Paretian optimality tends to be satisfied under perfect competition. Most neoclassical economists, however, recognize that market failure may provide a basis for government intervention. Factors making for market failure include externalities, pure public goods, economies of scale, and so on. Nevertheless, economists vary in their assessment of the importance of market failure. For example, there is disagreement over the extent of market failure. Furthermore, some argue that even if market failure exists, government interference may add to economic inefficiency, either because of X-inefficiency in government organizations, because of the transaction costs involved in government intervention (Mishan, 1981, Chapter 60) or because of various failures expected to arise from political and administrative mechanisms of resource allocation (Tisdell, 1982, Chapter 16 and references given there).

'DYNAMICS' AND NON-ALLOCATIVE INEFFICIENCIES

A serious limitation of static Paretian efficiency is that its achievement can interfere with economic growth. Schumpeter (1942) argued that greater economic growth may occur when Paretian efficiency is not achieved. Schumpeter thought that imperfect competition might provide some of the necessary slack for greater technical progress and innovation in the economy. In the long term an imperfectly competitive economy may be more productive than a perfectly competitive one.

A system operating continuously at full efficiency is likely to have a poorer long-run performance than one allowing some slack. This may be a rather general principle. Slack may be conducive to (but is, of course, not sufficient for) superior long-run performance. Managers, for example, may require slack periods and time for speculation or creativity. Running a business with full short-term efficiency may leave little room for slack. However, if full efficiency or effort is continuously necessary for business survival, harassed managers may be unable to propose and manage creative change and economic improvement. However, there are also other reasons for reassessing the productive importance of organizational slack.

Indeed, it has been suggested that perfect competition and Paretian efficiency are inconsistent with the presence of entrepreneurship (Gurzynski and Abraham, 1984, p. 19). Consequently, in the words of Gurzynski and Abraham (1984, p. 21), perfect competition 'should not be taken as a standard of perfection in achieving economic efficiency. ... We need an economy where change and growth come from within, under the impulse of entrepreneurial innovations which includes, of course, the application of inventions'.

X-EFFICIENCY AND ORGANIZATIONAL SLACK

Harvey Leibenstein (1966) sees the concept of efficiency as being at the core of economics and claims that microeconomic theory is solely concerned with allocative efficiency. While this is too narrow a view of microeconomic theory, this theory has concentrated on allocative efficiency. He argues that 'microeconomic theory focuses on allocative efficiency to the exclusion of other types of efficiencies that, in fact, are much more significant in many instances. Furthermore, improvement in "non-allocative efficiency" is an important aspect of the process of growth' (Leibenstein, 1966, p. 392). All types of efficiency other than allocative efficiency are termed X-efficiency. Corresponding non-allocative inefficiency can be called X-inefficiency.

Although motivation is a major element of X-efficiency, it is not the only element, according to Leibenstein. He suggests that the main factors leading to X-inefficiency and different degrees of economic performance by firms are (a) incomplete specification of labour contracts; (b) incomplete knowledge of production functions (for example, incomplete knowledge of available technology); and (c) the non-marketing of some inputs such as market information. 'For these and other reasons it seems clear that it is one thing to purchase or hire inputs in a given combination; it is something else to get a predetermined output out of them' (Leibenstein, 1966, p. 408). Hence, a mechanical view of economic production is inappropriate.

X-inefficiency does occur and in many cases scarcity could be considerably reduced and economic growth increased by eliminating or attending to some of its causes. However, to eliminate X-inefficiency completely may not be optimal. Some slack within economic organizations can add to overall efficiency because information collection, transmission and control involve costs (Tisdell, 1984 or see Chapter 9). In addition, some X-inefficiency, as mentioned previously, may be important for experimentation and spontaneity in organizations. It can provide individuals within organizations with some freedom of action and thereby help to motivate them. Furthermore, it may allow the organization flexibility in a changing and uncertain world. Some types of X-inefficiency or organizational slack are optimal given the inherently imperfect nature of the world.

In a world of uncertainty, decisions that appear inefficient *ex post* may nevertheless be optimal in the prospective sense. Hart (1942), for example, has pointed out that it may be efficient for an organization to build in flexibility (at a cost) so that it can respond more easily to new information (compare Tisdell, 1970). For example, it may carry larger cash reserves than normal to allow flexibility. Again, an organization may well employ less job-specific equipment or try to employ techniques with low fixed or unavoidable costs relative to variable or avoidable costs. Whether these are techniques which give rise to a relatively flat average variable cost curve is debatable (compare Stigler, 1939; Tisdell, 1968, Chapter 6). A firm that does not make such allowances for uncertainty may well look to be more efficient after the event than one that does, but on average it is not efficient at all. This is so even though on occasion fortune may favour the organization not making allowance for uncertainty.

In a world of changing technology, there are further problems in the *ex post* assessment of the productive efficiency of a firm (Johansen, 1972, and Førsund and Hjalmarrson, 1974). For every firm in an industry to adopt the best-practice technique available may not be optimal. Whether or not an individual firm should replace an existing technique depends upon the vintage of the technique and other considerations. In an industry in which technology is changing and techniques embodied in capital, a dispersed structure of techniques can be optimal and the optimal structure depends upon expectations about future technological change. This will be discussed when Farrell's approach to productive efficiency is considered.

Various methods have been suggested for measuring the economic efficiency of firms. These include the level of profits, survival techniques, and Farrell's measurement of efficiency using best-practice isoquants. Each of these will now be considered.

PROFITABILITY

Profit as a measure of economic efficiency has several limitations. To the extent that firms are involved in an imperfectly competitive market, profit is not a satisfactory measure of efficiency from a social viewpoint. (This is also true if various types of market failure are present.) However, differences in the efficiency of firms in similar situations will be reflected in differences in their profits, at least in the short run. In the long term, those factors of production responsible for greater efficiency and profitability of a firm can be expected to earn additional rents if they are reasonably mobile. For example, where managers are responsible for the superior performance of a firm, long-term competition for their services will raise their salaries and reduce residual profit for the firm originally employing such managers. In the long term, perfectly competitive firms can all be expected to earn normal profit or return on capital. This limits the long-term value of profits as an indicator of efficiency.

Limitations of profit as a measure of efficiency arise in another context, namely that of a divisionalized firm. If there are costs involved in using an outside market, the profits imputed to a division of the firm using optimal transfer prices may not reflect the true worth to the company of a division. This can be illustrated by considering a vertically integrated firm (see also Chapter 11).

Assume that a primary division of the firm is supplying the secondary division of the firm with a component for its production that can also be sold by the primary division on an outside market or purchased by the secondary division from outside the company. Let P_S represent the price that the primary division can obtain by selling its component on the outside market and let P_B represent the price at which the secondary division can purchase the component from outside the company. The difference between these two prices represents cost of using outside markets.

In Figure 15.1, curve ABC represents the marginal cost experienced by the primary division in producing the component and curve DBF illustrates the net marginal revenue obtained by the secondary division in using the component. It does not pay the company to trade in the outside market for the component. The optimal transfer price for the component is $\bar{P}$ and the profit-maximizing throughput of the component is $\bar{x}$.

Figure 15.1 Market transaction costs limit profit as an indicator of economic efficiency

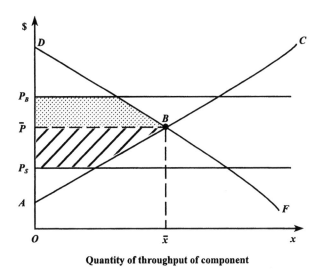

Quantity of throughput of component

Given the transfer price $\bar{P}$, the imputed profit of the primary division of the company is shown by the cross-hatched area. However, the cross-hatched area understates the true value to the company of the primary division. In the absence of the primary division the total profit of the company would be reduced by the cross-hatched area plus the dotted area. Consequently, imputed profit based upon optimal transfer prices is not an entirely satisfactory guide as to whether or not to close down a division of a firm. A division may make an imputed loss yet it may be profitable to retain it if there are costs involved in trading in outside markets.

SURVIVAL AND EFFICIENCY

It is tempting to suggest that those organizations and individuals which survive and prosper are most efficient. The survivor technique has been used in industry economics by Stigler (1954), Saving (1961) and others to estimate optimal plant or firm scales within industries. While Saving and Stigler were circumspect about the use of the technique for evaluating efficiency, other economists, such as Weiss (1964) claim that it has been used as an indicator of competitive effectiveness and therefore 'as one basis for evaluating the efficiency of an industrial organization in terms of resource use' (Weiss, 1964, p. 246). However, inefficient organizations (from a social point of view) may survive in an economy because of monopoly elements. If there are barriers to entry, a firm may survive even though it is relatively inefficient. Again, efficient firms may be driven out of an industry by such practices as predatory pricing or unusual events.

Those surviving unusual catastrophes are not necessarily those who can be expected on average to contribute most efficiently to the economy. The survivor technique does not, of course, claim that this is so but suggests that on average survivors are most efficient. For this to be tested, however, it would seem that one would need reasonably stationary and repetitive probability conditions.

Individuals or organizations prepared for an unusual and improbable event may well be very inefficient on average. However, if the event occurs, they may be the only ones to survive. For instance, take the hypothetical case of derelicts who sleep in the open in San Francisco. Suppose they are the only survivors of an earthquake. It would be nonsensical to conclude that they are the most efficient individuals in the city. We need a prospective concept of efficiency rather than a retrospective one. In an uncertain world, efficient firms in a prospective sense may fail to survive whereas some that are relatively inefficient are able to overcome unusual circumstances. In the economy, as in nature, the efficient are sometimes struck down, if efficiency is considered in terms of average probabilities of long-term success. Yet it is not always easy to decide who are efficient since probability distributions of events in the social environment (if not in the natural environment) are rarely stationary.

The probability of survival and economic growth is influenced by the average degree of X-inefficiency in the industry or society. In societies or industries where X-inefficiency is the custom, relatively inefficient organizations in comparison to the level of efficiency attainable are able to prosper.

FARRELL'S APPROACH TO PRODUCTIVE EFFICIENCY

Farrell presented his approach to the measurement of productive efficiency in 1957. The main purpose of his approach is to use cross-sectional data from an industry to estimate isoquants for firms based upon most efficient production practices in the industry. Suppose that a number of firms in an industry are producing the same level of output using two factors of production, say labour, *L*, and capital, *K*. The scatter of the observed values of (*L, K*) of different firms in the industry producing the same level of output, *X*, might be as shown in Figure 15.2 by the crosses. Farrell proposed that the apparent envelope of these points (represented in Figure 15.2 by the curve *QQ*) be used as an indicator of the best-practice isoquant at the level of the firm. Such an isoquant should belong to the efficient production function. It is not an 'average' function based on industry experience but an envelope type function (Aigner and Chu, 1968).

Figure 15.2 Productive efficiency is indicated by Farrell by an envelope of productive efficiencies

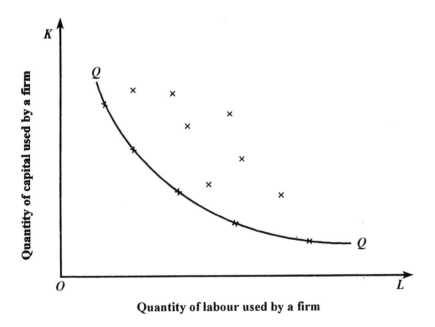

Quantity of labour used by a firm

Farrell suggests measures of both technical and price efficiency. The technical efficiency of a firm is assessed in relation to the 'efficient' or best-practice isoquant corresponding to its output. Thus in Figure 15.3 if a firm produces an output corresponding to isoquant *QQ* but uses the factor combination at *N* its technical efficiency is measured by the ratio *OM/ON*. This firm's efficiency is less than 1 (or 100 per cent) whereas a firm using the input combination at M to produce the same output has an efficiency of 1.

However, the combination of inputs at M may not minimize costs. Costs at M', given that AM' is the relevant factor price line, are only the fraction OR/OM of those at M. Farrell uses this to measure price efficiency and the ratio OR/ON to measure overall efficiency.

Figure 15.3 Illustration of Farrell's measures of both technical and price efficiency

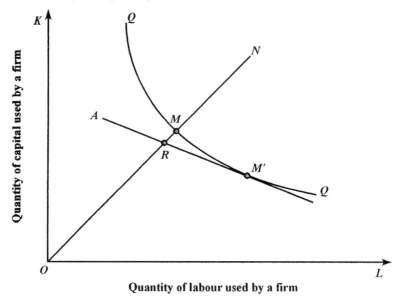

A number of 'technical' difficulties arise in applying Farrell's approach. In his original formulation, Farrell assumed constant returns to scale but methods for taking account of other than constant returns to scale have been suggested (Farrell and Fieldhouse, 1962; Førsund and Hjalmarrson, 1979). The randomness in observations adds to the difficulty of estimating a frontier production function. Methods for taking account of such randomness have been formulated (Lee, 1983), but even in the absence of these difficulties, fundamental problems remain. Let us consider some of them.

From the previous discussion concerning optimal allowances for uncertainty, a combination such as N in Figure 15.3 is not necessarily inefficient. Because of uncertainty, it may be optimal to build in flexibility at a cost. It may also be beneficial, as pointed out earlier, to have some slack in the organization. This may mean that the best-practice technique is, in fact, not on the frontier identified by Farrell.

Learning by doing is important for productivity in many industries and Farrell does not allow for this. Different firms, either because they have produced greater quantities of a product, or have been involved in production for longer periods of time, may have different productivities. However, this does not mean that their efficiency or productivity is fundamentally different. For example, suppose that two firms have the same productivity progress curve *OABC* as indicated in Figure 15.4 but are producing the same quantity of output in the period under consideration. Suppose that firm 1 is at point *A* on its productivity progress curve and firm 2 is at point *B*. Firm 2 will appear most efficient but this is only because it is at a different stage in its life cycle. If, in fact, firm 1 is on the productivity progress curve *OADF* (or a similar one), it will be more efficient over its life cycle.

Figure 15.4 Learning by doing or productivity progress should be taken into account (as illustrated) in assessing the relative efficiencies of different firms

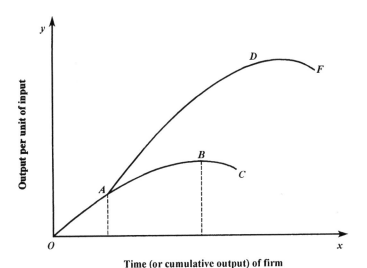

Time (or cumulative output) of firm

Given that productivity progress functions are important because of learning or other factors (see Chapter 7), a case can be made for assessing the relative efficiencies of different firms in terms of comparisons between their productivity progress functions, or (more generally) production functions, that include cumulative production or elapsed time as variables in the production function (Kibria and Tisdell, 1985). Of course, difficulties continue since if one is to consider efficiency in a prospective rather than a retrospective sense, one has to predict the productivity progress curves of firms in relation to their future production. Despite the difficulties, this could be a worthwhile attempt.

Problems of embodied technology as raised by Salter (1969) should be taken into account. The scrapping of an old plant is not always efficient when new technology comes along. If existing plant has no resale value, decisions about whether to retain it should be based on profitability in relation to its operating cost only. The economics of retaining existing plant (even though this type of plant is not efficient if new capacity has to be created) is not as widely appreciated as it could be, despite the useful guidance of Salter in this regard.

The presence of embodied technology and *ex post* rigidity of resources limits the normative significance of Farrell's measures of efficiency (Johansen, 1972, p. 238). As Førsund and Hjalmarsson (1979, p. 295) point out:

> If a vintage capital effect is the cause [of efficiency differences between firms] it is not economically relevant to pursue a policy of bringing all units up to the standard of the most efficient vintage. Differences in measured efficiency might correspond to differences in the age of equipment, and still be economically efficient. In this case the unit's optimization problem is dynamic and its success can only be evaluated over a number of replacement cycles.

Førsund and Hjalmarsson (1974) point out that the optimal path of replacement of techniques in an industry depends on the existing pattern of adopted techniques and capacity in an industry. Industries are subject to constant structural development. They say (1974, p. 148) that

> At a given point in time one can look backwards in time deriving an unconditionally optimal path perfectly anticipating all the relevant past developments. The concept of the optimal path can be extended into the future, *conditional* upon information about future techniques, prices and demand development, perfect foresight being the limit. Usually the optimal path is based upon the best available forecast existing at the respective investment dates. When at a future point in time one is looking backward this latter path may differ from the one based on perfect foresight. Inefficiency can then be assessed with reference to such an optimal development.

The view that efficiency should be assessed with reference to the perfect foresight alternative is debatable. Efficiency should rather be assessed in the light of the knowledge available at the time that a decision about resource use has to be made. After the event, allowances for flexibility, for example, frequently appear inefficient but no inefficiency is involved *ex ante*.

Given the embodiment problem, can a Farrell-type efficiency frontier be used to indicate best practices in relation to new investment? Johansen (1972, p. 238) suggests that it might be of some use as a guide to optimal replacement investment and the efficiency of production involving new investment. However, even in this case learning by doing and productivity progress could pose complications similar to those mentioned earlier.

We need at least to be aware that the above-mentioned problems may be of significance. Studies done so far indicate considerable differences between best-practice estimates of efficiency and those based on average performance in an industry (compare Førsund and Hjalmarrson, 1979). Farrell's approach has been useful in highlighting such discrepancies.

CONCLUDING COMMENTS

The subject of economic efficiency is a wide one. Different types of institutional arrangements for controlling resource use may reflect variations in efficiency. Coase (1937) suggests, for example, that the existence of firms themselves can be ascribed to costs involved in using outside markets for transactions. If a firm were to use markets to the maximum extent possible in carrying out its activities, this could add considerably to its costs and uncertainty. Williamson (see Dugger, 1983) argues that when market transaction costs are taken into account, large firms may very well be more efficient than small ones because larger firms make relatively more decisions about resource use without recourse to the market. Issues of this type are taken up in the next chapter.

The question has also been posed whether it is likely to be more efficient from an optimizing viewpoint to use a centralized approach to policy formulation or a decentralized interactive grassroots approach (see Lindblom, 1977, for instance). Views on this question remain unsettled. However, I do have doubts about the value of a centralized approach, relying, for example, on general equilibrium techniques and econometrics which purport to model the whole situation (compare Tisdell, 1981, especially Section 1.5).

The above discussion illustrates that economic efficiency has many dimensions. In the past some of these dimensions have been lost sight of by economists, particularly in their efforts to measure economic and productive efficiency. One suspects that this is because economists have been overly influenced by mechanical or engineering analogies. The organic element in economic organizations and the experimental and exploratory nature of resource use has been subject to considerable neglect, as for example suggested by Gurzynski (1976) and by Gurzynski and Abraham (1984).

REFERENCES

Aigner, D. and Chu, S.F. (1968), 'On Estimating the Industry Production Function', *American Economic Review*, 58, 826–39.

Coase, R.H. (1937), 'The Nature of the Firm', *Economica*, 4, 386–405.

Dugger, W.M. (1983), 'The Transactional Cost Analysis of Oliver E. Williamson: A New Synthesis?', *Journal of Economic Issues*, 17, 95–114.

Farrell, M.J. (1957), 'The Measurement of Productive Efficiency', *Journal of the Royal Statistical Society*, 120, 254–81.

Farrell, M.J. and Fieldhouse, M. (1962), 'Estimating Efficient Production Functions under Increasing Returns to Scale', *Journal of the Royal Statistical Society*, 125, 152–267.

Førsund, F.R. and Hjalmarrson, L. (1974), 'On the Measurement of Productive Efficiency', *Swedish Journal of Economics*, 76, 141–54.

Førsund, F.R. and Hjalmarrson, L. (1979), 'Generalized Farrell Measures of Efficiency: An Application to Milk Processing in Swedish Dairy Plants', *The Economic Journal*, 89, 294–315.

Gould, J.R. (1964), 'Internal Pricing of Firms when there are Costs of Using an Outside Market', *Journal of Business*, 37, 61–7.

Gurzynski, Z.S.A. (1976), 'Entrepreneurship – The True Spring of Human Action', *South African Journal of Economics*, 44, 1–23.

Gurzynski, Z.S.A. (1984), 'The South African Economy: The Decade Ahead', copy of an address given on the 10th Anniversary of the School of Economics, University of Cape Town.

Gurzynski, Z.S.A. and Abraham, H. (1984), 'The Entrepreneur: A Reconstruction of the Theory of the Firm', School of Economics, University of Cape Town.

Harberger, A.C. (1954), 'Monopoly and Resource Allocation', *Proceedings of the American Economic Association*, 77–87.

Hart, A.G. (1942), 'Risk, Uncertainty and the Unprofitability of Compounding Probabilities', in Lange, O., McIntyre, F. and Yntema, F. (eds), *Studies in Mathematical Economics and Econometrics*, Chicago: University of Chicago Press, 110–18.

Johansen, L. (1972), *Production Functions*, Amsterdam: North-Holland.

Kamerschen, D. (1966), 'On Estimation of "Welfare Losses" from Monopoly in the American Economy', *Western Economic Journal*, 3, 221–36.

Kibria, M.G. and Tisdell, C.A. (1985), 'Operating Capital and Productivity Patterns in Jute Weaving in Bangladesh', *Journal of Development Economics*, 18, 133–52.

Lee, Lung-Fei (1983), 'A Test for Distributional Assumptions for the Stochastic Frontier Functions', *Journal of Econometrics*, 22, 245–67.

Leibenstein, H. (1966), 'Allocative Efficiency vs "X-Efficiency", *American Economic Review*, 61, 392–415.

Lindblom, E.C. (1977), *Politics and Markets*, New York: Basic Books.

Mishan, E.J. (1981), *Introduction to Normative Economics*, New York: Oxford University Press.

Salter, W. (1969), *Productivity and Technological Change*, 2nd edn, Cambridge: Cambridge University Press.

Saving, T.R. (1961), 'Estimation of Optimum Size of Plant by the Survivor Technique', *Quarterly Journal of Economics*, 75, 569–607.

Schumpeter, J. (1942), *Capitalism, Socialism and Democracy*, 2nd edn, New York: Harper Brothers.

Stigler, G.J. (1939), 'Production and Distribution in the Short Run', *Journal of Political Economy*, 47, 305–28.

Stigler, G.J. (1954), 'The Economies of Scale', *Journal of Law and Economics*, 1, 61–7.

Tisdell, C.A. (1968), *The Theory of Price Uncertainty, Production and Profit*, Princeton, New Jersey: Princeton University Press.

Tisdell, C.A. (1970), 'Implications of Learning for Economic Planning', *Economics of Planning*, 10, 177–92.

Tisdell, C.A. (1981), *Science and Technology Policy: Priorities of Governments*, London: Chapman & Hall.

Tisdell, C.A. (1982), *Microeconomics of Markets*, Brisbane: John Wiley.

Tisdell, C.A. (1984), 'Slack and Strain in Efficient Budgeting and Resource Allocation by Organizations', *Managerial and Decision Economics*, 5, 54–7.

Weiss, L. (1964), 'The Survival Technique and the Extent of Suboptimal Capacity', *Journal of Political Economy*, 72, 246–61.

16. Market Transaction Costs, Economic Welfare and Management

INTRODUCTION

Practically all forms of social organization, including economic types of such organization, are subject to transaction costs. These constitute impediments to or frictions involved in social exchange and control of activity, that is, in social organization. Market exchange as pointed out by Max Weber[1] is one possible form of social organization. It is subject to transaction costs, the level of which varies with the circumstances.

Already we have been able to consider, in Part III, some transaction costs within organizations and have touched in Chapter 11 upon the influence of market transaction costs as an influence on the management of multidivisional firms using transfer pricing as a managerial device. The purpose of this chapter is to consider market transaction costs in more detail: identify them more precisely, trace out their economic welfare consequences (which involves a consideration of their impact on economic efficiency) and, as alluded to in the previous chapter, explore their consequences for the size of the firm and extend the discussion of their application to the multidivisional firm.

The view is now widely accepted that economic exchange and transacting involves, or can involve, significant costs which, although ignored in neoclassical theory, have important institutional consequences (Demsetz, 1968; Williamson, 1975, 1979; De Alessi, 1983). These factors influence the extent to which firms use outside markets and have implications for economic welfare and the optimal management structures of firms. Indeed, as pointed out in Coase's seminal article (1937), these costs help explain the very existence of firms. The specific purposes of this chapter are: (1) to identify the sources of market transaction costs, (2) to explore their consequences for economic welfare, (3) to outline briefly some implications of market transaction costs for the size of the firm, (4) to consider efficient management structures in large-sized firms, including the role of transfer pricing as a management device, (5) to specify limitations of transfer pricing as a management mechanism in multidivisional (*M*-form) firms, and in particular (6) to highlight the retardation problems which transfer pricing can pose for the process of innovation and adoption of new technology in the firm.

SOURCES OF MARKET TRANSACTION COSTS

The costs of using outside markets to satisfy the economic requirements of an organization for commodities, that is, the actual cost of transacting outside by an economic entity such as a firm (a household or any other organization for that matter), may arise from a number of sources. The origins of market transaction or exchange costs are rarely identified specifically in the economic literature so it is worthwhile highlighting some of these here. Market transaction costs can arise from:

1. Agency fees which could reflect the costs of search, recording and so on.
2. Government taxes or charges levied on market transactions such as sales tax.
3. Direct search costs for suitable suppliers and/or the costs of choosing between them.
4. Residual uncertainty involved in supply of services or inputs from outside the economic entity due to the fact that contracts (because of costs involved in complete specification) are usually imperfectly specified and knowledge about the supplier is usually less than that about supply from an internal source (Cheung, 1969). This problem is exacerbated by the fact that contracts may be costly to enforce and the remedies for non-compliance uncertain. Remedies such as the non-promotion of employees, their dismissal and or assignment of non-preferred tasks within an organization are easier (Alchian and Demsetz, 1972). However, the use of outside markets is not always more risky than supply from within the firm. For example, in Australia a firm by employing labour may encounter trade union restrictions which limit possibilities for dismissing this labour whereas provision of service on contract is not subject to this difficulty.
5. Use of a source of supply outside the firm may involve extra transport or communication costs because of greater distances to be covered.

6. Use of a source of supply outside the enterprise can involve extra physical, chemical and other productive processes which can be avoided by internal supply. For example, if metal is purchased from outside a firm it will have to be reheated for moulding purposes but if it is moulded where it is smelted and in an already molten state this cost is avoided.

7. Market exchange may require the issue of government permits or certificates. This can add to costs and cause delays.

It should, however, be observed that the cost to a firm or organization of using outside markets can also depend to some extent on its internal organization and procedures. Some procedures (for example, of a hierarchical nature, for instance for purchasing) can add considerably to the costs of using outside markets and deter units within the firm from making use of these.

WELFARE CONSEQUENCES OF MARKET TRANSACTION COSTS

Market transaction costs are usually seen as an impediment to maximizing economic welfare. They result in incomplete markets and, compared to their absence, result in an economic loss which can be substantial. This hypothetical loss can be divided into two components: (1) the extra cost imposed by market transactions that actually occur and (2) stemming losses as a result of transactions not undertaken because of the presence of transaction costs. This is illustrated in Figure 16.1. There, line AS represents the supply curve of a commodity, X, in the absence of market transaction costs and line BS_T represents the market supply after market transaction costs are taken into account. In the case shown, market transaction costs result in an economic loss equivalent to the area of quadrilateral $AFGB$. This consists of a stemming component equal to the dotted triangle plus one for actual transactions equal to the hatched area. A similar type of loss can be shown for other market forms, such as monopoly. Of course, it may not be possible to reduce market transaction costs to zero. However, in terms of this model any reduction in market transaction costs will increase economic welfare.

Another source of market transaction costs is asymmetry of information between buyers and sellers. This asymmetry might be smaller within organizations. Such asymmetry of information can lead to market failure. As a consequence, the markets for some commodities may completely fail, or the market for the higher-quality products may

Figure 16.1   Market transaction costs cause a welfare loss compared to a situation in which they are absent

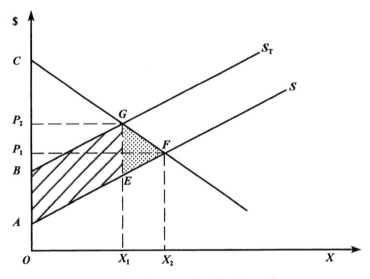

Quantity of commodity X exchanged

collapse as in the 'lemons' versus 'plums' example from the used-car market (Akerlof, 1970; Varian, 1993, Chapter 34; Mansfield, 1994, Chapter 6). When products of better quality are excluded from exchange due to imperfect information, adverse selection is said to occur. Moral hazard can also be a source of market failure, for example, when as a result of insurance, those insured reduce their standard of care so causing risks and premiums to rise and the insurance market to collapse or forcing those with lower risks to give up purchasing insurance. The costs and difficulties involved in the insurer monitoring the compliance of the insured with the condition of the insurance is the main problem.

To some extent, barriers to entry into an industry may also be considered as costs of transacting in a market. However, in this regard, note the importance of historical precedence in affecting the evolution of a market. Take the case illustrated in Figure 16.2. On the left hand-side $S_1 S_1$ represents the supply curve of commodity X in country or region 1 and on the right-hand side, $S_2 S_2$ represents that of country 2. External economies of scale exist. DD is the demand curve for the commodity.

Figure 16.2 Prior expansion or growth of an industry in a higher-cost region may prevent the evolution of a lower-cost industry in a lower-cost region

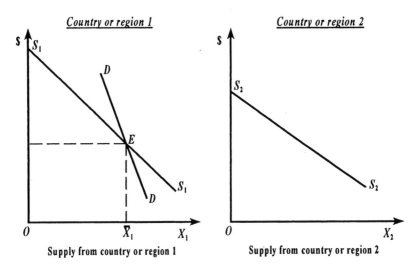

Suppose that the industry first evolves in region 1 because *initially* the costs of production in region 2 exceed those in region 1 and that the industry in region 1 develops to reach the equilibrium at *E*. Imagine that subsequently the supply curve $S_2 S_2$ becomes achievable in region 2. Even though costs would be lower by producing all output in region 2, the industry is unlikely to develop there because it cannot expand in an incremental manner and be competitive with region 1. A large jump in production in region 2 is required to displace region 1 in the market. Without non-market intervention, the potentially more-efficient but later-developing region, 2, is unlikely to establish its industry because of the scale barriers involved in its competitive entry into the market.

However, market transaction costs need not always have adverse welfare consequences. Sometimes they may increase the stability of markets. Bonding of symbiotic relationships between businesses (for example, preferred lists of sellers or purchasers) as explained in Chapter 13 may be economically advantageous to the parties concerned. At the same time, such bonding can constitute a barrier to the entry of new businesses into industry. Nevertheless, because of the positive effect of business bonding in providing businesses with opportunities for learning by helping them survive in an industry for longer than otherwise might occur, in reducing market transaction costs and in enabling advantage to be taken of favourable external economies between partners, it may be to the advantage of consumers. A completely open competitive system, especially if it fosters rapid entry into and exit from an industry, will result in many 'rolling stones' and it is likely that the adage 'rolling stones gather no moss' will apply.

MARKET TRANSACTION COSTS AND THE SIZE OF THE FIRM

The greater the transaction costs involved in obtaining the supply of an input from the marketplace, the more incentive (other things being equal) a firm has to supply the input from internal sources rather than purchase it in the marketplace. This increased sourcing of supply from internal sources as a result of market transaction costs is commonly believed to result in firms of increased size (Galbraith, 1967). Where transaction costs increase generally in an economy as a whole this may be the outcome, but theoretically the picture is quite complicated. For example, while transaction costs may result in more activities being sourced from within the firm, the greater costs involved as a result of not finding it worthwhile to use the market may reduce a firm's total volume of production and in terms of the quantity of production the size of firms could fall.

Consider the simple case shown in Figure 16.3. Suppose that a firm produces a final product, Y, which requires one variable essential (intermediate) input X, which can be produced and supplied from internal sources by a unit of the firm or purchased on an outside market. Let the firm's net marginal revenue productivity from this input, X, be as indicated by the curve marked *MRP* in Figure 16.3 and let the curve marked *MC* represent its marginal cost of supplying the input internally. Let the line AB represent the market price of the input. In the absence of market transaction costs, the firm would maximize its profit by using x_3 of the input. Of this quantity, x_1 would be supplied from internal sources and $x_3 - x_1$ from the external market. However, if market transaction costs amount say to AD per unit of input X, it will no longer pay the firm to use the outside market for some supply of the input. A greater quantity of the input, namely quantity x_2, will be supplied from internal sources but (other things equal) total production (the level of final output Y) will decline.

Figure 16.3 The presence of market transaction costs may result in a reduction in the size of a firm as judged by the volume of its output

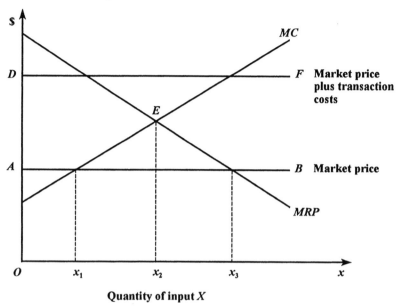

Quantity of input X

Thus, on the basis of some measures of size, such as number of employees or level of assets, the firm may be larger but on the basis of other measures, such as volume of final output, it may be smaller after market transaction costs are taken into account. On the other hand, if all firms in the industry experience similar market transaction costs and this is reflected in a higher equilibrium market price for the final product, their *MRP* curves are likely to move upwards as a result of greater market transaction costs. This 'market compensation effect' will reinforce any tendency towards larger-sized firms.

Nevertheless, it is clear that social economic welfare tends to be lower the higher are market transaction costs since they reduce the extent of market operations. Among other things, economies from and advantages of specialization in production tend to be lost as the operation of markets becomes more constricted.   However, it is not true in all circumstances that reduced use of markets for the purpose of economic production reduces economic efficiency. In some circumstances and for a variety of reasons such a trend can increase economic efficiency or economic welfare (compare Williamson, 1982, 1983; Jones, 1982, 1983 and see above).

EFFICIENT MANAGEMENT STRUCTURES IN LARGE-SIZED FIRMS AND TRANSFER PRICING

A number of factors may favour large-sized firms. Market transaction costs appear to be just one of the possible contributing factors. Whatever the exact reasons for their emergence, large firms are characteristic of the current era. However, whether or not they are of an optimal size which satisfies Coase's (1937) optimality rule, is unclear. Coase suggested that a firm should be expanded in size to the point where 'the cost of organizing an extra transaction within the firm becomes equal to the costs of an exchange in the open market or the costs of organizing in another firm'. While the use of outside markets involves costs, organizing transactions within firms also involves cost. Costs within the firm are affected by the *bounded rationality* of individuals which limits their effective span of control, information storage and processing abilities (Simon, 1961). Among other things, bounded rationality may allow opportunism to flourish, that is, provide considerable scope for individuals to pursue their own self-interest within an organization at the expense of the organization's collective goals. Williamson (1975) claims that such factors have important implications for the most efficient way to organize a firm as it grows in size.

Williamson (1975) argues that the larger a firm becomes the more likely it is to find it an economic advantage to organize itself in a multidivisional form (*M*-form) rather than in a unitary form (*U*-form). Williamson points out that large and often single-product enterprises organized along functional lines emerged in the later 1800s in the Western world. The principal operating units in such *U*-form firms are the functional divisions – sales, finance, manufacturing.

> Specialization by function not only was then, but, in organizations of only moderate size at least, is now the 'natural' way by which to organize multifunctional activities. ... Specialization by function permits both economies of scale and an efficient division of labor to be realized. (Williamson, 1975, p. 133)

However, with expansion in the size of the *U*-form enterprise (1) 'control loss' increases and reduces internal efficiency, and (2) strategic decision making alters because participants increasingly favour their own sub-goals at the expense of the firm's overall goal. The administrative load on top executives increases and it becomes difficult for them to operate effectively. They have reduced time available for strategic planning. Opportunism and information compactedness become significant. Managers may perceive that stresses in the U-form provide greater opportunities for discretion and permissive attitudes towards slack may develop.

Given the problems associated with the centralized U-form, companies such as the Du Pont Company and General Motors in the United States introduced multidivisional (or M-form) organizational structures once their size increased. This involved 'substituting quasiautonomous operating divisions (organized mainly along product, brand, or geographic lines) for the functional divisions of the U-form structure as the principal basis for dividing up the task and assigning responsibility' (Williamson, 1975). Of course, operation divisions themselves might be internally organized on functional lines.

Williamson (1975) claims that this administrative change to an M-form organization is more significant than might appear to be so at first sight. It decentralizes decision making and makes it possible for the general office of the firm (the peak coordinator's office) to concentrate on strategic decision making. This office may also play an important role in distributing capital most efficiently within the organization.

It has been suggested that divisions in multidivisional firms should be encouraged to maximize their profits independently either on the basis of market prices or optimal transfer prices which take account of the market transaction costs (Hirshleifer, 1956; Gould, 1964; Naert and Janssen, 1971). Let us consider this by taking a firm which could potentially be vertically integrated and has two divisions. Division A, the primary division, produces an intermediate product used by Division B, the secondary division, to produce a finished product. However, suppose also that an outside market exists for the intermediate product.

In the absence of market transaction costs and assuming that the firm does not influence market prices for the intermediate product, the firm maximizes its overall profit by each division maximizing its profit on the basis of the market prices for the intermediate product. As illustrated in Figure 16.4, this means that the secondary division would purchase the intermediate product, X, to some extent from outside the company if the market price of the intermediate product is less than the value for which the marginal cost of production by the primary division equals the secondary division's net marginal revenue from use of the input. On the other hand, if this market price of X is above the intersection point, E, of the line marked NMR and that marked MC, then the primary division sells on the outside market. For example, in Figure 16.4, if the market price of the input is OA, the primary division produces x_1 of the intermediate product which it may sell to the secondary division or on the outside market. The secondary division finds it optimal to use x_3 of the input and of this quantity at least $x_3 - x_1$ is obtained on the outside market. Alternatively, in Figure 16.4, if OD is the market price of X the primary division sells at least some of its output (at least, $x_4 - x_2$) to the outside market and the secondary division uses x_2 of the intermediate product. In this case, optimal transfer prices are market prices and the management problem of the multidivisional firm is simple. But this is not so when market transaction costs are present.

Figure 16.4 In the absence of market transaction costs (and internal market failure), a multidivisional firm maximizes its profit by adopting transfer prices equal to market prices

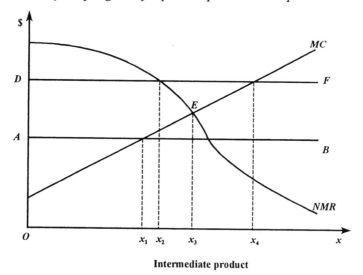

Intermediate product

TRANSFER PRICING AND MARKET TRANSACTION COSTS

When market transaction costs are important, the optimal transfer price within a multidivisional company depends on the level of market transaction costs. Market transaction costs cause the effective price received by a seller of a commodity to diverge from the effective price paid by a buyer even when all traders are price takers. The price

effectively paid by a buyer will be in excess of that effectively received
by the seller and the spread represents total market transaction costs.

*Figure 16.5 A case in which a multidimensional firm finds that it does
not pay to trade its intermediate product on the outside
market due to the existence of market transaction costs;
imputed profits based on optimal transfer prices
underestimate the value of both divisions to the firm*

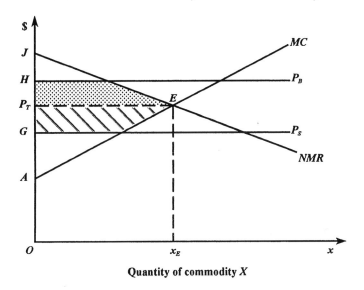

Quantity of commodity X

In the type of firm under consideration, market transaction costs may be
such that optimally (a) no external trading takes place by any of the
divisions or (b) only the secondary division trades in the outside market
or (c) only the primary division trades in the outside market in the
intermediate product.   In Figure 16.5, let P_B represent the effective
buying price of the intermediate product, X, as far as the secondary
division is concerned and let P_S represent the effective selling price
obtainable by the primary division if it sells its product X on the outside
market.   Also let E represent the value for which the net marginal
revenue of the secondary division from using input X equals the
marginal cost to the primary division of producing X.   It corresponds to
the intersection point of the lines identified by *NMR* and *MC* in Figure
16.5.

If $P_B > E$ and if $P_S < E$, it does not pay the company to trade X on
the outside market.   The optimal transfer price of X corresponds to E.
We shall call this the straddle case.   This is illustrated in Figure 16.5

where the optimal transfer price is indicated by P_T. In this case, the primary division should produce x_E and supply this at price P_T to the secondary division. A profit equal to the area of $\triangle AEP_T$ is then imputed to the primary division and a profit equal to the area of $\triangle P_T EJ$ is imputed to the secondary division. Figure 16.6 illustrates the situation where the appropriate transfer price is P_S, the price that would be effectively received by the seller of X, and Figure 16.7 illustrates the case where the optimal transfer price is that effectively paid by a buyer of X, that is P_B. In the case in Figure 16.6, the primary division sells $x_2 - x_1$ on the outside market and supplies x_1 to the secondary division. In the case shown in Figure 16.7, the primary division supplies x_3 of X to the secondary division which also buys $x_4 - x_3$ of X on the outside market.

Figure 16.6 Case in which the primary division of an M-form firm producing intermediate product, X, finds it optimal to sell some of its product on the outside market; in this case, due to the presence of market transaction costs, the value of the primary division to the firm is underestimated by its imputed profit based on the optimal transfer price

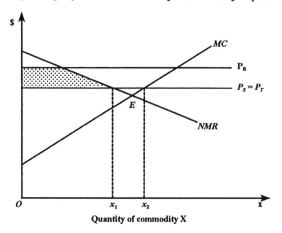

Quantity of commodity X

Note that imputed profit using transfer prices underestimates the value to the company of its divisions. In the 'straddle case' (Figure 16.5) the value of both divisions is underestimated. Although profits equal to the area of triangle $P_T EJ$ are imputed to the secondary division an additional amount of profit equal to the hatched area depends on the existence of the secondary unit. Similarly an extra amount of profit (to that imputed to the primary division) shown by the dotted area depends on the existence of the primary division. If the fixed costs of one of the divisions just exceeded its imputed (operating) profits, this would not be a sufficient case for closing it down. Thus, the central office of the firm has to be very careful in using imputed profit to guide it in decisions about whether or not to close down a division or dispose of it.

In the type of situation illustrated in Figure 16.6, the case where the global profit of the firm is maximized by the primary division selling X to some extent on the outside market, imputed (operating) profit *underestimates the value of the primary division* by the dotted area. Imputed (operating) profit *underestimates the value of secondary division* by the hatched area when the type of situation illustrated in Figure 16.7 applies, that is, the case where the global profit of the firm is maximized by the secondary division purchasing X to some extent on the outside market.

Figure 16.7 Case where the secondary division of an M-form firm finds it optimal to purchase some of the intermediate product, X, on the outside market; in this case, the value of secondary division to the firm is underestimated by the imputed profit based on optimal transfer price because of the presence of market transaction costs

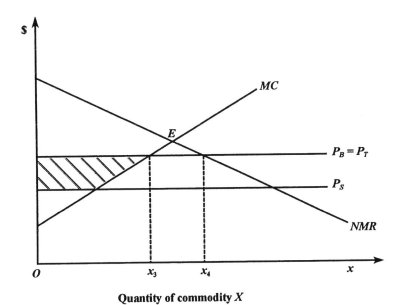

Quantity of commodity X

The amount of information required to determine optimal transfer prices in the types of situation illustrated in Figures 16.6 and 16.7 seems to be small. However, more information is required in the straddle case illustrated by Figure 16.5. In principle, the internal market equilibrium might be found by trial and error along similar lines to that suggested by Lange (1938) and Taylor (1938) in another context. However, one difficulty that can arise is that one of the divisions may engage in strategic behaviour designed to raise its imputed profit. For example, the primary division may withhold some supplies at a P_T (transfer price) value equal to E to force up the transfer price and take advantage of its monopoly position in relation to the secondary division.

There is the further possible problem in that the appropriate value of the transfer price, P_T, may change over time as cost and demand conditions alter. This may mean that peak coordinators or managers of a multidivisional firm will have considerable difficulty in predicting optimal transfer prices. Furthermore, transfer pricing being an internal market method of management, is subject to many of the types of market failure identified in standard microeconomic theory (see, for instance, Tisdell, 1982, Sections 13.3 and 13.4; Koopmans, 1957). For example, externalities may exist between divisions. Such effects are well known. Furthermore, as is discussed in the next section and as raised in Chapter 11 but considered in more detail here, a system of transfer prices can discourage innovation or technical progress within an organization.

TECHNICAL PROGRESS, INNOVATION AND TRANSFER PRICING

If bonuses are paid to divisional managers on the basis of the imputed profits of their division or if their performance is assessed on the basis of imputed profit of their division, this can retard innovation and the adoption of new technology which would be profitable for the firm as a whole. This can arise in the straddle case in which essential input, X, is not traded by the firm in the outside market. It can occur when the main impact of the innovation or technical change is either on marginal values of the primary divisions marginal cost or on marginal values of the secondary division's net marginal return. This can be illustrated by Figure 16.8 for an innovation by the primary division.

If the technology of the primary division initially is such that marginal costs are as indicated by line $AEMC_1$, the optimal transfer price is P_T. Should an innovation be possible that alters the marginal cost curve

from $AEMC_1$ to $ABMC_2$, the primary division's imputed profit is reduced by the difference between the dotted area and the hatched area in Figure 16.8 as the production of X expands from x_1 to x_2. The innovating division loses imputed profit and the secondary division gains imputed profit without innovating. Some types of shift in the marginal cost curve will of course raise imputed profits of the primary division, for example, a shift of the marginal cost curve to the right by a constant.
(See in another context, Duncan and Tisdell, 1971; Lindner and Jarrett, 1978).

Figure 16.8 A case in which the adoption of new technology by the primary division of an M-form firm results in an increase in the firm's global profit but reduces the imputed profit of the primary division when transfer pricing is used

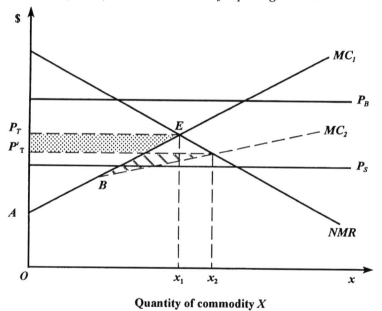

Quantity of commodity X

Similarly, innovation, or the adoption of new technology by the secondary division, need not increase its profit in the straddle case even when the global profit of the firm is raised by this. This is illustrated by Figure 16.9. A shift in the secondary division's net marginal revenue curve from that indicated by $FENMR_1$ to $FGNMR_2$, for example, reduces the imputed profit of the secondary division. Before the adoption of the new technology, which shifts the net marginal revenue productivity curve, the optimal transfer price is P_T but afterwards it is P'_T and use of input X rises from x_1 to x_2. Hence the secondary division's imputed profit falls by the difference between the hatched and the dotted area in Figure 16.9.

On the other hand, if the straddle case does not apply and the optimal transfer price either remains equal to P_B or to P_S the innovating division appropriates the full extra profit from its innovation or adoption of new technology. There is no disincentive to the innovation or adoption of

Figure 16.9 A case in which the adoption of new technology by the secondary division of an M-form firm results in an increase in the firm's global profit but reduces the imputed profit of the secondary division when transfer pricing is used

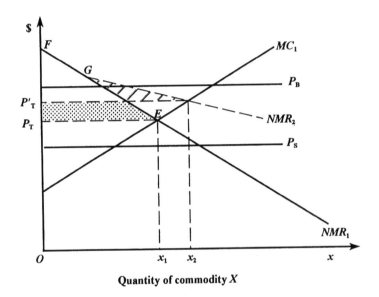

Quantity of commodity X

new technology. In effect, each division faces a perfectly elastic demand curve (or supply or factor curve) at the transfer price (within limits). This is, for example, illustrated in Figure 16.10. If the primary division's marginal cost curve is as indicated by MC_1 the optimal transfer price is $P_T = P_B$. Should an innovation alter the marginal cost curve to that indicated by MC_2 the optimal transfer price remains unchanged. However, the primary division's profit rises by the equivalent of the hatched area and it 'appropriates' all the profit from the new technology.

CONCLUDING COMMENTS

The existence of market transaction costs and the presence of internal transaction costs within firms has contributed to the emergence of multidivisional firms. The organizational structure of *M*-form firms results in decentralization of decision making within the firm. In various

Figure 16.10 A case in which the adoption of new technology by the primary division of an M-form firm increases the profit of the firm and of the division despite the existence of market transaction costs and the use of transfer pricing

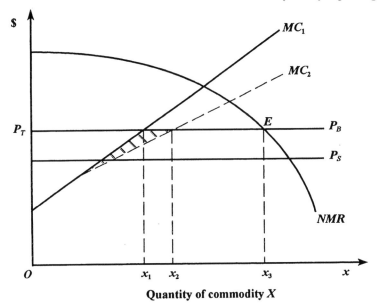

Quantity of commodity X

circumstances when market transaction costs are important, coordination and economic efficiency in an *M*-form can be achieved by the central managerial office of the firm adopting a system of transfer pricing and setting transfer prices so as to promote overall profit maximization by the firm. However, transfer pricing can encounter difficulties as a result of internal market failure. Furthermore, the imputed profits (losses) of divisions based upon optimal transfer prices are not always a satisfactory basis to determine whether or not to close down divisions. When market transaction costs are important, the imputed profit (loss) of a division based on optimal transfer prices may fail to measure the value of the division to the firm in terms of the division's contribution to the global profit of the firm.

In addition, it has been shown that the use of transfer pricing within a multidivisional firm can retard innovation and the adoption of new technology by divisions even when the adoption of the new technology would add to the global profit of the firm, and increase economic welfare generally. Even though static economic efficiency within the *M*-form firm can in various circumstances be achieved through transfer pricing, there is no guarantee that an optimal rate of technological progress will be achieved. Some central intervention may be needed to ensure this. Note also that the results have obvious implications for the economic optimality of decentralized socialist systems making use of transfer pricing (compare Lange, 1938; Taylor, 1938; Koopmans, 1957). While these might achieve optimality in economic allocation, there is no guarantee of them doing so in relation to technological change. On the other hand, there can, of course, be no guarantee that a centralized administrative system will promote an optimal pattern of technological progress.

In criticism of the above it might be argued that the problem concerning the distribution of gains from innovations advantageous to the global profit of a multidivisional company can be overcome by negotiation and bribes or side payments in the case where an innovating division would have a reduction in its imputed profit. The division(s) gaining could bribe the innovating division. This, however, may not occur because (i) of the bilateral monopoly aspect of the situation and the uncertainties and difficulties of negotiation and (ii) the central coordinating body controlling the firm· may not find side payments acceptable. If side payments could be costlessly arranged without risk and uncertainty, the innovation problem identified in this chapter would disappear. However, we should not underestimate the difficulties involved in obtaining Paretian optimality of maximization of collective gain even in the small numbers case (compare Tisdell, 1966, or see Chapter 8).

NOTES

1. For an edited translation of Max Weber's work, see Parsons (1947).

REFERENCES

Akerlof, G. (1970), 'The Market for Lemons: Quality Uncertainty and the Market Mechanism', *The Quarterley Journal of Economics*, 84, 488–500.

Alchian, A.A. and Demsetz, H. (1972), 'Production, Information Costs and Economic Organization', *American Economic Review*, 62, 777–95.

Cheung, S.N.S. (1969), 'Transaction Costs, Risk Aversion and the Choice of Contractual Arrangements', *Journal of Law and Economics*, 1(12), 23–42.

Coase, R.H. (1937), 'The Nature of the Firm', *Economica*, New Series 4, 386–405.

De Alessi, L. (1983), 'Property Rights, Transaction Costs and X-Efficiency: An Essay in Economic Theory', *American Economic Review*, 73, 64–81.

Demsetz, H. (1968), 'The Cost of Transacting', *Quarterly Journal of Economics*, 82, 33–53.

Duncan, R.C. and Tisdell, C.A. (1971), 'Research and Technical Progress – The Returns to Producers', *Economic Record*, 47, 124–9.

Galbraith, J.K. (1967), *The New Industrial State*, London: Hamish Hamilton.

Gould, J.R. (1964), 'Internal Pricing in Firms Where There Are Costs of Using an Outside Market', *Journal of Business*, 37, 61–7.

Hirshleifer, J. (1956), 'On the Economics of Transfer Pricing', *Journal of Business*, 29, 172–84.

Jones, S.R.H. (1982), 'The Organization of Work: A Historical Dimension', *Journal of Economic Behaviour* and Organization, 3, 117–37.

Jones, S.R.H. (1983), 'Technology and the Organization of Work: A Reply', *Journal of Economic Behaviour and Organization*, 4, 63–6.

Koopmans, T.J. (1957), *Three Essays on the State of Economic Science*, New York: McGraw-Hill.

Lange, O. (1938), 'The Guidance of Production in a Socialist State', in Lippincott, B. (ed.), *On the Economic Theory of Socialism*, Minneapolis: The University of Minnesota Press, 41–54.

Linder, R.K. and Jarrett, F.G. (1978), 'Supply Shifts and the Size of Research Benefits', *American Journal of Agricultural Economics*, 60, 48–58.

Mansfield, E. (1994), *Microeconomics: Theory and Applications*, 8th edn, New York: Norton.

Naert, P.A. and Janssen, C.T.L. (1971), 'On Suboptimization in Decomposition Approaches to Transfer Pricing', *Journal of Industrial Economics*, 3(19), 220–30.

Parsons, T. (1947), *Theory of Social and Economic Organization*, New York: Free Press.

Simon, H. (1961), *Administrative Behaviour: A Study of Decision-Making Processes in Administrative Organization*, New York: The Macmillan Company.

Taylor, F.M. (1938), 'On the Economic Theory of Socialism', in Lippincott, B. (ed.), *On the Economic Theory of Socialism*, Minneapolis: University of Minnesota Press, 55–142.

Tisdell, C.A. (1966), 'Some Bounds upon the Pareto Optimality of Group Behaviour', *Kyklos*, 19, 81–105.

Tisdell, C.A. (1982), *Microeconomics of Markets*, Brisbane: John Wiley.

Varian, H. (1993), *Intermediate Microeconomics: A Modern Approach*, 3rd edn, New York: Norton.

Williamson, O.E. (1975), *Markets and Hierarchies: Analysis and Antitrust Implications*, New York: The Free Press.

Williamson, O.E. (1979), 'Transaction-cost Economics: The Governance of Contractual Relations', *Journal of Law and Economics*, 12, 233–62.

Williamson, O.E. (1982), 'The Organization of Work', *Journal of Economic Behaviour and Organization*, 35–8.

Williamson, O.E. (1983), 'Technology and the Organization of Work: A Reply to Jones', *Journal of Economic Behaviour and Organization*, 4(1), 57–62.

17. Incomplete Markets for Science, Technology and Knowhow: Problems Raised by Transaction Costs and Policy Implications

Market transaction costs were discussed in some detail in the previous chapter. This chapter pays particular attention to their influence on the supply and exchange of science, technology and knowhow. Such supply and exchange is extremely important for the development of modern economies and for the survival and growth of many industries, as has been emphasized by Schumpeter (1942). But even if problems associated with technological and scientific spillovers or externalities are ignored, market transaction costs make it impossible to establish perfect markets for science, technology and knowhow. At least, there is no apparent economic method of establishing such complete and perfect markets in reality.

Significant limits to market-making and to the economic provision of private property rights exist (particularly in relation to science, technology and knowhow) because of the presence of transaction costs. The appropriate form of property ownership is primarily determined by economic factors. As will be illustrated for product and for cost innovations, market transaction costs lead to significant economic welfare losses as a rule both when marketing takes place and when it does not. Market transaction costs are usually very high for trade in science, technology and knowhow. The presence of asymmetric information leads to market failure in information markets and signalling of information, rather than increasing economic efficiency, may reduce it. An example is given in which the competitive contracting out of research adds to inefficiency in resource use because signalling by researchers or consultants does not result in a separating equilibrium. Increased market-making and specialization need not overcome such difficulties and may result in economic loss if pursued at length. Size of market (or of an economy), size of firms and economies of scope have implications for the supply of knowhow and its marketing. For example, because of the nature of market transaction costs it may, as is illustrated, be uneconomic to market knowhow in an industry consisting of many small firms. However, if symbiotic institutional arrangements between large and small firms are fostered, some of these problems may be overcome. Problems faced by small economies in marketing knowhow are given particular attention. Furthermore, doubts are expressed about the economic wisdom of existing 'competitive' mechanisms for allocating academic research funds because they add significantly to transaction costs and may encourage socially inefficient signalling, with the consequence that the mediocre tend to drive out the gifted.

SOME BACKGROUND LITERATURE – MARKET FAILURE, PROPERTY RIGHTS AND TRANSACTION COSTS

Pioneering theories of market failure (Pigou, 1938) left the way open for considerable government intervention, and in the past the economic analysis of science and technology policy has mostly relied on the established body of economic theory dealing with market failure (compare Bator, 1957 and Tisdell, 1981). This theory ignored transaction costs. But since Coase (1937), a strong body of economic theory has developed (and possibly has become dominant since the early 1970s) to take account of transaction costs and the importance of property rights. The older theory (Pigou, 1938, and more recently, Mishan, 1981) has been associated with those economists favouring some direct public intervention in resource allocation to counteract market failure, whereas the newer theory is associated with those favouring deregulation, improvements in and extension of conditions for market operation and for voluntary exchange – an approach identified with the 'Chicago School'. The latter approach takes the optimistic view that if institutional conditions for the operation of markets are sufficiently improved, either market failures may disappear or be reduced to such an extent that no direct public intervention can be justified on economic grounds. Consequently, until recently, those looking at technology policy tended to take a Coasian approach and to press for market-making as the correct efficiency promoting device. Here, I argue that this is often not an appropriate policy. It is shown that when due account is taken of transaction costs and the different types of firms and markets for products, the making of markets is not necessarily as efficient as some writers suggest.

Mishan (1981, p. 403) says that 'the term transaction costs is a fairly generic term that has been much used in the literature since about 1960 to include all costs incurred in negotiating terms or in discovering, correcting or defending any change in economic organisation, particularly a change towards an optimal position'. In the absence of transaction costs, most market failures would not exist. For instance, Mishan (1981, p. 380) points out that externalities (an important consideration in science and technology policy) would be optimally corrected or 'internalized' into the economy in the absence of transaction costs.

Transaction costs exist both within organizations and in their dealing with the outside world, including their dealings with the outside world through markets (see Chapters 11 and 16; Williamson, 1975). Indeed, Coase (1937) suggested that market transaction costs largely explain the existence of firms and that the optimal size of the firms might be determined by optimally balancing the cost of transacting within the firm with that of using outside markets.

In the real world, transaction costs exist and give rise to traditional market failures, such as externalities, and to administrative failures. For this reason, market failures and administrative failures remain of interest (compare Mishan, 1981, p. 403). On economic-efficiency grounds (if the Kaldor–Hicks or Pareto potential improvement criterion is adopted) market failure (and/or voluntary exchange failure) is a necessary but not sufficient condition for government intervention, because the costs involved in the remedy itself must also be taken into account. This is so for science and technology policy as well as for other policies.

Those economists who are influenced by the Pigovian tradition usually see externalities as an important source of market failure and believe that on the whole significant favourable externalities arise from research and development (R & D) effort which will be undersupplied in a free market situation. They have generally argued that a government subsidy is likely to be justified for R & D effort because of the presence of favourable externalities (Nelson, 1959; Tisdell, 1971, 1973). In addition, they often claim that other sources of market failure (Tisdell, 1981, p. 4), such as the comparatively high levels of risk or uncertainty associated with R & D (Arrow, 1962) provide grounds for government intervention in the economy in support of R & D. In general, the 'Pigovian group' favours positive government support for R & D.

More recently some economists of a pro-conservationist persuasion, such as Pearce et al. (1989), have by implication given their support to knowledge creation as a meritorious activity. Pearce et al. (1989) have argued that at this historical stage of development on the planet, the existing natural environmental stock should as a rule be held constant. (See discussions by Arndt, 1993, Chapter 24; Tisdell, 1993a, Chapter 8.)

However, in certain special circumstances some depletion in this stock might be allowed, for example if it would result in knowledge expansion of an acceptable type. Thus investment in R & D may be encouraged (at least in some circumstances) as an acceptable substitute for conserving the natural environment.

Needless to say neither of these policy approaches is acceptable to those with an anti-interventionist point of view, popularly associated with the Chicago School of Economics. Non-interventionists usually argue that (1) sources of market failure are exaggerated by the Pigovians; (2) government failure occurs and is likely to be much worse than market failure; and (3) if any sources of market failure exist, this is because in most cases the government has created impediments to markets or has not promoted institutions supportive of market-making. Government laws may hamper the operation of markets or the government may fail to establish an appropriate institutional framework for the operation of markets or voluntary exchange. For example, private property rights may not be clearly established. Some Chicago economists put great faith in the ability of private property creation to create perfect or near perfect markets or ideal conditions for voluntary exchange (Coase, 1960). This view influences not only environmental policy but also science and technology policy.

One of the problems that the neoclassical market-making school has encountered in recent times is that market transaction costs are significant. How can these be integrated into theory so as to be compatible with the free trade position of this school? This has been an especially felt need because Coase (1937, 1960, 1988) has contributed to both lines of development of economic thought. He has contributed to the idea that market and other transaction costs are important (Coase, 1937) and the view that voluntary exchange can be a powerful force for economic efficiency if private property rights are clearly established (Coase, 1960). In general, pro-marketeers argue that while market transaction costs exist, they would be very much smaller if government was smaller and more supportive in terms of the law and institutional arrangements of private property and markets. The science policy implication of this view is that in general government should not support research and development to any great extent but further extend systems of private property rights to intellectual knowledge. Furthermore, the government should reduce the transaction costs involved in the registering and enforcement of these rights and institute reforms to reduce the cost of exchanging or trading in such knowledge. In those circumstances, very little or no government support for R & D is needed according to this viewpoint.

The applicability of this argument, however, depends upon the economic practicality of establishing and enforcing private property rights. As North

(1981), of Chicago University but not belonging to the market-making group, points out, the optimality of creating private property rights is largely an economic matter. It depends upon the benefits and costs of establishing and of enforcing such rights which often alter in an historical context, for example because of changes in demand or in available technology. Indeed, on the basis of this view, 'forced' creation of private property by governments can be uneconomic or unworkable depending upon the historical stage reached. North (1981) and Demsetz (1967, p. 350) claim that in general societies develop appropriate institutional arrangements for the ownership of property as they evolve.   This intellectual position in many ways is more *laissez-faire* than that of market-making economists. As for markets for intellectual knowledge, North's view suggests that when and if it is economic for markets to develop for the supply and exchange of such knowledge, they usually will do so, and in those cases where markets do not exist, it is highly probable that this is because private property rights and markets are uneconomic (compare Field, 1986).

In opposition to this view, market-makers argue that the difficulties of creating markets are exaggerated. Technological change can greatly reduce the cost of exclusion and reduce market transaction costs to very low levels. However, in most cases these forces are thwarted by government attitudes and restrictions on trade and failure of the government to confer and define private property rights clearly (Furubotn and Pejovich, 1972, p. 134) and to provide efficient legal mechanisms for the protection of such rights. Therefore, an important part of the pro-market agenda is to search for means of reducing market transaction costs, as well as reducing the costs of conferring and protecting private property rights.

In relation to research and development, market-makers will tend to favour creation of private property rights such as those conferred by patents, copyright and trade marks. From a policy perspective they are likely to concentrate on ways to reduce the costs of obtaining these rights (for example, by the introduction of systems of petty patents), the period for which the property rights should be conferred, whether the costs of enforcing rights can be lowered and the ways in which trading using these rights can be improved. In addition, they are likely to search for ways to extend intellectual private property rights, for example, to rights in new varieties of plants or, in relation to biological conservation, the establishment of private property rights in genetic material.

Market transaction costs can take many forms, some of which have been detailed in Tisdell (1990) and in Chapter 16. Casson (1982) has developed a useful list of factors which may contribute to market transaction costs and (as is argued later) are important for trade in knowhow. Furthermore,

Teece (1977) and other authors have established that these costs are empirically substantial when it comes to technology transfer.

WELFARE LOSSES IN TECHNOLOGY TRADING DUE TO MARKET TRANSACTION COSTS

Let us analyse the magnitude of economic welfare forgone as a result of such costs in relation to trade in science and technology.[1] Take the case of a purely competitive industry and suppose that each market transaction involves a cost of a. This market transaction cost includes both that of the buyer and the seller. Particularly in the case of technology transfer, both parties incur substantial costs for the transfer process alone. Suppose for simplicity that the knowhow to be transferred is essential to the production of a product X for which each firm in the industry can produce one unit (has an optimal unique scale of one unit) but that increasing costs are present in the industry in the sense that some firms have higher costs of production than others. Thus in a one-period model (like that illustrated by Figure 16.1), equilibrium supply of X depends on demand for X and the transfer of knowhow for its production to producers. The knowledge concerned is assumed to be in the public domain but this does not mean that the exchange of it is costless.

Let $f(X)$, where X is the quantity supplied of product X, represent the supply curve for industry X in the absence of market transaction costs and let $h(X)$ represent the market demand curve for X. Both functions are assumed to be normal. Suppose that the market equilibrium occurs for $X = X_1$. However, because the transfer of knowledge involves costs, transaction costs result in a supply curve not of $f(X)$ but one of $a + f(X)$ if a is the cost of transferring knowhow to each firm. A market equilibrium supply of $X = X_0$ is assumed to result which is less than X_1 given that $a > 0$. Consequently, transaction costs result in an economic welfare loss (potential economic welfare forgone) of $aX_0 + \int_{X_0}^{X_1} [f(X)dX - h(X)dX]$. If the demand and supply curves are linear, this welfare loss becomes $aX_0 + 0.5a(X_1 - X_0)$. This is an application of the case illustrated by Figure 16.1 and the surrounding discussion.

From the above, it can be seen that the total welfare loss consists of an 'economic loss' on the transactions undertaken due to their transactions costs plus a loss stemming from those transactions which are not economic and not completed because of the presence of transaction costs. Clearly the total welfare loss involved as a result of technology transfer costs will increase, other things equal, with the level of per-unit transaction costs, with the size of the market and with the size of the stemming loss. The last mentioned loss will usually be greater the more elastic are the supply and demand curves for the product. However, this assumes that per-unit transaction costs are independent of the market size. They may in some markets or exchange situations decline with volume for reasons mentioned by Casson (1982). Therefore, if $g(X)$ represents transaction costs per transaction, $g(X)$ may not be a constant but a declining function of X. Nevertheless, transaction costs are likely to involve large economic welfare loss because they are incurred on all transactions, not just at the margin. Thus, these economic welfare losses are likely to be much greater than those arising from static allocative economic inefficiency.

To take another example, assume that the relevant knowhow is not in the public domain. Suppose that an inventor has a patent on a product which provides him or her with an absolute monopoly but that his or her expertise in producing and marketing the product is such as to make it relatively uneconomic for him or her to do so. The optimal policy of the inventor is to license his or her invention. Suppose that a large group of producers are able to produce the product at a cost of a per unit using the invention and consider the economics of licensing its use. While some simple mathematics is used to explain this case, note that it is also easy to illustrate diagrammatically.

The patent-holder in the absence of transaction costs will be able to exploit fully his or her monopoly position. Where $h(X)$ is the market demand curve for the product, the patent-holder will wish to determine his or her licence fees so that the quantity of the product produced in the industry equates marginal cost, a, to marginal revenue. Let this occur for $X = X_1$. Consequently, the optimal licence fee per unit of production from the inventor's point of view would be $h(X_1) - a$.

However, monitoring and other transaction costs can be expected to occur in the collection of licence fees. Assume for simplicity that these are b per unit of production. Because b is positive, there is likely to be a significant loss of economic welfare. In the new situation, the patent-holder will need to adjust his or her licence fee so that $a + b$ (marginal production costs plus marginal transaction costs) equals the marginal revenue from production. This will occur for a level of output say of X_0 which is less than X_1. The licence fee will rise and the price of the final product will increase with a consequent reduction in consumer's surplus because of the presence of transaction costs. In addition, the patent-holder's royalty income will decline, and especially so after deduction of transaction costs. Thus a considerable reduction in economic welfare occurs compared to a situation in which transaction costs are of no significance. The loss in total economic welfare will tend to be greater the more inelastic is the demand curve for the product and the higher are per-unit transaction costs.

Both of these theoretical examples underline the likely importance of market and exchange transaction costs from an economic welfare point of view. Let us now consider factors which are likely to influence the level of these costs, particularly in relation to the exchange of knowhow.

INFLUENCES ON MARKET TRANSACTION COSTS AND THEIR RELEVANCE TO TRANSFER OF KNOWHOW

Casson (1982) has identified the following factors as being important generally in raising market transaction costs:

1. Small numbers of potential buyers and/or sellers – this may add to negotiation costs.
2. Novelty of the product – this makes for limited knowledge by buyers.
3. Complexity of the product's functions – this may limit knowledge of buyers.
4. Difficulty of inspecting for quality before use – this limits knowledge of buyers.
5. Lag in evaluating performance after use – this reduces opportunities to take advantage of limited warranties.
6. Difficulty of metering or monitoring – this results in asymmetric information and provides scope for dishonesty and cheating.

Most of these factors are important in the marketing of knowhow, especially for the marketing of unpatented knowhow. Consider the relevance of each of these.

Often there are a few potential buyers and sellers of new technology. Where a new technology or product is patented there may be only one seller. Furthermore, some technologies can only be used in particular industries and then only by firms with the necessary complementary skills and so this can limit potential buyers, especially if the technology is being transferred to a small economy.

Much new technology is relatively novel to potential buyers and some types are extremely complex. Inspection prior to sale is a problem for transfer of much knowhow because in the process of inspection the knowledge can be revealed to the potential buyer. Once the potential buyer has this knowledge, the prospective buyer may no longer be prepared to pay for the knowledge and could use it without payment. So market failure occurs. Learning to use new technology can take a long time. Therefore, warranties need to be exceptionally long to overcome problems arising from asymmetry of information and buyers of new technology tend to become locked into its use and costs associated with this. Hence, asset specifity becomes a problem.

In addition, sellers of knowhow can have difficulties in metering and monitoring its use. This, for example, is relevant if the licence or royalty fee is based on the amount of use of the knowhow. It may be difficult for sellers to enter the premises of users of their technology and meter the volume of production and sales which buyers are obtaining by using the knowhow transferred. Even without such complications, the costs of transferring technology are high because of the bounded abilities of human beings to comprehend complex, and novel relationships and in most cases, learning by doing and trial and error are required in the process of technology transfer.

The costs of selling or exchanging technology or knowhow can in practice be very high as indicated, for example, by empirical studies of international technology transfer (see for example Teece, 1977 and Dosi, 1988, p. 1133). As pointed out by Welch (1983), the costs and amount of time required to transfer technology are much greater than is usually realized because continuing direct contact and commitment on the part of the originator are frequently required for its transfer (Welch, 1983). Quite often these costs are so high that licensing of the knowhow does not occur. Knowhow may be kept secret and not exchanged or it may be exchanged or transferred by non-market means (Tisdell, 1993b, Chapter 4).

A major problem in the exchange of science and technology is asymmetry of information. As pointed out by Dunning and McQueen (1982, pp. 81–2), new technology and knowhow can often be classified as 'experience' rather than search goods. If potential buyers are able to inspect the new technology or knowhow thoroughly it may become known to them to a significant degree. Consequently, the knowledge revealed by inspection may be used to replicate the technology and it may not be purchased from the prospective vendor. Inspection subjects the vendor to moral hazard. Nevertheless, even extensive inspection in some cases is inadequate to reveal all relevant information needed to make successful use of the technology. Sometimes, this information will only be obtained once the buyer has purchased the technology and had experience with it for some time.

As in the well known 'plums and lemons' example (Akerlof, 1970; Varian, 1993), the sets of information of parties to the potential transactions are asymmetric, with sellers of the technology usually having much better knowledge about it than buyers. Consequently, if there is more than one potential seller of technology, it is possible for those providing inferior technological or knowhow packages to drive out the superior one. Thus market failure occurs along the same lines as that considered theoretically for the used-car market by Akerlof (1970). Economic welfare is reduced by the bad driving out the good. Indeed, the problem of buyers not being able to identify accurately the quality of the good which is being considered for purchase, may result in the complete collapse of a market (the bad not only drives out the good but also the bad) when the existence of a market would be in the social interest (Varian, 1993, Section 34.2). In the present context, no trade in the relevant knowhow may occur even though a Paretian improvement could be achieved through trade in quality knowhow 'packages'.

It should also be noted that many contracts or agreements for the supply of knowhow are inevitably incomplete in their specifications. Usually the provider of knowhow has scope for opportunistic behaviour. Thus a considerable amount of trust and goodwill is needed to ensure the functioning of such markets. In practice, potential traders may only be able to establish their credentials over a long period of time.

While signalling might be used to overcome some of the information problems indicated above, it does not always result in a separating equilibrium (Varian, 1993, p. 612) and the type of signalling used is not always efficient from a resource-use point of view. For example, in relation to contract research, signals may fail to distinguish between poor and good performers or do so to only a limited extent. Consequently, the cost of the signalling may exceed the extra economic benefits obtainable from increased discrimination available as a result of the signals.[2]

Take an example of the above. Assume that applications are to be called for contract research for which a flat fee is payable and suppose if given the contract all potential contractors could make equal profit from it, G. Whether or not an individual tenderer gets the contract may depend upon the strength of his or her signal relative to others. Suppose that two signals are available, a weak signal involving virtually no cost and a strong signal costing k to each individual using it. Furthermore, imagine that those using the strong signal will always be preferred to those using the weak signal. Selection is made only among those using the strong signal. So it will always be used in the competitive situation by those who tender or bid.

When x represents the number of strongly presented bids made for a research or consulting contract the likelihood that a bidder obtains the contract is $1/x$. Therefore the expected profit or gain of the bidder is G/x. Given open access and a large pool of potential bidders, the number of bids in equilibrium will be such that $G/x = k$. It will be such that the expected gain of each bidder equals the cost of bidding, if we suppose expected net gain maximization motivates bidders. Any potential rent is dissipated by an increased number of bids in an analogous way to the open-access fisheries case. The number of bids received, therefore, will be $x = G/k$. The number of bids, x, will be greater in number the higher is the gain from the contract and the lower is the cost of making a bid. However, if the bidding system fails to distinguish between the able and the less competent, it involves wasteful transaction costs. A system which, for example, reduced the number of bidders would be more efficient.[3] It is important to search for cost-effective and relatively efficient screening devices when it comes to offering research or consulting contracts. Open-access bidding is usually not efficient. Note that the discussion in Chapter 13 suggests that this is likely to be true for a much wider range of supply of commodities than appears to be usually realized and for additional reasons to those adduced here.

Contracting out of research by government departments may encounter the above problem. Furthermore, it is possible that in some cases the bad drive out the good in contracting for research. Those able to provide superior consulting services may require a slightly higher price for this than inferior consultants. However, the party calling tenders may not be able to differentiate accurately between inferior and superior consultants and some of the inferior consultants may also charge the higher price. Consequently, as in the 'lemons' and the 'plums' case (Akerlof, 1970) the market fails, and only 'inferior' consultants may tender. Alternatively, it is possible that the tenderer can identify very poor consultants but cannot differentiate between those of moderate and superior ability. Consequently, those of moderate ability may drive out both those of superior and those of inferior ability. Hence, procedures for contracting out research can result in economic loss as a result of simulated market competition. This matter seems to have been overlooked in reform processes which have encouraged market-making or market simulation.

Casson (1982, pp. 31–2) makes the point that:

> economic efficiency calls for the specialisation of the resources used in market-making activities, and also for the specialisation of the bearing of market-making risks. However, specialisation is effected using markets, and the greater is the degree of specialisation the more markets are required. It must then be recognized that transaction costs will be incurred not only in the markets where the original obstacles to trade were encountered, but also in the markets for market-making services, and the markets for the allocation of market-making risk.

This indicates that no amount of market-making may be able to eliminate market transaction costs entirely and that 'excessive' market-making can be economically inefficient. Casson (1982, p. 32) states that specialization of market-making activities and markets for the bearing of risk should only be extended up to the point where the additional transaction costs incurred as a result of greater specialization equals savings in transaction costs achieved elsewhere. However, this rule is not always followed by government policy makers.

SIZE OF MARKETS, SIZE OF FIRMS, ECONOMIES OF SCOPE AND MARKET TRANSACTION COSTS

Casson's observations suggest that in larger markets and economies, market transaction costs per transaction are likely to be less than in smaller ones. In larger markets and economies, there is more scope for specialization in the provision of marketing services and economies of scale in making market transactions are likely to be available. Other things equal, this is likely to put smaller economies and markets at an economic disadvantage compared to larger ones. Trade in most commodities is likely to be affected, but more so for those commodities for which market transaction costs are a larger component of total costs, such as in the case of trade in science and technology.

This issue can be illustrated Figure 17.1. Suppose that the supply curve

Figure 17.1 Per-unit market transaction costs may be lower in larger markets and this may provide a competitive advantage to firms located in such markets

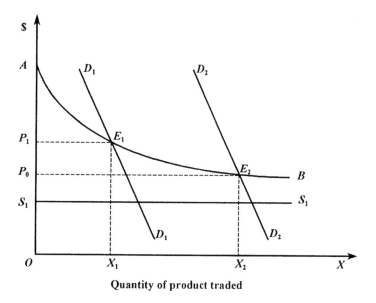

Quantity of product traded

of product X, ignoring market transaction costs, is as indicated by the line marked S_1S_1 in Figure 17.1 and that after market transaction costs are added it is as indicated by curve AE_1E_2B. If market demand is as shown by line D_1D_1, market equilibrium is achieved at E_1. However, if the market is larger and D_2D_2 represents the market demand curve, equilibrium is achieved at E_2. Hence, a larger market results in competitive advantage via economies in market transaction costs.

This market transaction element can be expected to affect international specialization in production and exchange. Larger and more central economies are likely to have a comparative cost advantage in the supply of commodities for which transaction costs are a relatively large component of total costs. Since this is especially likely to be so for intellectual property and knowhow, centre countries may be advantaged in the marketing or supply through exchange of these commodities. Thus even when intellectual knowledge is created in a small economy such as Australia, it may be marketed though a larger one, for example, the European Union.

In addition to the element of a small market, spatial factors are likely to influence market transaction costs. The greater the distance between buyers and sellers, the higher market transaction costs are likely to be. This may be expected for the following reasons:

1. Market transactions generally require communication between buyers and sellers and the greater the distances between them the higher normally are communication costs.
2. Particularly in the case of exchange of non-standard commodities, communication may be very important with inspection before final purchase or delivery by the buyer being essential. In the case of a standard commodity, this inspection may be more easily left to an agent.
3. Transport of the commodity being exchanged is usually higher the greater is the distance between the seller and the buyer.
4. After-sales advice or service may be a significant element in market transactions involving non-standard products, for example, those incorporating new technology and follow-up may be essential in the transfer of knowhow. Costs of providing these are likely to be raised if the distance of the seller from the buyer increases.
5. Sellers more distant from centre countries may find it more difficult and costly to access information networks (both formal and informal). These networks often play an important role in the sale of non-standard technologies or knowhow.

Small economies may be at a particular disadvantage in marketing and making use of their knowhow. Small countries, such as Australia and New Zealand, distant from major world markets face the following difficulties:

1. Relative lack of specialist agents able to assist in marketing knowhow (partially a result of their small markets).
2. Because of the small home markets of these countries, the commercial success of their new knowhow is likely to depend more heavily on their sales of it abroad than in the case of countries with a large home market. Transaction costs involved in selling to foreign markets may be substantially greater than at home. This problem is likely to be acute when a country has few multinational corporations capable of exploiting its knowhow abroad.[4] In that case, the alternative is one of direct export or licensing, both of which can involve considerable transaction costs.
3. Transaction costs can also be experienced by buyers. Transaction costs can be high for small and distant countries wishing to buy knowhow. For instance, they usually have relatively few observers or contact points abroad so it may be more difficult for them than for centrally located countries to find the optimal knowhow which they are seeking.

Consideration should also be given to the costs involved in protecting property rights in intellectual knowledge. These are likely to be much higher for the owner of such rights when he or she is distant from the region of use of the knowledge, which is likely to be the case when Australian intellectual knowledge is widely used in Europe and America, for example. This requires attention to be given not only to the costs of detecting infringement but also to the costs of enforcing rights, for instance, through the courts. In this respect, note that it is virtually impossible to determine whether some types of knowledge discovered by others have been used, for example, relatively abstract principles. This is one reason why these principles are not afforded patent protection.

Where an invention or method can be readily copied and replicated by many small and scattered firms for their own use, enforcement of patent rights may be unprofitable. This is so for a number of methods or techniques of production used by the farming community, and provides a reason for government intervention in research of value to agricultural industries.

The structure of markets and the size of firms within them clearly have an influence on market transaction costs for knowhow. In general, small firms appear to be at an economic disadvantage in marketing knowhow, and the marketing of knowhow in an industry consisting of many small firms is frequently uneconomic. The latter problem can be seen from the following example: suppose that each market transaction involving the sale of knowhow to a firm, consists of a fixed cost to the seller of $A irrespective of the size of the firm. Suppose that the potential benefits to firms in the industry as a whole are $B, that all sellers are of equal size and the benefits would be shared equally by them. Suppose further that there are n-firms in the industry. Clearly, transactions in knowhow will only occur if $A \leq B/n$. Or transactions will only occur if $n \leq B/A$. Thus if the benefit to sellers is 100 units (that is B = 100) and the cost of each transfer is 10, the number of firms must be less than or equal to 10 for technology transfer to be economic.

In practice, of course, the transaction costs of exchange of knowhow may involve fixed and variable costs. However, even in the case where a variable cost is involved, this may very well decline per unit as the quantity of use of knowhow transferred to each firm increases.

Small firms find it difficult to appropriate gains from new technology invented by them not only because of their difficulties in marketing knowhow, but also because they can obtain little comparative benefit by using it themselves, if their supply accounts for only a small share of the market. In other words, ability to appropriate gains from any knowledge advantage which a small firm temporarily acquires is limited by the small size of its market (Dosi, 1988, p. 1139).

Sizes of firms and market structure have important implications for the appropriation of benefits from R & D, and for incentives and motivation to perform R & D. Large firms in monopolistic market structures, and especially if they are multinational, have greater scope for appropriating gains from R&D than small firms in purely competitive industries.

Diversity of size of firms having some degree of economic interdependence can also have implications for exchange of knowledge. Such diversity can lead to symbiotic exchange of knowhow.[5]

Baumol et al. (1982) suggest that economies of scope can be important in the modern world. Economies of scope refer to a situation where economies are achieved not by increasing the scale of an activity but by increasing the range of activities undertaken. Economies of scope may, for instance, be achieved by carrying out diverse research activities or for, instance, by carrying out quality control plus research in the same laboratory.

Economies of scope, scale and transaction costs have practical consequences for relationships between small and large firms, as the research of Dr Tse (1985), in relation to Marks & Spencer, illustrates (see also Chapter 13). This British retailer is not just a shopkeeper or retailer but has a symbiotic relationship with its suppliers. Its policy is to carry out product research and analysis of market demand, and assist its suppliers to take advantage of this knowledge in supplying products. This has been of mutual advantage to it and to its suppliers, many of whom have been associated with Marks & Spencer for more than 50 years. As a result of this arrangement, small suppliers obtain appropriate market information and technological knowledge from Marks & Spencer. Given this relationship, practically all of the supplies of Marks & Spencer come from UK sources, which is surprising given the potential competition from abroad.

Scope for economic symbiosis between firms and for business cooperation exists in a diversity of fields, as far as information and knowhow are concerned. Opportunities for mutually valuable information and knowhow flows seem very likely:

1. from a large user (retailer, manufacturer and so on) to small suppliers of inputs, and
2. from large suppliers of inputs or products to small users of these.

Case (1) is beautifully illustrated by the (legal) Australian heroin poppy industry where two large users supply a substantial stream of new technology to approximately 600 farmers producing opium poppies.

Franchising arrangements may also provide for economies of promotion and research (see Chapter 13). The scope for symbiosis and business cooperation in relation to intellectual property and knowhow deserves more consideration. In fact, the new transaction cost theories point to the importance of arrangements such as those fostered by Marks & Spencer.

MISCELLANEOUS OBSERVATIONS ABOUT TRANSACTION COSTS AND SCIENCE AND TECHNOLOGY

It seems pertinent to make a couple of miscellaneous observations about transaction costs and science and technology. This author (Tisdell, 1989, 1990) has considered technological change in multidivisional firms faced by significant market transaction costs and in which management adopts transfer pricing as a management technique. Among other things, it was found that transfer pricing can deter managers of divisions from adopting new technology when the salaries of the managers of divisions are positively related to the imputed profits (based on transfer prices) of their divisions, even when the adoption of such technology will increase the overall profit of the firm (see also Chapters 11 and 16). In some cases, the adoption of new technology reduces the profit imputed to a division on the basis of the optimal transfer price but raises the profit of the firm as a whole. This comes about because the optimal transfer price may be reduced in certain cases when a division adopts new technology. As a result, there is a serious problem in relying entirely on transfer pricing as a management technique.

As suggested above, competitive contracting out of research may reduce rather than increase economic efficiency. There are reasons for doubting, for example, whether the contracting out of government research by the creation of markets is in fact always efficient. Similarly, one should seriously question whether procedures for allocating funds for academic research are economically efficient, for example, allocation of research funds to academics in Australia through the Australian Research Council, or in Britain through the Research Councils. There is a need to examine how effective the signals used (or elicited by the system) are in allocating funds and whether or not the transaction costs being imposed by competition are too high. There is a risk that if the costs involved in transmitting a relatively effective signal (application) become too high in relation to the probability of an award then the better researchers may withdraw from the race, since the opportunity cost of their time is high. The mediocre could push out the better researchers. Furthermore, the additional benefits in terms of status, income, and so on, to be obtained by more capable researchers (or a set of them) may be low relative to the less competent. For this reason, also, better researchers may refrain from bidding. Hence, in academic research there is a risk of the mediocre driving out the gifted in a bidding situation even though the incompetent may be rejected by the system. This suggests that a change in allocation mechanisms are needed if real merit is to be encouraged, for example, funding heavily related to past productivity with less emphasis on detailed applications for research funding. This is one of the mechanisms for funding available to academic researchers in the United States, for example.

Partha Dasgupta (1988, p. 6) has expressed a related point of view to mine. He says: 'The avenues along which basic knowledge grows are many and varied, and typically unpredictable. It is for this reason that one hears the argument that a part of the public subsidy for research should be earmarked for creative persons rather than projects. Creative persons can be relied upon to choose promising problems'. Dasgupta goes on to provide an example in which this policy has worked very well and argues that centralized mechanisms for choice of research projects are usually inefficient, especially in relation to basic research.

While it is not a major purpose of this chapter to discuss mechanisms of 'bidding' for Australian Research Council (ARC) grants and of evaluating methods of selection of successful applications, it is noted that in a recent evaluation of ARC grants for economics by Jarrett et al. (1993), little attention is given to the transaction costs involved in ARC applications and mechanisms to reduce these costs. Indeed, in the light of the above discussion, it is disappointing to read that one of their recommendations is 'the ARC continue to rely on peer group mechanisms rather than mechanical application of performance indicators until the reliability of the latter improves' (Jarrett et al., 1993, p. 62). The economic and academic advantage of peer-group selection mechanisms is far from apparent. Why are they superior to mechanisms relying on a combination of performance and peer-group selection? My predilection is towards putting greater weight on performance indicators as selection mechanisms for research awards and as means to reduce transaction costs.

There is also another intriguing element that would be worthy of further investigation. The Economics Review Panel rightly points out that a successful ARC application is regarded as a prestigious award (Jarrett et al., 1993, p. 8). A number of institutions are now subsidizing ARC applications because of this prestige element and because of the fact that an Australian university's quality ratings may be improved by the university obtaining more ARC grants, which in turn means more government funding for it. However, is such subsidization in the public interest, and meritorious from an economic point of view? This matter does not appear to have been addressed by the review panel. Future analysis of this could be worthwhile, making use of the modern economics of selection and signalling mechanisms (Varian, 1993, Chapter 34).

CONCLUDING COMMENTS

Transaction costs clearly play a major role in determining the supply of science, technology and knowhow as well as its exchange. This chapter indicates that it is a false hope to expect extension of property rights and more widespread market-making or market simulation to result invariably in economic efficiency or improvements in economic efficiency in the production and use of knowhow. Greater scrutiny is required of prescriptions or institutions which fail to appreciate the capacity of transaction costs for causing economic losses. Furthermore, the presence of bounded rationality and transaction costs strongly suggests the relevance of considering technological change and knowledge creation as evolutionary processes (Nelson, 1987; Dosi, 1988; Tisdell, 1994). This matter is taken up in the next chapter.

NOTES

1. Economic loss or economic welfare forgone is being measured here by the hypothetical loss in consumers' plus producers' surplus which would occur compared to a situation in which transaction costs are zero (see also Figure 15.1 and discussion of it). It may, of course, be impossible to reduce transaction costs to zero just as it may in many physical situations be impossible to reduce or eliminate friction. Nevertheless, the frictionless and no transaction costs limiting cases provide a valuable and definitive benchmark against which to compare possibilities. Traditional neoclassical theory has been based on the assumption of zero transaction costs. This limits its empirical relevance but still it remains important as a theoretical benchmark.
2. Solutions, or economical solutions, to the above problems are not always possible in a pure market context but call for institutional arrangements, many of which nevertheless still remain imperfect in the Kaldor–Hicks sense but which do lead to a Kaldo—Hicks improvement. Those selling technology may, for example, use guarantees as signalling devices. The value of these, however, depends on the credibility of the guarantor, the terms and conditions of the guarantee, the ability and willingness of the guarantor to pay compensation, and the degree of ease, cost and uncertainty involved in legal enforcement if this is required. Demonstration of the use of technology can send valuable signals but, as discussed in this chapter, it provides hazards for the vendor in that it may reveal the vendor's intellectual knowledge to a prospective purchaser and consequently the exclusion condition for marketing (involving transfer of property only on payment) may be violated. This condition helps to explain the prevalence of multinational corporations and the use of joint-venture arrangements (Tisdell, 1993b) in industries in which new technologies are important. Similar problems help to explain the prevalence of in-house research rather than the contracting out of research and development activity by business corporations (Teece, 1988). As for contract R & D or consulting, examples of previous reports, previous research results, academic qualifications and so on, may be used for signalling. If tenders are called for contract research, the field of those invited to tender may be limited by preconditions or only initial expressions of interest may be called for in the first instance. This is used as a way to reduce the numbers tendering with a view to reducing transaction costs. Reductions in transaction costs are likely to benefit both parties to exchanges.
3. Systems of tendering and selecting between tenders are not costless. As discussed in note 2, filtering systems which limit those allowed to tender or to provide a full tender can be economically desirable because they can reduce the transaction costs of the parties involved.
4. One of the many possible functions of multinational companies is to act as relatively efficient vehicles for the international transfer of technology. Very often they transfer their own technology but they may also acquire the technology of others and once they prove it in one country, transfer it internationally if it is successful. Both host and originating countries can benefit from this institutional process even though there are complex matters to be considered in assessing it (Tisdell, 1993b, Chapter 4). Multinational companies with their headquarters in Australia (such as BHP) may do much to assist the transfer of Australian technology abroad and the import of appropriate technology. The same may also be the case for multinationals with branches in Australia. Note also that companies originating in centre countries may find it easier to become multinational than those that originate in and retain their headquarters in peripheral economies.
5. The importance of symbiotic business relationships was discussed in Chapter 13. Note that the scope for fostering symbiotic business relationships (relationships which often depend heavily on close personal contacts) may as a rule be less in small distant economies than in larger centrally located ones. For example, the range and diversity of firms present in smaller economies may be less than in larger ones. Such factors may favour the growth of the economic centre at the expense of the periphery.

REFERENCES

Akerlof, G. (1970), 'The Market for Lemons: Quality Uncertainty and the Market Mechanism', *Quarterly Journal of Economics*, 84, 488–500.

Arndt, H.W. (1993), *50 Years of Development Studies*, The National Centre for Development Studies, Canberra: Australian National University.

Arrow, K.J. (1962), 'Economic Welfare and the Allocation of Resources for Invention', in Nelson, R.R. (ed.), *The Rate and Direction of Economic Welfare*, Princeton, New Jersey: Princeton University Press.

Bator, F.M. (1957), 'The Simple Analytics of Welfare Maximisation', *American Economic Review*, 47, 22–59.

Baumol, W.J., Panzer, J.C. and Willig, R.D. (1982), *Contestable Markets and Theory of Industry Structures*, New York: Harcourt, Brace & Jovanovich.

Casson, M.C. (1982), 'Transaction Costs and the Theory of the Multinational Enterprise', in Rugman, A. (ed.), *New Theories of the Multi-National Enterprise*, London: Croom Helm, 22–43.

Coase, R.H. (1937), 'The Nature of the Firm', *Economica*, New Series 4, 386–405.

Coase, R.H. (1960), 'The Problem of Social Cost', *The Journal of Law and Economics*, 3, 1–44.

Coase, R.H. (1988), *The Firm, the Market and the Law*, Chicago: University of Chicago Press.

Dasgupta, P. (1988), 'The Welfare Economics of Knowledge Production', *Oxford Review of Economic Policy*, 4(4), 1–12.

Demsetz, H. (1967), 'Towards a Theory of Property Rights', *American Economic Review*, 57, 347–59.

Dosi, G. (1988), 'Sources, Procedures and Microeconomic Effects of Innovation', *Journal of Economic Literature*, 26, 1120–71.

Dunning, J.H. and McQueen, M.L. (1982), 'The Eclectic Theory of Multinational Enterprise and the International Hotel Industry', in Rugman, A. (ed.), *New Theories of Multinational Enterprise*, London: Croom Helm, 79–106.

Field, B.C. (1986), 'Economic Development and Property Rights Institutions', mimeo, Department of Agricultural Economics and Resource Economics, Amhurst, Mass.: University of Massachusetts.

Furubotn, E.G. and Pejovich, S. (1972), 'Property Rights and Economic Theory: Survey of Recent Literature', *Journal of Economic Literature*, 10, 1137–62.

Jarrett, F., Shapiro, P. and Trevor, R. (1993), 'Report of a Panel to Review Australian Research Council Funding of Economics Research 1986–1990', in National Board of Employment, Education and Training, *Reviews of Grants Outcomes No. 1: Economics 1986–1990*, Canberra: Australian Government Publishing Service, 9–71.

Mishan, E.J. (1981), *Introduction to Normative Economics*, Oxford: Oxford University Press.

Nelson, R.R. (1959), 'The Simple Economics of Basic Research', *Journal of Political Economy*, 67, 297–306.

Nelson, R.R. (1987), *Understanding Technical Change as an Evolutionary Process*, Amsterdam: North-Holland.

North, D.C. (1981), *Structure and Change in Economic History*, New York: Norton.

Pearce, D., Markandya, A. and Babier, E.B. (1989), *Blueprint for a Green Economy*, London: Earthscan Publications.

Pigou, A.C. (1938), *Economics of Welfare*, 4th edn, London: Macmillan.

Schumpeter, J.A. (1942), *Capitalism, Socialism and Democracy*, 2nd edn, New York: Harper Brothers.

Teece, D. (1977), 'Technology Transfer by Multinational Firms: The Resource Cost of Transferring Technological Know-How', *Economic Journal*, 87, 242–61.

Teece, D. (1988), 'Technological Change and the Nature of the Firm', in Dosi, G., Freeman, C., Nelson, R., Silverberg, G. and Soete, L. (eds), *Technical Change and Economic Theory*, 256–81, London: Pinter.

Tisdell, C.A. (1971), 'Commonwealth Industrial Research and Development Grants – An Economic Evaluation', *Economic Analysis and Policy*, 2(2), 27–50.

Tisdell, C.A. (1973), 'The Australian Research Subsidy to Overseas Firms and Other Aspects of the Distribution of Research Grants', *Economic Record*, 49, 194–210.

Tisdell, C.A. (1981), *Science and Technology Policy: Priorities of Government*, London: Chapman & Hall.

Tisdell, C.A. (1989), 'Transfer Pricing: Technical and Productivity Change within the Firm', *Managerial and Decision Economics*, 10, 253–6.

Tisdell, C.A. (1990), 'Market Transaction Costs and Transfer Pricing: Consequences for the Firm and for Technical Change', *Revista Internazionale di Scienze e Commerciali*, 37, 203–18.

Tisdell, C.A. (1993a), *Environmental Economics*, Aldershot, UK: Edward Elgar.

Tisdell, C.A. (1993b), *Economic Development in the Context of China*, London: Macmillan.

Tisdell, C.A. (1994), 'Government Support for Research and Development and Evolutionary Economics: Economic Justification', in Australian National University and Bureau of Industry Economics, *1994 Conference of Industry Economics: Papers and Proceedings*, 58–81, Canberra: Australian Government Publishing Service.

Tse, K.K. (1985), *Marks & Spencer: Anatomy of Britain's Most Efficiently Managed Company*, Oxford: Pergamon Press.

Varian, H. (1993), *Intermediate Microeconomics: A Modern Approach*, 3rd edn, New York: Norton.

Welch, L.S. (1983), 'The Technology Transfer Process in Foreign Licensing Arrangements', in Macdonald, S., Lamberton, D. and Mandeville, T.D. (eds), *The Trouble with Technology: Explorations in the Process of Technological Change*, London: Pinter.

Williamson, O.E. (1975), *Markets and Hierarchies: Analysis and Antitrust Implications*, New York: The Free Press.

18. Science and Technology Policy, and Evolutionary Economics

INTRODUCTION

This chapter is based on the assumption that evolutionary factors play a large role in the process of innovation by firms. It is argued that taking account of differences in human capacities, limitations set by the organization of firms and the presence of bounded rationality, it is unlikely to be economic for all firms to strive to be technological leaders. Usually optimality requires different firms to fill different niches in an industry, especially in relation to technological change. This diversity of businesses within an industry can be economically optimal and it is possible for a diverse group of businesses in the same industry to co-exist in a changing world.

Technological progress has been identified as a major factor in economic growth, international trade and the improvement of economic welfare. Furthermore, the superior technologies of particular nations have been important factors in gaining and maintaining their international political dominance. It is, therefore, not surprising that nations have taken a considerable interest in whether and how the government should support R & D for the purpose of increasing national economic benefit.

Conventional market failure analysis has traditionally been used to provide an economic rationale for government intervention in and support of R & D effort. Basically, this involves application to policy of the type of welfare analysis developed by Marshall and Pigou and formalized in the Kaldor–Hicks welfare principle relying on the concept of a potential Pareto improvement. In recent years, these models have been modified by detailed consideration of transaction costs (for example, Williamson, 1986; Teece, 1977, 1988) and of property rights, that is, so-called neo-institutionalism factors. For the most part, these models are in the comparative static tradition. However, developments in 'new industrial economics' (for example, Dasgupta and Stiglitz, 1980) and in evolutionary economics have been designed to model the dynamic processes set in train by R & D, invention and innovation. The full implications of their developments for government R & D policy are still being worked out, and in particular the theories of evolutionary economics are still developing.

Rather than provide here an in-depth review of conventional equilibrium-type theories justifying government support of R & D, I shall merely recapitulate the main points of conventional analysis and concentrate on evolutionary economic analysis, the importance of encouraging diversity in R & D effort, and some other possible policy implications of evolutionary economics.

CONVENTIONAL ECONOMIC EQUILIBRIUM TYPE MODELLING AND GOVERNMENT SUPPORT OF R & D

Traditionally, as discussed in Tisdell (1981), the following three main market failure grounds for government intervention in R & D have been put forward:

1. *Favourable externalities* It is argued that those engaged in R & D capture only a (small) fraction of the economic benefits generated by their effort (Nelson, 1959). Thus R & D effort will tend to be undersupplied from a Kaldor–Hicks viewpoint and the degree of rectification involved will vary with the 'extent' of the favourable externality. This, however, all assumes that such externalities are significant in magnitude, that they are Pareto relevant (either actually or potentially in the Kaldor–Hicks sense, as discussed by Tisdell (1973, 1993a) and Walsh and Tisdell (1973)) and that government agency/transaction costs involved in intervention do not outweigh potential economic benefits from this.

2. *Risks and uncertainty* Because of its very nature, the outcomes of R & D effort are uncertain. Arrow (1962) argued that because of the prevalence of risk aversion, this factor is liable to lead to an undersupply of R & D effort. This uncertainty may evidence itself, for example, by an undersupply of funds for R & D from the capital market, especially non-equity capital. However, this failure can easily be exaggerated given the existence of companies, the scope for purchasing shares in companies involved in R & D and the general possibilities for spreading risk by diversification of portfolios of assets.

3. *The presence of non-marginal externalities and myopic mechanisms for economic change* The possibility of an economy which relies on gradualism and myopic mechanisms of adjustment failing to reach a 'global economic' optimum has long been recognized in the economic literature. The infant industry argument is one example. There appears to be at least three possible sources of such market failure:

a. industry-wide economies *external* to individual economic agents caused by the expansion of an industry; a possibility recognized by Alfred Marshall (1925). Such economies may also arise for a region or a collection of productive agents not necessarily in a single industry (Tisdell, 1993b, Chapter 6).

b. Extra-marginal favourable externalities from the activities of individual economic units (Walsh and Tisdell, 1973; Tisdell, 1993a, Chapter 4). These favourable externalities only come into force when the economically relevant activity of the economic unit exceeds some threshold value.

c. The dynamics of economic adjustment in markets and regions may be such as not to cause convergence to an optimum or may do so in an unsatisfactory manner (compare Tisdell, 1993b, Chapter 6).

Even though many economists are prepared to entertain the above possibilities, most remain rather conservative in drawing inferences from these for government support of R & D. These above types of relationships suggest that selective uneven government support for R & D effort could be optimal, that 'big pushes' may be necessary and desirable and that thresholds of support need to reach at least critical minimum values in many cases to be effective. Conservatives point out that big leaps requiring major support by government provide scope for big mistakes and, given the amount of faith involved, leave considerable room for rent-seeking behaviour.

The Common Pool Problem

Although the above arguments suggest that there is likely to be an undersupply of R & D in a market economy, neoclassical economic theory also points to possible oversupply of R & D effort from a Kaldor–Hicks point of view in one set of circumstances: when private property rights are assured in the output of R & D, for example, inventions resulting from it, for instance through the patent system, oversupply is a possibility. The situation then is that ideas and their embodiment are as 'open access' fish in the sea – common property until captured, whereupon they become private property. As is well known, those fishing in these circumstances will to a considerable extent be guided by expected or average returns from their effort. An excessive amount of resources flows into the exploitation of open access resources and the allocation of resources is unfavourably biased in favour of fields offering above-average returns (Tisdell, 1977). This possibility was elaborated on by Dasgupta and Stiglitz (1980) using a Cournot-type model.

It remains an open question as to whether the open access phenomenon offsets, or more than offsets, undersupply from the other sources mentioned. It will certainly not do so where inventions or new ideas cannot be patented or when patents in practice provide limited property rights, as many empirical studies indicate is often the case.[1]

MARKET STRUCTURE, TRANSACTION COSTS AND R & D

Market Structures

Using either comparative static models, or simple deterministic dynamic models, mainstream economists have engaged in lively debate during the last few decades about the influences of market structure on R & D and the consequences of transaction costs for R & D. Arrow (1962) using a very simple model, suggested that R & D is likely to be more profitable when markets are perfectly competitive rather than monopolized, and in doing so expressed a thesis at variance with Schumpeter (1942). He considers the case of a cost-reducing invention, and shows that the inventor can obtain a higher reward from it if the product market making use of the invention is purely competitive rather than monopolized. In doing this, however, he ignores the difficulties involved in enforcing patent rights and transaction costs involved in R & D. Inventions and inventors appear to be divorced from firms involved in the production process whereas, as Teece (1988) observes, in-house R & D has become more the norm than the exception as far as industrial R & D is concerned. This may partially be due to transaction costs involved in marketing knowhow. Furthermore, synergies may exist between problems identified in the production process or by customers so making in-house connections with R & D more effective than would be the case if R & D is organized as a 'stand alone activity'.

A second set of issues is one taken up by Dasgupta and Stiglitz (1980). They criticize Arrow's assumption that market structures are given and independent of R & D effort and success, and Arrow's view that no matter whether the market is perfectly or imperfectly competitive, R & D effort will tend to be undersupplied from a social viewpoint. They argue that in several circumstances, competition via R & D effort results in increasing market concentration, and in winner-take-all models to excessive investment in R & D due to the common pool problem. However, as Stiglitz (1991, p. 27) points out: 'depending on the precise assumptions, patent races [or more generally races for the acquisition of knowledge] can result in excessive expenditure on research and development' (Dasgupta and Stiglitz, 1980) or 'insufficient expenditures' (Dasgupta and Stiglitz, 1988; Stiglitz, 1988).

Endogeneity

The view that a certain amount of endogeneity exists between market structure and R & D effort is not all that novel. It is at least explicit in Schumpeter's theories (Schumpeter, 1942) and it appears to follow naturally in terms of evolutionary theory. As Nelson and Winter (1982, p. 281), taking an evolutionary approach, point out:

> whereas most analyses of the connections between market structure and innovation have viewed the causation as flowing from the former to the latter, under Schumpeterian conditions there is a reverse flow as well. Successful innovators who are not quickly imitated may invest their profits and gain in relation to their competitors. Similarly, a firm that plays an effective 'fast second' strategy may come ultimately to dominate the industry. Market structures should be viewed as endogenous to an analysis of Schumpeterian competition, with the connections between innovation and market structure going both ways.

Transaction Costs, Property Rights and R & D

Despite the fact that Coase (1937) pointed out several decades ago the significance of transaction costs for economic organization, their importance has only been widely recognized in recent decades and many of their consequences are yet to be appreciated fully. Market transaction costs are extremely important in relation to R & D and the exchange of knowhow and help to explain the presence of a number of types of institutional phenomena, for example, the prevalence of in-house research by industrial enterprises, the widespread occurrence of multinational companies, joint ventures and the occurrence of symbiotic rather than competitive relationships (for example, close networks) between groups of firms. As Coase (1937) observed, the costs of transacting are important both within the firms and in using the market. These aspects have been explored in some depth by Williamson (1986) and by Teece (1977, 1988).

Coase (1960) pointed out that a clear specification of property rights can often be valuable in reducing the costs of transacting and in achieving economic optimality, or in approximately doing so. However, while a clear specification of property rights can help, it may not be sufficient to achieve 'economic optimality'. As North (1981) observes, it may be uneconomic to enforce private property rights or to do so fully. This is often the case in relation to knowhow even when intellectual property rights are established. Nevertheless, the establishment of intellectual property rights by government may reduce market transaction costs and promote voluntary agreement about the production and exchange of knowhow. Yet it will not overcome the common pool problem and in some cases the right will be of no economic value because the cost of enforcing it will exceed the benefit. There are limits to the value of the economics of making markets by the establishment of private property rights and by reliance on the use of market-type mechanisms, for example, contracting out of government R & D by open competitive tender. Nevertheless, this is not to be interpreted as meaning that market systems are never optimal.

Mixed Hierarchical and Market Systems in R & D

Taking into account transaction costs and the bounded (limited) rationality of individuals, mixed hierarchical and market systems are likely to be optimal and the policy challenge is to get the 'correct' institutional mix. The appropriate mix has become an important policy issue.

It is one, for instance, that has been taken up by Weder and Grubel (Weder and Grubel, 1993, p. 507). They argue:

> that according to Coasean economics, the externalities from R & D should result in the development of institutions which internalise them. We postulate that industrial associations, company structures, industry clusters and other contractual agreements represent such private market responses to the existence of externalities from R & D and that they reduce the potential under-investment in R & D considerably. We note that a number of different contracts and organisational forms of companies have evolved to take advantage of the low marginal cost of using the information obtained by the fixed investment in R & D. Industrial clusters and the concentration of population both encourage and increase the effectiveness of industrial associations and other forms of cooperation.

These institutional arrangements, in their view, will arise naturally and they will capture benefits from information spillovers and externalities. Consequently, one should exercise 'great caution with regard to the desirability of public subsidies to private R & D' (Weder and Grubel, 1993, p. 508). They argue that governments should be supportive of industry associations which facilitate the capture of favourable information externalities from R & D but should also be aware of the possible rent seeking of such associations. Competition in product markets should be kept free and they recommend governments to enter into international free trade agreements to control such rent seeking (Weder and Grubel, 1993, p. 510). They claim that it is not necessarily in the public interest in the United States to break up cartels and associations, especially if international trade is free, because they internalize information externalities. However, their international free trade argument is at odds with the infant-industry-type of argument (compare List, 1904; Dosi and Soete, 1988) and the views of centre periphery theorists.

Romer (1993) specifically explores the role which government might play in promoting the formation of voluntary R & D associations. In doing so, he adds weight to the view that some combination of hierarchical and market forms of economic organization might constitute the best achievable economic systems.

EVOLUTIONARY ECONOMICS AND R & D

Many evolutionary economists consider much of the transaction costs literature to be relatively static and have expressed doubts about whether the type of neo-institutionalism expounded by Williamson (1986) represents a significant advance on neoclassical equilibrium-type analysis. Despite this, it can be contended that the presence of transaction costs and bounded rationality on the part of individuals adds to the plausibility of non-deterministic evolutionary economic models. As pointed out by Hodgson (1993, pp. 4–45), evolutionary economic models may be deterministic or non-deterministic, and may or may not gravitate towards a final resting point or some final state of consummation. Most modern evolutionary economics is at least to some extent non-deterministic in nature.

The evolutionary economics approach is especially well suited to a consideration of the economics of technological change because the progress of R & D activity and the techniques thrown up by R & D activity are uncertain and variable, as are mutations in biological evolution. However, it should be observed at the start that the models of evolutionary economics are not blind copies of those of biological science, nor are the arguments advanced by evolutionary economists just based upon analogies with biological evolution. Evolutionary economics is a method of study in its own right, sharing a paradigm which has been found to be useful in other sciences (Metcalfe, 1993). Many evolutionary economists have contributed to thought in the modelling of technological change and innovation, especially since Nelson and Winter began contributing to it in the 1970s (see Nelson and Winter, 1974, 1977, 1980, 1982).

Non-determinism and Diversity in Technological Change

The following is the type of non-deterministic model that generates most current interest in relation to the evolution of technology. It involves:

1. The occurrence of new diversity or variety in the population of available techniques.
2. Selection mechanisms ensuring survival or persistence of some mutations (new techniques) in the population set and their multiplication and the elimination of some varieties of techniques with the passage of time.

In such a system, non-determinism (or varying degrees of uncertainty) can occur either because of randomness in the occurrence of 'mutations' or because of randomness in the occurrence and operation of selection mechanisms. Without changing variety, many systems would proceed to a stationary state. Changing patterns of diversity are the life-blood of most evolutionary systems, and in relation to technological change the value of economic systems may be judged by their ability to create suitable changing arrays of technological variety and to select from these arrays in a socially desirable way. Technological change is essentially a trial and error process involving learning by experimentation.

Variety may occur in the evolution of innovations due partially to design and partially to chance. This may be true both in relation to the production of new techniques and their selection from the resulting array of techniques. Sources of variation could include:

1. Variability in motives of economic agents.
2. Variety in organizational structures with, for instance, the bounded rationality element resulting in a degree of randomness in organizational behaviour.
3. Chance happenings in search and learning procedures, especially in relation to scientific discoveries.

Selection and Survival of New Techniques

The survival of a new technique (or mutant) rarely depends just upon the 'fitness' of the individual technique. It is greatly influenced by factors external to the agent having knowledge of it, such as whether there are other groups with which the agent can form a symbiotic relationship. So the economic survival of a technique (even though it may be an advantageous technique) will depend upon the population of other techniques and of industries able to provide support for its survival. Symbiotic relationships therefore become extremely important. Some are of the type described by Marshall (1925, pp. 266, 314, 441) in relation to external economies and the expansion of industry but others may be fostered by particular arrangements made between firms (for example, the relationship of the British retailer Marks & Spencer to its suppliers). There are many examples of R & D cooperation between firms and institutions for mutual benefit. Survival of a new technique in a location at a particular time may depend upon whether suitable complementary institutional arrangements and economic and technological structures are present. Complementaries must be considered not only in relation to the production of new technology but also in relation to the process of its selection and diffusion. In short, a 'fit' technique (or set of these) may fail to be selected because its surrounding environment at the time of its occurrence is unfavourable.

'Optimal' Techniques Do Not Always Survive

In addition to the above, there are sometimes other reasons why techniques superior to existing ones fail to survive and spread. Basically these arise from the barriers to entry and the need for the technique to be used on some minimum scale in society before it can prosper. Many examples of this aspect can be considered. Suppose that two similar new substitute products are developed, for example, different types of video systems, but one is somewhat better than the other. Due to chance or other circumstances, the inferior form may be used first commercially. Large economies of scale may be generated and complementary products developed. This is likely to provide insuperable barriers to the better technique and it may fail to survive (compare Arthur, 1990). Furthermore, the earlier adoption of an inferior technique may lead to further innovations improving it. Hence, the development process reduces the initial superiority of the superior technique and may eventually reverse the ordering of the techniques. This may happen even if the superiority of the initially superior technique would have been even further enhanced by its use. Thus under competition, the fittest do not always survive and prosper, even if they are 'born'. Selection mechanisms can sometimes be inefficient even in a bounded rationality sense.

Behavioural Assumptions of Evolutionary Economists

Evolutionary economics is still evolving and the theories of evolutionary economists often differ in assumptions about human behaviour and processes of selection. They differ, for example, in the extent to which their assumptions diverge from those of neoclassical theory. Nelson and Winter (1982) and possibly also Metcalfe (1989, 1993), concentrate on models which show a relatively low degree of divergence from the behavioural assumptions of neoclassical economics. Nelson (1987, pp. 20–21), for example, says:

> Technical innovation, and innovation more generally, is a critical   aspect of economic activity and ought to be modelled in terms of exploration of a choice set that is not fully known, and regarding which different actors have different beliefs. In our evolutionary models, as in neo-classical ones, the actors are viewed as purposive and intelligent, and as operating according to set decision rules. As in orthodox theory, these are the best actors know about at the time, and (metaphorically at least) some thought has been given to the matter. However, in our evolutionary theory we stress another aspect of decision rules. They are carried out as a matter of 'routine'.

It is not quite clear whether Nelson is embracing the optimal rules-of-thumb concept (Baumol and Quandt, 1964). In reality, it may be that human behaviour is even more varied than assumed by Nelson. Actors may not all be as purposive and as rational as Nelson assumes. Variety in actions and outcomes occur not only because information sets of actors vary and because they draw different hypotheses from these, but because the objectives of individuals can vary considerably. Hence variation in decision making arises from multiple sources.

Economic Competence

Carlsson and Stankiewicz (1991, p. 96) point out that: 'Evolution is the result of two seemingly contradictory processes: the creation of variety and its successive reduction through selection. Effective long term adaptation requires that these two processes be kept in balance'. Invention and innovation require not only the generation of technological variety but also aptitudes on the part of economic actors to take advantage of the information and possibilities generated. The ability of firms or actors to generate and take advantage of new opportunities is sometimes called their economic competence. Carlsson and Stankiewicz (1991, p. 107) state:

> The *economic competence* of a firm may be defined, then, as the sum total of its abilities to generate and take advantage of business opportunities. It includes the firm's competence in all areas of its activity, whether defined by function (such as R & D, engineering, production, marketing, service, and general administration), product, or market; it certainly includes the ability to perceive new opportunities, to read and interpret economic signals and adjust accordingly, to learn from success as well as failure, to coordinate activities, to take the appropriate risks, and to estimate correctly the limits of the competence of one's own firm and that of other firms.

Countries which are able to improve the economic competence of their firms are likely to be at an international economic advantage. However, Carlsson and Stankiewicz also point out that it is difficult to specify the content of economic competence. They state that

> it refers not so much to the set of maximising or optimising skills normally attributed to the firm in static theory as to the qualities that make for good performance in the long run: to generate opportunities, not just to react to exogenous changes; to make educated guesses and to take risks, to maintain flexibility and to learn. (Carlsson and Stankiewicz, 1991, p. 101)

Thus an element of entrepreneurship is involved.

Networks

In addition to the above, networks between individuals, firms and other organizations for communicating information are believed to be very important in influencing the progress of knowledge of economic value, its application to invention and the process of innovation (see von Hippel, 1988, Chapter 7). Such networks may provide mutual advantages to participants if two-way exchange of information is involved which improves the economic performance of the parties in areas in which they are not in competition. There will be a double incentive for exchange of such information when the activities of parties are complementary to one another, as often is the case between a user and supplier of commodities.

Sometimes communication networks are informal, but they may also be organized along formal lines. Costs of networking and information transfer and of economic symbiosis generally tend to be lower when parties are in reasonable proximity to one another and higher when they are spatially distant from one another. Thus many Australian firms, being spatially distant from counterparts in central countries such as the

United States or Europe, find it difficult to obtain equal access to similar firms in central countries. This, therefore, places Australian firms at some disadvantage. While techniques of communication have reduced these disadvantages, they still remain.

Clusters and Critical Mass

The above view suggests that clustering of resources or of businesses engaged in related (or complementary) forms of innovative activity is likely to be an advantage because it makes networking more efficient. Furthermore, a number of the types of external economies mentioned by Marshall (1925), for example, due to increased specialization, could increase the economic success of clustering. On the other hand, there is also a possibility that clustering will lead to consensus and uniformity, so reducing variability, an important ingredient in some theories for technological change.

At the same time, a number of evolutionary theorists (for example, Carlsson and Stankiewicz, 1991) introduce the concept of a critical mass in their discussion of industrial development and innovation activity. However, this in itself need not be regarded as a peculiarly evolutionary concept. The idea of a minimum critical mass of R & D activity by firms in order to achieve innovative success is inherent in a number of neoclassical microeconomic theories (for example, Nordhaus, 1969). In some circumstances, however, a critical mass may apply to group or collective effort.

When external benefits from clustering and agglomeration occur, optimal clusters may not arise naturally and clusters may grow beyond optimal sizes, as discussed in relation to regional developments (Tisdell, 1993b) and optimal city sizes (Tisdell, 1975a).

Persistence of Development Paths (Inertia)

In order to get sufficient clustering of resources and generate at least minimum critical masses in at least some industries, a selective approach to industrial development and supporting R & D effort may be required. The aggregate pattern of effort may require some organization by a coordinating body so as to provide greater economic benefit than otherwise would occur naturally for selected industries. It has been suggested that the Ministry of International Trade and Industry (MITI) has played this role in Japan (Freeman, 1988) and it has played an important role in networking. While there is some self-organization in economic systems, self-organization does not necessarily lead to optimality in an evolving world.[2]

A further consideration in relation to economic evolution and the production of new technology is the persistence of existing development trajectories (compare Dosi, 1988) or the presence of inertia in the system. Existing paths and old economic and social structures tend to persist even when mutations or variations in possibilities occur. Development paths not only exhibit irreversibility but also show resistance to deflection, for example, a new invention may not be adopted, even though it is superior to existing technology, because of barriers to its entry. Existing dominant industries tend to resist decline both by political means and where, for example, a roughly constant proportion of their sales revenue is ploughed back into R & D for the industry, because of bias in the pattern of R & D in favour of the status quo. Thus a superior new industry and its technology may not develop as quickly as is desirable, and an existing industry for which demand is falling may decline too slowly, being propped up by political lobbying, by large R & D expenditures and even in some cases by increasing intensity of R & D to avoid the decline. This is at least an aspect which government needs to be aware of. Japan has had policies through MITI not only to support the growth of promising new industries but also to assist the decline of industries no longer appropriate to Japan's economic condition. It has, for example, assisted some to move offshore. In general, technological and scientific policy cannot be sensibly divorced from industrial policy from an economic viewpoint.

The Changing Value of Communication Networks

The importance of communication networks in relation to technological change have been noted. It should also be noted that the appropriate networks often change as an industry develops. As pointed out by Nelson (1987, pp. 120, and 86–91) universities have played an important role in the development of many modern industries in the United States. In their early stages, many new industries have been highly dependent on advances in basic knowledge and its application made in universities, for example, computer development. But after a time, further development may be made primarily within firms. Today, industries based on biological engineering are very dependent on advances made within universities. So networks involving universities are or can be important for industrial development and the importance of universities in communication networks is likely to vary with the stage of development of an industry.

NOTES ON THE PRINCIPLE OF VARIATION OR DIVERSITY OF TECHNOLOGICAL POSSIBILITIES

The new theories of economic evolution depend heavily, as pointed out above, on the occurrence of variations in the economic system. Technological progress, for example, relies on the occurrence of changing sets of technological possibilities which are themselves varied or diverse in character. One of the advantages of the capitalist economic system is claimed to be its ability to generate diversity by supporting pluralism. For many, the advantages of capitalism and free societies are not seen so much in terms of the ability of perfectly competitive systems to achieve a Paretian optimum (if they can in fact do so) but in the capacity of the capitalist system to generate economic improvements by innovation in a dynamic context.

The Capitalist System and Pluralism

Nelson (Nelson, 1987, p. 118) elaborates at length on this theme. He argues 'that the most important advantage lent to the capitalist engine by its built-in pluralism and rivalry is in its mechanism to cope with the uncertainties innately involved in R & D, and to take advantage of, not repress, differences of opinion'. He praises the capitalist system for giving freedom to individuals to make choices without their having to rely on the judgement of committees of experts who, Nelson argues, are often unreliable judges.

> What the capitalist engine provides (at least in a mixed economy) are multiple sources of initiative, and competition among those who place their bets on different ideas. And it does so in a context where those that lay their bets have every incentive to attend to the market, and there is widespread access to the basic technological knowledge one needs to command in order to scan the possible solutions. The capitalist engine lets the market decide, *ex post*, what were the good ideas and what were the poor ones. (Nelson, 1987, pp. 121–2)

Nelson suggests that this is probably the best one can do.

Despite this, we cannot be sure that the system works to the best advantage (consider here Pelikan, 1988). We know that competitive conditions do not always create optimal variety but can lead to excessive bunching in types of product supplied and the places in which they are supplied (Hartley and Tisdell, 1981, Section 9.4) even when externalities are absent. Market failures such as externalities can in some cases reduce variety, as often do economies of scale and barriers to entry to an industry. Indeed, the development of market systems has sometimes been described as leading to excess uniformity and lack of variety (see Scitovsky, 1976).

Dasgupta and Stiglitz (1980, 1988), using neoclassical economic analysis, have provided us with examples of excessive competition resulting in lack of variety in research efforts by businesses and in conformity in R & D procedures. There is social waste because of excessive duplication of approaches to R & D by firms and any rents from R & D effort are dissipated by this. In this case, perfect market-making does not lead to economic efficiency and a system in which competition is less than perfect may perform in a superior economic way.

Conditions in Which Diversity is Advantageous

This raises the question of what is an optimal degree of diversity? Humans, by means of social changes, have the ability to influence the amount of variety generated in an economic system, and so the issue is worth thinking about. The first question to ask ourselves is under what conditions is diversity likely to be an advantage? The existence and creation of diversity is likely to make a positive contribution to society under several conditions, only some of which can be mentioned here.

Advantages of Diversity According to Dasgupta and Stiglitz (1980)

When the benefits to be had from an uncertain event are a strictly convex function of the magnitude of the event, then increasing the variation of the event will raise expected benefits if the average of the event remains constant. This was the basic principle used by Dasgupta and Stiglitz (1980) in considering the advantages of variety or diversity in their modelling. In their basic model, social economic benefits from a reduction in the per-unit costs of production in an industry increase at an increasing rate. The obverse relationship is shown in Figure 18.1 by curve *BGJ*. The curve *BGJ* shows that economic benefit declines at a decreasing rate as per unit costs of production in an industry increase.

Figure 18.1 Advantages of diversity as illustrated by Dasgupta and Stiglitz (1980)

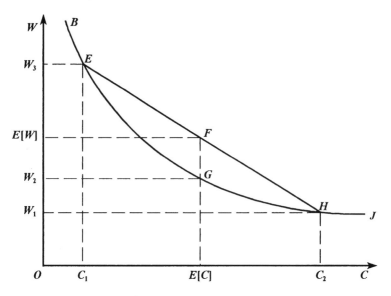

Per-unit costs of production in an industry

Basically, the relevant argument is that conformity in R & D effort may result in costs per unit being uniformly reduced to $E[C]$. But less conformity may result in, say, C_1 occurring with a probability of 0.5 and C_2 arising with a probability of 0.5. Therefore, the social economic benefit to be obtained on average rises from W_2 to $E[W]$. However, this supposes that the average of the probability distribution involved is independent of the spreading of the research effort. This is glossed over by Dasgupta and Stiglitz. One can imagine cases in which diversification of the effort reduces or increases the average. For example, if effort is spread too thinly, all experiments may fail. The matter is clearly much more complex than is apparent from the exposition of Dasgupta and Stiglitz.

Considering Diversity Differently

Also there may be advantages in considering the matter in a different way as far as innovation is concerned.[3] The creation of more variety or mutations provides greater scope for learning by trial and error. It extends the known possibilities. The wider the extended set of known possibilities, the greater the chance that a possibility superior to the existing known ones will be discovered. If there is no variation or little variation in the set of known possibilities, there is virtually no scope for improved economic choice.

Costs and Benefits of Diversity

Creating greater diversity in R & D effort is likely to involve extra costs. Therefore, from an optimality point of view, diversity should be extended until the expected extra benefit equals its extra cost. Often the extra costs of diversity are small, but the potential extra benefits are very large. This is not to say that we are in a position to specify precisely the optimal degree of diversity. We most likely cannot do so because of our bounded rationality. However, this does not prevent us from developing relevant hypotheses about the rationality of different procedures (Tisdell, 1975b, 1976).

Difficulties of Measuring Diversity

The matter is made even more complicated by the fact that diversity or variety does not have a simple measure. To specify the distribution of variety by a single parameter is usually unsatisfactory. Thus variety could occur by spreading a characteristic evenly or by spreading it by means of clustering along a spectrum. In the first case, the distribution tends to be continuous but in the second discontinuous with concentrations. Evolutionary and related theories introducing the concept of clusters and critical masses would appear to suggest that diversity of the latter type could be optimal.

Generation of New Ideas to be Balanced against their Selection

Note that in assessing systems for economic development, account must not only be taken of the ability of a system to generate varied new sets of possibilities but also of its ability to select between the possibilities. Thus a system which generates many possibilities but poorly selects from them will function poorly. In extreme cases, overload from new possibilities generated may reduce abilities to select because of the 'boundedness' of economic agents. Thus paradoxically 'excessive' generation of variety can in some cases reduce the performance of a system. In any case, more attention needs to be given to processes of selection, and both the generation of varied new possibilities and mechanisms for their selection need to be kept in balance.[4]

Problem in Designing Optimal Diversity of R & D Effort

There appears to be some conflict in the design of optimal economic and social systems for technological change. Given uncertainty, spreading seems desirable, but given the occurrence of economic thresholds and the presence of economies of concentration and agglomeration, some key points of concentration are needed. Selection of these key points, then, becomes an important policy question because externalities are frequently involved. Furthermore, in the real world as far as international trade is concerned, leads and lags in technological advance must be considered so as to maximize monopoly profits or rents from such trade. The type of considerations raised by new technology theories are important (Posner, 1961; Vernon, 1966; Tisdell, 1981).

Freedom in Structures

It seems that science and technology policy from a national point of view needs both to structure R & D effort as well as leave it unstructured. Policies which provide government support for R & D generally but with extra support for selected areas provide a compromise between the two considerations. However, the important policy problem is to select appropriately the key areas to obtain special support, bearing in mind that the choice involves decision making under uncertainty. Research is needed to identify the principles which might best be used for such a choice for a small peripheral economy such as Australia.[5] In the past, the principles used by the Japanese seem to have been reasonably successful, but one cannot transfer these without modification and the relevant criteria need to be spelt out explicitly. There is little doubt that one has to rely on a combination of markets and suitable hierarchies to obtain substantial benefits from industrial development and science and technology policies. Substantial dangers exist in relying exclusively either on hierarchies or on markets.

SOME POSSIBLE POLICY CONSEQUENCES OF EVOLUTIONARY ECONOMICS FOR GOVERNMENT SUPPORT OF R & D

Because evolutionary economics is not a settled body of thought and a variety of evolutionary types of economic models exist, it is rather difficult to generalize about the implications of evolutionary economics for government policy and support of R & D. However, it is known that evolutionary systems do not necessarily result in the occurrence, the survival and spread of that which is economically best. It may, therefore, be possible in some circumstances for these situations to be identified in advance and for the government to modify organizational mechanisms so as to improve the chances of superior techniques being discovered, surviving and spreading. However, policies need to be designed taking into account dynamics, the relatively non-deterministic nature of evolution and the bounded rationality of government.

Inertia and Policy

In addition, in actual economies, strong forces favour the persistence of established economic patterns. Such economic inertia may arise from transaction costs, bounded rationality, the attractions of local equilibria especially in a world of externalities, persistence of adaptive behaviour, difficulties in changing perceptions and the decision-making procedures of organizations and the political power of 'the establishment'. These 'frictions' do not necessarily have unfavourable economic consequences in all circumstances but they can have and this should be taken into account in policy making. On occasions, there may even be a case for governments to intervene to jolt the economic system out of one path of development towards another instead of reinforcing persistence, as they sometimes do.

Concepts which appear to be of particular interest to a number of evolutionary economists as far as innovation policy is concerned are the competence of economic actors, diversity and variety in the economic world and the importance of thresholds, networks and externalities. However, one does not have to be an evolutionary economist to find such concepts of interest.

Economic Competence, Policy and Market Competition

Competence has to do with the effectiveness of economic actors not only in choosing between existing economic possibilities but also in generating and choosing between new possibilities. Thus there is a change in emphasis compared to traditional economic analysis which tends to concentrate on existing sets of possibilities. This suggests that there could be a role for government in trying to increase competence. But how can it be done? Presumably provision of education has been one of the main means tried for this purpose. However, depending upon their content, educational systems may reduce competence or increase it. For instance, education which concentrates on set answers and the transmission of set rules may very well reduce competence. There may also be a link between the level of economic competence and the degree of market competition. In very protected markets competence may decline. However, this could also be true in highly competitive markets where survival in the short term becomes the imperative, leaving no leeway for the development of long-term competence. So it is probably in some intermediate state of competition that competence is best fostered. Account needs to be taken also of the 'maturity' of economic agents and economic developments as implied by infant industry arguments. Some writers (Hall, 1993) have suggested that reduced protection for Australian industry in recent times has been a factor resulting in rising competence among Australian business managers.

Thresholds, Networks, Externalities and Small Economies

Thresholds, networks and externalities in R & D have received considerable emphasis recently from evolutionary economists, as well as some non-evolutionary economists. Nevertheless, a difference of opinion exists about the implications of these factors for government support of R & D. Many who see these factors as important suggest that they may provide a case for relative concentration of R & D effort by locality or by industry or by field of inquiry and that 'optimality' in that regard may require government intervention. While there is considerable evidence that information externalities are important, the prevalence of thresholds and the size of external economies from agglomeration and concentration are less well established. In relation to this matter Carlsson and Stankiewicz (1991, pp. 115–16) suggest:

> In the light of what has been said here about the importance of variety, clustering of resources, and critical mass for the creation of effective technological systems, it may be claimed that small countries find themselves in a position of hopeless disadvantage compared with large ones. Indeed, if technological systems are locked into the relatively closed national systems, small countries such as Sweden or Switzerland could never achieve the same level of technological and economic performance as, say, the United States or Japan, and they would be progressively 'squeezed out' of the international markets for technologically advanced goods and services. Yet it is an empirical fact that, at least up to now, some of the smaller industrial nations have been remarkably successful in holding their own, technologically and economically, against larger and more powerful competitors.

However, their point of view really does not draw exclusively on evolutionary economics and emphasizes the importance of networks and institutions.

They argue that there may now be fewer technological disadvantages for small economies than previously because small economies are becoming more open and international. They also suggest that some small countries may be in an advantageous situation relative to larger ones because they may have less of a nationalistic tendency towards autarky and several have developed 'organizational and cultural patterns which make them particularly effective operators in the international system'. They mention Sweden, Switzerland and the Netherlands as having cultural and organizational advantages, pointing out that they are characterized by (i) a high ratio of exports to GNP; (ii) great importance in their economies of domestically based multinationals; (iii) integration of companies into the international industrial networks; and (iv) scientific and technical communities well linked to international centres of excellence (Carlsson and Stankiewicz, 1991, p. 196).

The Role for the Government in Networking

Given the apparent value of networks, one might ask if the government can play a useful role in networking. While there is undoubtedly value in government being involved in some networks and even fostering some, all networks need to be subjected to cost–benefit analysis. Most are not costless and it is probably true that some sponsored by government departments and international agencies have little economic value. Nevertheless, some governments, such as the Japanese government, appear to have used networking very effectively for economic gain.

Limits to the Generation of Technological Diversity

The significance of generation of variety or diversity has been stressed by evolutionary economics. Mechanisms which encourage diversity of research may well be worth fostering as far as government support for R & D is concerned, and in general types of peer review system which favour conformity should be discouraged. However, there may be limits to the benefits to be reaped by spreading research subsidies more widely in an attempt to generate greater diversity of ideas, for example, dispersion of funds may lead to research effort falling below critical thresholds across the board. Appropriate mechanisms for generating diverse new ideas need further exploration, and one must keep a balance between generating new ideas, choosing from this set and making use of these for economic purposes.

Diversity in Behaviour, Roles and Vintages of Business Practices is Optimal

There is another aspect of diversity that may well be worth further investigation. It is unlikely to be optimal for all firms in an industry to try to fill the same niche. There may in any industry be an optimal composition of technological leaders, followers and laggards. One can envisage an optimum distribution of behaviours or roles for firms. Such a situation avoids wasteful duplication of R & D effort (not that duplication of such effort is always wasteful), may make better use of varied human personalities and organizational structures (that is, encourage specialization by roles according to natural comparative advantage) and make better use of non-frontier or older vintage equipment which, as pointed out by Salter (1969), may still be worthwhile using from an economic point of view. To have all firms operating at the technological possibility frontier is likely to be economically wasteful of resources and government policies that encourage all firms to be technological leaders may be unsound from an economic point of view. Diversity in roles, behaviours, degrees of competence and in use of techniques within an industry rather than uniformity may be the ideal. This aspect appears to have been insufficiently explored in neoclassical economics and in a number of approaches to specifying the economic efficiency of industries.

CONCLUDING COMMENTS

There are circumstances where traditional arguments in favour of government support for R & D are sufficient to justify such support, for example, the presence of favourable externalities, which are expected to flow from much research conducted in universities. However, the skein is tangled as far as market failures and the economic justification for government support of R & D are concerned. As yet, the implications of evolutionary economics (or some types of it) for government support of R & D seem to have been little developed but, as indicated in this chapter, its attention to processes and diversity raises new policy issues and perspectives on economic policy.

While some evolutionary economists consider economic competence, thresholds (critical masses), networks and externalities to be important for R & D, the appropriate role for the government is not always transparent. Important questions needing further consideration are: to what extent does market competition generate economic competence? What role does or can eduction play? Are thresholds or levels of critical mass really important or always important?   Where is the evidence?   Can the government play an economically valuable role in networking or may many government-sponsored networks be an economic waste?   How do we best deal with externalities?

The optimal diversity issue is far from settled, but some existing mechanism for allocating R & D funds may generate too much conformity.   In addition, it seems clear that it is not necessarily optimal for all firms in the same industry to try to fill the same technological niche, for example, to be technological leaders.   Diversity in roles, behaviours, degrees of competence and use of techniques within an industry rather than uniformity may be ideal.

NOTES

1. In some cases, it could be preferable to have a common pool problem than to have no R & D or little R & D in the absence of property rights or government support for the R & D.
2. However, it does not follow that 'the government' is competent to organize.   For example, it may try to establish economically wasteful networks, or try for a critical mass without any solid evidence of what that mass is, or on mere faith, pursue a selective industry approach aimed at obtaining economies of concentration and agglomeration.
3. In fact, I believe that my conception below deals with the essence of the problem, whereas the view of Dasgupta and Stiglitz is too narrow.
4. In relation to new technologies, it is important to select reasonably well between the possibilities generated by R & D and to ensure their economic use.
5. Adequate directed Australian research seems not to have been done in this regard partly because of the derivative character of much Australian inquiry, for example, Australia's dependence on knowledge from central countries and on academic leadership from these. Consequently, as in the case of New Zealand, important issues may be overlooked, and policies more appropriate to larger central economies may be pursued in small peripheral economies like the Australian one.   It would seem unwise to embark (at least, on a major scale) on selective or strategic policies in Australia until the principles are reasonably well worked out within the Australian context and debated.   Appropriate research may need to be funded by the government for exploration of the possibilities in the Australian context, and it would be desirable for diverse views to be explored.

    There are many examples of strategies or selective industrial policies which have not worked, as well as others which have been an apparent success.

    This raises the question of who should take the risk when such policies are pursued. Certainly a case can be made out for industry bearing at least some of the risk and being involved in the decision process if strategic R & D and industrial policy is to be pursued. A symbiotic or cooperative approach may be needed in industry with the government acting as a catalyst rather than as a substitute for industry decision making.

REFERENCES

Arrow, K.J. (1962), 'Economic Welfare and the Allocation of Resources for Invention', in Nelson, R. (ed.), *The Rate and Direction of Industrial Activity*, Princeton, New Jersey: Princeton University Press.

Arthur, W.B. (1990), 'Positive Feedback Mechanisms in the Economy', *Scientific American*.

Baumol, W. and Quandt, R. (1964), 'Rules of Thumb and Optimally Imperfect Decisions', *American Economic Review*, 54, 23–46.

Carlsson, B. and Stankiewicz, R. (1991), 'On the Nature, Function and Composition of Technological Systems', *Evolutionary Economics*, 1, 93–118.

Coase, R.H. (1937), 'The Nature of the Firm', *Economica*, New Series 4, 386 *et seq.*

Coase, R.H. (1960), 'The Problem of Social Cost', *Journal of Law and Economics*, 3, 1–44.

Dasgupta, P. and Stiglitz, J. (1980), 'Industrial Structure and the Nature of Innovative Activity', *Economic Journal*, 90, 268–93.

Dasgupta, P. and Stiglitz, J. (1988), 'Potential Competition, Actual Competition and Economic Welfare', *European Economic Review*, 32, 569–77.

Dosi, G. (1988), 'Sources, Procedures and Microeconomic Effects of Innovation', *Journal of Economic Literature*, 36, 1126–71.

Dosi, G. and Soete, L. (1988), 'Technical Change and International Trade', in Dosi, G., Freeman, C., Nelson, R., Silverberg, G. and Soete, L., *Technical Change and Economic Theory*, London: Pinter, 401–31.

Freeman, C. (1988), 'Japan: A New System of National Innovation?', in Dosi, G., Freeman, C., Nelson, R., Silverberg, G. and Soete, L., *Technical Change and Economic Theory*, London: Pinter, 330–48.

Hall, P. (1993), 'Strengths and Impediments Affecting the Nature, Scale and Application of Australian Science and Technology: Economic Context', in de Laeter, J., *International Dimensions of Australian Scientific and Technological Development*, Canberra: Australian Government Publishing Service, 34–82.

Hartley, K. and Tisdell, C.A. (1981), *Microeconomic Policy*, Chichester, UK: John Wiley.

Hodgson, G.M. (1993), *Economics and Evolution*, Cambridge: Polity Press.

List, F. (1904), *The National System of Political Economy*, London: Longman. A translation of the German edition of 1844.

Marshall, A. (1925), *Principles of Economics*, 8th edn, London: Macmillan.

Metcalfe, J.S. (1989), 'Evolution and Economic Change', in Silbertson, A., *Technology and Economic Progress*, London: Macmillan, 54–85.

Metcalfe, J.S. (1993), 'The Economic Foundations of Technology Policy: Equilibrium and Evolutionary Perspectives', Department of Economics, University of Manchester, mimeo.

Nelson, R. (1959), 'The Simple Economics of Basic Scientific Research', *Journal of Political Economy*, 67, 297–306.

Nelson, R. (1987), *Understanding Technical Change as an Evolutionary Process*, Amsterdam: North-Holland.

Nelson, R. and Winter, S. (1974), 'Neoclassical vs. Evolutionary Theories of Economic Growth', *Economic Journal*, 84, 866–905.

Nelson, R. and Winter, S. (1977), 'Dynamic Competition and Technical Progress', in Balassa, B. and Nelson, R. (eds), *Economic Progress, Private Values and Public Policies: Essays in Honour of William Fellner*, Amsterdam: North-Holland.

Nelson, R. and Winter, S. (1980), 'Forces Generating and Limiting Concentration under Schumpeterian Competition', *Bell Journal of Economics*, 11, 524–48.

Nelson, R. and Winter, S. (1982), *An Evolutionary Theory of Economic Change*, Cambridge, Mass.: Harvard University Press.

Nordhaus, W. (1969), *Invention, Growth and Welfare*, Cambridge, Mass.: MIT Press.

North, D.C. (1981), *Structure and Change in Economic History*, New York: Norton.

Pelikan, P. (1988), 'Can the Imperfect Innovation Systems of Capitalism be Outperformed?', in Dosi, G., Freeman, C., Nelson, R., Silverberg, G. and Soete, L., *Technical Change and Economic Theory*, London: Pinter, 370–400.

Posner, M. (1961), 'International Trade and Technical Change', *Oxford Economic Papers*, 13, 323–41.

Romer, P.M. (1993), 'Implementing a National Technology Strategy with Self-Organizing Industry Investment Boards', *Brookings Papers: Microeconomics 2*, 345–99.

Salter, W. (1969), *Productivity and Technological Change*, Cambridge: Cambridge University Press.

Schumpeter, J.A. (1942), *Capitalism, Socialism and Democracy*, 2nd edn, New York: Harper Brothers.

Scitovsky, T. (1976), *The Joyless Economy: An Inquiry into Human Satisfaction and Consumer Dissatisfaction*, New York: Oxford University Press.

Stiglitz, J. (1988), 'Technological Change, Sunk Costs and Competition', in Bailey, N.N., and Winston, C. (eds), *Brookings Papers on Economic Activity*, Special Issue on Microeconomics, Brookings Institute, Washington, DC, 883–967.

Stiglitz, J. (1991), 'The Invisible Hand and Modern Welfare Economics', in Vines, D. and Stevenson, A. (eds), *Information, Strategy and Public Policy*, Oxford: Blackwell, 12–50.

Teece, D. (1977), 'Technology Transfer by Multinational Firms: The Resource Cost of Transferring Technological Know-how', *Economic Journal*, 87, 242–61.

Teece, D. (1988), 'Technological Change and the Nature of the Firm', in Dosi, G., Freeman, C., Nelson, R., Silverberg, G. and Soete, L., *Technical Change and Economic Theory*, London: Pinter, 256–81.

Tisdell, C.A. (1973), 'The Australian Research Subsidy to Overseas Firms and other Aspects of the Distribution of Research Grants', *Economic Record*, 49, 194–210.

Tisdell, C.A. (1975a), 'The Theory of Optimal City-sizes: Some Elementary Considerations', *Urban Studies*, 12, 61–70.

Tisdell, C.A. (1975b), 'Concepts of Rationality in Economics', *Philosophy of Social Sciences*, 5, 259–72.

Tisdell, C.A. (1976), 'Rational Behaviour as a Basis for Economic Theories', in Benn, S.I. and Mortimore, G.W. (eds), *Rationality and the Social Sciences*, London: Routledge & Kegan Paul, 196–222.

Tisdell, C.A. (1977), 'Research and Development Services', in Tucker, K.A. (ed.), *Economies of the Australian Service Sector*, London: Croom Helm.

Tisdell, C.A. (1981), *Science and Technology Policy: Priorities of Governments*, London: Chapman & Hall.

Tisdell, C.A. (1993a), *Environmental Economics*, Aldershot, UK: Edward Elgar.

Tisdell, C.A. (1993b), *Economic Development in the Context of China*, London: Macmillan.

Tisdell, C.A. (1994), 'Transaction Costs and Markets for Science, Technology and Knowhow', *Discussion Paper*, 149, Brisbane: Department of Economics, University of Queensland.

Vernon, R. (1966), 'International Investment and International Trade in the Product Cycle', *Quarterly Journal of Economics*, 80, 190–207.

von Hippel, E. (1988), *The Sources of Innovation*, Oxford: Oxford University Press.

Walsh, C. and Tisdell, C.A. (1973), 'Non-Marginal Externalities: As Relevant and as Not', *Economic Record*, 49, 447–55.

Weder, R. and Grubel, H. (1993), 'The New Growth Theory and Coasean Economics: Institutions to Capture Externalities', *Weltwirtschaftliches Archiv*, 129, 488–513.

Williamson, O.E. (1986), *Economic Organizations: Firms, Markets and Policy Controls*, Brighton: Wheatsheaf.

19. Concluding Observations on Economic Evolution, Diversity and Rationality

While there are many different views about what evolutionary economics is, in this book I have assumed that its main focus is on dynamic disequilibrium processes, the consequences of which are usually not perfectly predictable. Concern with the lack of complete predicability of the outcome of economic processes is a feature of much modelling in evolutionary economics. Bounded rationality in economic affairs is both a possible source of disequilibrium and a circumstance resulting in incomplete predicability of economic phenomena. Thus evolutionary economics and bounded rationality are closely linked.

Diversity of behaviour of individuals and groups is of central interest in evolutionary economics. Reasons for such diversity have been outlined in this book. In the case of individuals, such diversity reflects differences in knowledge sets and in motivations, all of which are influenced as a rule by experience, sometimes in irreversible ways. In the case of groups and organizations, behaviour may be varied not only because of the divergent behaviour of individuals comprising different groups and their collection into groups in different mixtures but also because organizational and management structures and social rules and customs often vary between groups, as do their information sets. Organizational and cultural structures evolve usually in a collective manner (that is, rarely as a result of complete control by one individual) and they are not easily reversed or altered. They are a significant source of inertia in socio-economic systems. While such institutional structures can be an asset to society, they sometimes become a liability for it.

Nelson (1987) has suggested that the institutional structures of organizations, such as business firms, may be regarded as the genetic material of socio-economic systems. They may programme the response of an organization to its changing environment. If institutional or organizational structures are relatively stable, they 'contain' the coding for socio-economic responses to changing environmental conditions.

Because of various types of inertia, such structures may be relatively stable, even though they may change more quickly than their counterparts in biological evolution.

Just as genetic information in biology does not permit perfect prediction about the future populations of species because environmental experiences also play a role, so too can one expect absence of perfect predicability in the process of business selection considered by Nelson (1987).

Economic selection on the supply side of markets may operate in different spheres. In the literature, the greatest emphasis has been on the process of selection in relation to innovation, generally interpreted as the introduction of new techniques of production. This is an important field of enquiry, but the process of selection operates more widely because the success of a business usually depends upon much more than its production techniques. In some cases, marketing and distributional techniques will be very important, as will be managerial techniques, that is, the methods and practices involved in organization.

As environments change, those organizations unable to adapt their organizational structures and techniques appropriately can be expected to be left behind in the 'competitive struggle' and in all probability will eventually fail to exist. This is not to say that competitive selection always results in the survival or advancement of the fittest. It does not. As observed in the literature, a superior technology is sometimes unable to establish itself because of the barriers to entry created by an earlier technology. As pointed out in the two previous chapters, a similar situation can come about for regional specialization in production. From this, however, we should not conclude that evolutionary processes are of no economic value but rather that they cannot be expected to lead always to a perfect economic outcome. Because of bounded rationality and path dependence, it is over-optimistic to expect a perfect economic world to evolve.

Evolutionary economists are interested in diversity of behaviour and organizations, both from a positive and a normative point of view. Diversity of behaviour is believed to be important in practice. By taking account of its diversity, predictions of economic models can be improved. Most current economic models are based on uniformity of behaviour. Secondly, from the normative standpoint, it is believed that diversity in the economic behaviour of economic agents and groups, in economic techniques adopted and in search patterns can give positive social benefits from an efficiency and an evolutionary standpoint in comparison to uniformity of behaviour. It might be argued that the static outlook of neoclassical economics concentrating on equilibrium has led it to promote the notion that uniformity of economic behaviour is ideal.

For example, in the neoclassical ideal welfare situation all economic agents act on the same prices and maximize their self gain. Divergences in expectations or behaviour are seen as involving a loss in economic welfare. But this is only tenable in an equilibrium situation involving unbounded rationality.

Furthermore, neoclassical economic theory suggests that all firms in the same industry should adopt best-practice techniques and efficiency-frontier analyses, as discussed in Chapter 15. However, apart from not allowing for different vintages of techniques, this view fails to take account of the fact that it may not be economic for all organizations to adopt the 'best' practice technique because the actual and potential abilities and capacities of individuals and organizations differ. It may be more efficient in a world of change for specialization by firms to occur according to their abilities. Some firms may concentrate on the role of technological leadership, others may be close followers and still others laggards in innovation. This may mean specialization by comparative advantage in terms of innovatory and managerial abilities of different economic agents. This means that different economic agents are exploiting different niches. Consequently their overall relationship may be more symbiotic than competitive, given that continued change is occurring.

Even if there were no differences in the 'coping' capacities of firms or economic agents, some specialization by type of industry function may be desirable. If all were, for instance, to try to be technological leaders, it could result in wasteful duplication of research activity, notwithstanding the fact that some duplication could be optimal, given the uncertainty of outcomes. Research effort in a field that extends the variety of search procedures can be worthwhile since it is impossible to know in advance exactly what procedure will succeed or how quickly it will succeed.

Diversity of organizations may also enable society to adjust quickly to changing environments. As environments change, particular types of organizations may be favoured and others fall into disfavour. The former may expand and be imitated whereas the less favoured may decline. The greater the variety of organizations available, the wider is the range over which the forces of socio-economic selection can operate.

Furthermore, diversity of behaviour may play a role in stabilizing economic markets and social behaviour. In some circumstances, mixed reactions and motivations have a dampening effect on markets. Thus, in contrast to neoclassical theory I want to stress the economic advantages of diversity of behaviour and organizations.

Neoclassical economic theory tends to assume that frictions in economic systems generally lead to economic inefficiency. It has been argued in this book that in a dynamic setting involving learning, market transaction costs and so on, this is not necessarily the case. Finely tuned highly sensitive systems are rarely optimal in a world of bounded rationality and evolution. This was argued, for instance, in relation to rules versus discretion in micro- and macroeconomic policy formation but is also the case in relation to management *within* organizations. For instance, it was shown that in some cases slack within organizations (this involved a degree of insensitivity) is optimal.

Again, systems involving intense myopic economic competition (and, therefore, highly sensitive to change) are very often suboptimal. In many cases, symbiotic business relationships (see Chapter 13) increase the long-term prosperity and survival of a business group. In addition, positive business preference or discrimination favouring particular economic agents may be important in fostering symbiotic business relationships. Intensive competitive short-run pressures, as observed by Schumpeter (1942) in relation to monopolies, do not necessarily lead to optimal long-term economic results. In fact, they seem rarely to do so. Thus, as pointed out in Chapter 17, government policies which aim to imitate theoretical competitive markets by competitive bids or tenders for the supply of knowhow (including the provision of educational services) may in fact be inefficient.

Because of our changing knowledge, the need for current decisions to be adjusted to accommodate the range of future possible sets of information was stressed. Thus the precautionary or flexibility principle needs to be applied. This may require certainty bias in decisions about current controlled variables (for example, levels of conservation), in order to retain flexibility. At the social level, retention of diversity of organizations, for example, in an industry, is another way of retaining flexibility. Retention of flexibility in an uncertain world can be economic, even though costs are involved.

Some social disorder can be beneficial for the generation of new ideas and the creation of new institutions and organizations, thereby potentially adding to economic diversity. From an evolutionary point of view, completely ordered socio-economic systems are likely to be less than ideal. On the other hand, social systems containing a very high degree of heterogeneity or diversity of actors and with little structure could result in social chaos and collapse of a society. There may, therefore, be a need from the point of view of the survival and development of a society to achieve an appropriate balance between socio-economic order and disorder (between social harmony and disharmony) with neither extreme being ideal.

This book has stressed limits to rationality both as a predictor of individual and social behaviour and as a guide to policy. A study of the theory of games has highlighted serious obstacles to social groups using principles of unbounded rationality to organize themselves. In the case of games of strategy for which mixed strategies are a possible solution, no certain outcome can be predicted. Knowledge by players does not help in this case. It also transpires that many multiperson games have no rational solution. Their core is empty. Thus, unbounded rationality is incapable of providing a social solution in many cases. In this regard, customs or rules in society may play a positive role in eliminating or considerably reducing social uncertainty and so prevent a possible social impasse from occurring. In addition, bounded rationality (for example, limited knowledge by the actors) may assist a social solution.

In conclusion, in a dynamic, uncertain and evolving world, the occurrence or design of socio-economic structures and institutions is very important from a policy point of view. Furthermore, one suspects that the appropriate socio-economic structures will usually be decentralized and diversified. In addition, the ideal system (if such a system exists) would be unlikely to be as fluid or sensitive as that suggested by some economic models based upon (almost) unbounded rationality: for example, the perfectly competitive model and rational expectation models. Thus, it follows that bounded rationality and evolutionary economics provide a different perspective on management and economics from that arising out of neoclassical economics.

REFERENCES

Nelson, R. (1987), *Understanding Technical Change as an Evolutionary Process*, Amsterdam: North-Holland.

Schumpeter, J. (1942), *Capitalism, Socialism and Democracy*, 2nd edn, New York: Harper & Brothers.

ACKNOWLEDGEMENTS

Most of the chapters in this book are based on a selection of my previously published articles, the originals of which have been modified or extended. These are specified below. In several cases substantial new material has been added. I am grateful to the appropriate editors and publishers for their permission to me to draw on, or reproduce these works, where permission was required. The chapters in which this material is used is indicated below.

Chapter   Article

2.   'Concepts of Rationality in Economics', *Philosophy of the Social Sciences* (5), 1975, 259–72.
3.   'Rational Behaviour as a Basis for Economic Theories', in Benn, S.I. and Mortimore, G.W. (eds), *Rationality and the Social Sciences: Contributions to the Philosophy and Methodology of the Social Sciences*, Routledge & Kegan Paul, London, 1976, 196–222.
4.   'Economic Policy, Forecasting and Flexibility', *Weltwirtschaftliches Archiv*, 106(1), 1971, 34–5.
4.   'Comments on Muth's Note on Economic Policy, Forecasting and Flexibility', *Weltwirtshaftliches Archiv*, 110(1), 1974, 176–7.
5.   'Implications of Learning for Economic Planning', *Economics of Planning*, 10(3), 1970, 177–92.
6.   'Certainty Equivalence and Bias in the Management of Production', *Review of Marketing and Agricultural Economics*, December 1973, 3–15.
7.   'Productivity Progress Parameters for Manufacturing in an LDC: The Startup or Learning Phase in Bangladesh Jute Mills', *Australian Economic Papers*, 24, 1985, 370–79. (with Kibria, M.G.).
8.   'Some Bounds upon the Pareto Optimality of Group Behaviour', *Kyklos*, 19(1), 1966, 81–105.
9.   'Slack and Strain in Efficient Budgeting and Resource Allocation

by Organizations', *Managerial and Decision Economics*, 5(1), 1994, 54–7.

10.   'Slanting Advice and Biasing Recommendations for Welfare Gains in an Imperfect World', *Information Economics and Policy*, 1, 1984, 229–37.

11.   'Transfer Pricing: Technical and Productivity Change within the Firm', *Managerial and Decision Economics*, 10, 1989, 253–6.

12.   'Rational Behaviour as a Basis for Economic Theories', in Benn, S.I. and Mortimore, G.W. (eds), *Rationality and the Social Sciences: Contributions to the Philosophy and Methodology of the Social Sciences*, Routledge & Kegan Paul, London, 1976, 196–222.

13.   'Lessons about Technology Transfer and Economic Co-operation for Hong Kong, China and the other Countries from Dr K.K. Tse's Study of Marks & Spencer', *The Hong Kong Manager*, 23(1), December 1986/January 1987, 38–45.

14.   'Dissent from Value, Preference and Choice Theory in Economics', *International Journal of Social Economics*, 10(2), 1983, 32–43.

15.   'Conceptual Issues in the Measure of Economic and Productive Efficiencies', *South African Journal of Economics*, 53(1), 1985, 55–66.

16.   'Market Transaction Costs and Transfer Pricing: Consequences for the Firm and for Technical Change', *Rivista Internazionale di Scienze Economiche e Commerciali*, 37(3), 1990, 203–18.

17.   'Transaction Costs and Markets for Science, Technology and Know-How', *Australian Economic Papers*, 34, 1995, 136–51.

18.   'Evolutionary Economics and Research and Development', in Dowrick, S. (ed.), *Economic Approaches to Innovation*, Edward Elgar, Aldershot, 1995, 120–44.

Index